STREETWISE®

CRASH COURSE
MBA

Learn the Fundamentals of Finance, Marketing, and
Management—Without Going to Business School

LITA EPSTEIN, M.B.A.

Adams Media
Avon, Massachusetts

A Streetwise® Publication.
Streetwise® is a registered trademark of F+W Publications, Inc.

Published by Adams Media, an F+W Publications Company
57 Littlefield Street, Avon, MA 02322 U.S.A.
www.adamsmedia.com

ISBN: 1-59337-210-8

Printed in the United States of America.
J I H G F E D C B A

Library of Congress Cataloging-in-Publication Data
Epstein, Lita.
Streetwise crash course MBA / Lita Epstein.
p.   cm.
ISBN 1-59337-210-8
1. Master of business administration degree—United States—Handbooks, manuals, etc.
2. Business education—Curricula. I. Title.

HF1131.E67 2004
650'.071'173--dc22

2004013278

This publication is designed to provide accurate and authoritative information with regard to the subject matter covered. It is sold with the understanding that the publisher is not engaged in rendering legal, accounting, or other professional advice. If legal advice or other expert assistance is required, the services of a competent professional person should be sought.
— From a *Declaration of Principles* jointly adopted by a Committee of the American Bar Association and a Committee of Publishers and Associations

This publication is intended to provide current and prospective business owners with useful information that may assist them in preparing for and obtaining business capital loans and investment funding. This information is general in nature and is not intended to provide specific advice for any individual or business entity. While the information contained herein should be helpful to the reader, appropriate financial, accounting, tax, or legal advice should always be sought from a competent professional engaged for any specific situation regarding your enterprise.

Many of the designations used by manufacturers and sellers to distinguish their products are claimed as trademarks. Where those designations appear in this book and Adams Media was aware of a trademark claim, the designations have been printed in initial capital letters.

Cover illustration by Eric Mueller.
Graph on page 42 by Eric Andrews.

This book is available at quantity discounts for bulk purchases. For information, call 1-800-872-5627

Contents

Contents

Introduction

Today you can work toward your master of business administration (MBA) in a traditional full-time two-year program, or you can get one on weekends by attending an Executive MBA program. Maybe you'd prefer a part-time three-year evening program, or even one you can do primarily at home by taking courses on the Internet. Whichever way you choose, the time and monetary commitment are tremendous.

While I can't promise that this book will give you the same education you would get in a formal program, I can promise that it will give you an overview of what is being taught in business schools today and the basics you'll need to understand the core curriculum of all MBA programs—accounting, finance, management, and marketing. The intensity of the experience of actually attending a top business school can never be duplicated in any book.

I'll never forget my first year at Emory University's Business School. It was like boot camp where more work was assigned than could ever be completed, even if one worked twenty-four hours a day, seven days a week. Overloading students is a major part of most MBA programs, as they are trying to teach students both time-management skills and the ability to determine what must be done in order to get by. As any top manager has learned, more work piles up on a desk than can realistically be completed by one individual. A good manager learns how to sort through that work, determining what he or she must do personally and what can be shared by his or her team.

As a teaching assistant in financial accounting while I finished my MBA, I got a peek at the teaching techniques used, in addition to being one of the willing victims of those grueling methods myself. There were times when professors deliberately scheduled three exams on the same day or one day apart just to increase the pressure. Students had to depend on the teams they formed in order to succeed in the program. In many business schools, 25 to 35 percent of the students who start the program never finish.

Training managers for today's changing world is an ever-evolving task. Universities that offer MBAs teach the basics of the core curriculum but try to differentiate themselves by what they do in addition to those core courses or by their teaching methods. Let's look at the promises made by some of the top business schools on their Web sites:

Northwestern University's Kellogg School

"Along with learning how to navigate a financial statement, evaluate potential investments and motivate employees, students are now taught how to obtain capital for a start-up company, enter emerging markets and formulate strategy in technology-driven markets."

Harvard Business School

"We are educating students and building knowledge for a global community that is increasingly entrepreneurial and ever more reliant on technology—and therefore more dependent on its shifts. These times demand creative leadership."

MIT's Sloan School of Management

"In the MBA Program, we strike a balance between the science and art of management. We measure the facts—and we also dream. We innovate, yet we keep the fundamentals in sight."

Not all schools promise to train for the entrepreneurial marketplace. Some keep their focus on the fundamentals.

Stanford Graduate School of Business

"We focus on general management disciplines—accounting, finance, human resource management, management information systems, marketing, operations and strategy—with special emphasis on understanding functional relationships. Our philosophy is that only a general management education provides the strong foundation, perspective, and balance to lead effectively."

University of Chicago Graduate School of Business

"Essentially the Chicago philosophy holds that it is wasteful and inefficient for a university to try to provide a pale substitute for business experience. What the university can do well is develop the student's critical, analytical, problem-solving, and decision-making capabilities; it equips the student with the basic knowledge and analytical tools to cope most effectively with the situations that lie ahead in our constantly changing business environment."

As you can see from these promises, each school focuses on slightly different aspects of management training. In choosing a program, a student must determine which school will give them the best training for the type of management they plan to pursue. You won't have to face those choices here. I'll concentrate on giving you a complete grounding in the basics of the core curriculum. Once you understand the MBA basics, you can fine-tune your specific management-learning needs based on how you want to use these basics.

> **Chapter 1**

Defining a Business

Part One

Part Two

Part Three

Part Four

Part Five

Part Six

PART ONE   TODAY'S BUSINESS CULTURE
■ CHAPTER 1 **Defining a Business** ■ CHAPTER 2 Business Trends ■ CHAPTER 3 Business Ethics
■ CHAPTER 4 Economics

Business Basics

Dictionaries define the term *business* in several different ways—"the principal activity you do in your life to earn money," "the activity of providing goods and services involving financial and commercial and industrial aspects," or "a commercial or industrial enterprise and the people who constitute it." Whichever formal definition you choose, basically a business is offering goods or services to customers with the expectation of making a profit. Even a child who opens up a lemonade stand on his or her front lawn understands that aspect of business.

Running your own successful business is a lot more complicated than opening a lemonade stand, but the basics are still there: deciding what raw materials you need, deciding how you use those raw materials to make a marketable product or develop a marketable service, deciding what you need to charge for that product or service to make money, determining how best to market that product, and figuring out how to maximize your profits from the enterprise. In addition, you must determine how to staff your enterprise to succeed in that business and how to motivate your staff to perform at their peak levels.

Understanding Business Structures

Before you can even open the doors of your business, you must first determine how to structure that business: as a sole proprietorship, a partnership, a limited liability company, or a corporation. Let's look at the differences and how the choice will impact your accounting structure, your tax implications, and your legal exposure.

Sole Proprietorship

Many businesses start out in a small home office as a dream of one individual. Most of these businesses start as a sole proprietorship, owned and run by one person. This is the easiest form of business to start with the least complicated accounting and legal structures. In fact, the IRS will assume your business is a sole proprietorship unless you formally incorporate the business under state law.

You don't have to do anything special either legally or financially to get your business going as a sole proprietor in the eyes of the federal government, but you may need to do some research on local or state laws that regulate businesses. For example, local zoning laws may forbid operating any kind of business out of your home or may limit certain types of home-based businesses. Local limits are usually put in place if your business requires a considerable amount of customer traffic. State licenses may be required before operating many types of businesses.

If you live in a condominium or another community controlled by a homeowner's association, there could be limitations unique to that community structure. Before getting started on your home business be sure to consider any local limitations if you want to operate that business out of your home. The last thing you need to do is to develop a successful business and then be shut down just as the operation is getting off the ground.

The biggest disadvantage of a sole-proprietorship business is the legal exposure. You can be sued for any business activity, and your personal assets are put on the line. Any debts or other claims against your business entity are made against you as an individual, and you can lose your home and many of your possessions to make good on that claim. If you do operate your business as a sole proprietor, the best way to protect yourself is with business liability insurance.

Accounting processes for a sole proprietor are also simpler than for other forms of business. You have the choice of operating on a cash basis or an

The Majority of Businesses Are Home-Based

You may find this hard to believe, but more than 70 percent of businesses are home-based and filled by the ranks of the self-employed. Those statistics are based on data from the U.S. Department of Commerce. Most of these businesses are structured as sole proprietorships. Only about 6 percent are set up as corporations and about 5 percent as partnerships. More than 24 million Americans run home-based small businesses, according to the Association of Home-Based Businesses, and women own nearly 40 percent of these businesses. Many others were started by corporate executives and managers who were downsized from their companies and decided they did not want to return to the corporate rat race.

Choosing Your Accounting Method

You may wonder which accounting method—cash basis or accrual—makes more sense. Actually, both methods have their pros and cons. There is no doubt that the accrual method does a better job of matching your income and expenses, but it gives you only a partial view of your actual cash flow. This is how businesses get in trouble. They book their revenue but don't carefully monitor their actual cash receipts. As customers and clients get more behind in payments, the business develops a cash-flow problem and can't pay its bills. Chapters 5 and 6, on financial and managerial accounting issues, will discuss ways to avoid this. Most accountants recommend that you use the accrual method of accounting. If your business is truly a cash business with revenues and expenses closely matched, however, you might consider using the simpler cash-basis accounting for your small business.

accrual basis. *Cash-basis accounting* is based on cash flow. Revenues are only booked (entered into the accounting system) once the money is actually received, and expenses are booked when the cash is actually paid out. *Accrual accounting* does a better job of matching actual expenses to revenue. Revenue is booked when the transaction is complete, even if your company has not yet been paid for the work. Expenses are booked when they are incurred, even if you haven't yet paid the bill.

The accounting method you choose can impact greatly how you figure your profits and taxes at the end of the year. For example, if you just finished a big job at the end of December 2003 but aren't expecting payment until January 2004, the way you account for this payment is very different depending on the accounting method you use. For the cash-basis method you wouldn't include your payment in 2003, and your profits would be lower as would your taxes. The expenses for the project probably were incurred in 2003, so they too would lower your profit margin. If you are using the accrual method, you would book the income when the job was finished, which would increase your profits and your taxes for the 2003 tax year.

Most small businesses actually use a modified cash-basis accounting method. They do book revenues and most expenses as cash is received or paid out, but certain transactions that relate to major expenses incurred over time, such as the purchase and use of equipment, are booked over a number of years using a method called depreciation, which gradually reduces the value of the asset as its useful life diminishes. These accounting issues will be discussed in greater detail in Chapter 5.

Besides the possible tax consequences of the accounting method chosen, sole proprietors face other tax issues that are unique to this business structure. Their taxes are reported as part of their individual tax returns on Schedule C (Profit or Loss from Business) or Schedule C-EZ (Net Profit from Business). On both forms, the net profit or loss figure on the bottom line of the form is added to the front page of your 1040 where you calculate income. Taxes on your business profits are based on your current income tax rate.

Sole proprietors must also fill out one other tax form, the Schedule SE (Self-Employment Tax). They are responsible for paying both the employer and employee sides of the Social Security and Medicare taxes, which total 15.3 percent. These taxes are calculated using the net profit figure on the Schedule C. Those who pay self-employment taxes are allowed to subtract half of the taxes paid as an adjustment to gross income on the front page of the 1040.

Partnerships

If you start a business with a friend, then you would start up as a partnership rather than a sole proprietorship. The IRS considers any business started with more than one person a partnership unless you have incorporated the business under state law or have elected to be taxed as a corporation by filing IRS Form 8832 (Entity Classification Election).

There are two types of partners: general partners and limited partners. *General partners* are the ones responsible for the day-to-day activities of the business. They are subject to the same legal exposures for personal liability as a sole proprietor, even if the claim is against an act carried out by one of the other partners. Take this as a warning: If you do start a business with a friend or acquaintance, be sure that their methods of operating are both legal and ethical. Not only is your business reputation on the line but so are all your personal assets.

Partners who don't take an active role in the daily business operations, commonly known as silent partners, are considered *limited partners*. Their liability is limited. If the company is sued, their legal losses are limited to their actual investment in the business and any obligations they may be required to make in the future.

If you take on the responsibilities as the general partner with everyone else being limited or silent partners, you are the one who is exposed legally to any debt or other claims made against the business, even if the claims exceed your investment in the business. Again, as was recommended for a sole proprietor, be sure you are protected against legal claims with business liability insurance.

Accounting issues for partnerships are similar to those a sole proprietor faces. The major difference is in record-keeping for partners' contributions and withdrawals. Taxes for the partnership are filed on what is known as an information form—IRS Form 1065 (Partnership Return). Partnerships are not taxed separately. This form gives the IRS information about income, deductions, and other tax-related business information. The form must also include the name and address of each partner and designates each partner's share of the taxable income. The general partner signs the information form and takes responsibility for its contents.

In addition to filing the Form 1065, a partnership also files a Schedule K-1 (Shareholder's Share of Income, Credits, Deductions, etc.) for each partner. Each partner then uses the information on the Schedule K-1 to prepare his or her individual tax returns and to report any income or losses to the IRS. Partnerships, like sole proprietorships, are not a taxable entity. Even if you and the other partners decide to leave the profit in the business for future business use, you will still have to pay taxes on any profit made by the business.

A partnership can legally skip filing Form 1065 if there is no activity during a given tax year, but you may want to file the Form anyway. The IRS could send you a notice of a $50 penalty for a non-filing fee, and it would be your responsibility to prove you didn't need to file the form. It's easier just to file a Form 1065 and indicate there was no business activity for the year and avoid the potential IRS hassle.

You may wonder why anyone would choose to establish a partnership rather than organize as a corporation. One major reason is that partnerships are a much more flexible form of ownership. Income and losses can be distributed to the partners in any way determined by the owners as long as the distribution makes business sense, such as 30 percent for one owner and 70 percent for the other. For example, in order to minimize his or her personal tax bill, a silent partner may need the losses more than a general partner. To claim those losses, the silent partner may be willing to put more cash upfront to get the business started. Since the silent partner put up more additional cash, there would be a legitimate reason to designate more of the initial losses to that partner. The general partner has the expertise used to run the business daily, and his or her stake would gradually be increased in the company with the time and effort put into the business. As the business grows and turns profitable in later years, the distribution can shift, based on some formula initially designated in the partnership agreement.

Generally when you start a new business, you expect to have losses initially rather than profits because of start-up costs. You can't write off expenses that are greater than your actual cash investment against other income, but you can track those losses and write them off in future years as profits increase in the business.

This flexibility in ownership is the reason many partners decide to organize initially as a partnership. Corporations must distribute their income or losses based on a percentage of ownership or investment in the business.

Families frequently use partnerships to minimize their tax hits, and the IRS watches for this carefully. In reality, partnerships can be a great way to minimize a family's tax hit by paying salaries to the children, who are listed as partners. Since this has great potential as a tax-avoidance scheme, the IRS does have strict rules established for families.

For a family member to be recognized as a partner, he or she must meet one of these two criteria:

Capital is a material income-producing factor and the partners all got their ownership interest by buying into the business, even if it was a gift from another family member. The family member must also have a controlling interest in the business. What this means is that if your children are to be considered partners, you must gift them the money for their initial investment and you must allow them to be part of the decision-making. Can you imagine including your three-year-old in a business meeting? The IRS can't either, and they'll question you if you try to say you paid your toddler a salary and file an individual tax return for your child based on business income.

Capital is not a material income-producing factor and the partners joined together in good faith to conduct a business. Partnerships that fit into this category are usually service-based

Are You Operating a Business or Writing Off a Hobby?

Most businesses lose money in their early years. While you may enjoy the benefits of writing off those losses on your tax returns, eventually you will have to show a profit to the IRS. If the activity will never be profitable and is something you would choose to do even if you never earn a profit, the IRS could determine that business is a hobby and disallow your loss deductions. The key test for the IRS is that your business be profitable in at least three of the past five years. If you don't expect your business to be profitable in that time frame, then you will have to prove that you really do intend to run this business for profit. To prove you are building a business rather than writing off a hobby, you must keep accounting records and bank accounts separate from personal accounts and other records. Order business cards and develop a business plan. Document the time you spend on your business to prove you are putting in significant effort to get that business started.

businesses that do not require a huge start-up investment. Their income is generated primarily by fees or commissions for their services. Even though you don't have to worry about proving your child contributed to business start-up costs, a three-year-old will still not be considered a reasonable working partner. Obviously, you wouldn't send that three-year-old out on calls and probably wouldn't even trust him or her to handle phone calls that come into the house.

Legal liability is not the only critical legal issue to be determined when you set up a partnership. Other key legal issues include how the partnership will be sold, what will happen to the partnership if one of the partners dies, who will be responsible for what aspects of the business, and how to handle the division of the business assets if one of the partners decides he or she wants out of the business. There is no question that you should work with an attorney to sort out the legal issues for your business before opening its doors. We'll discuss business legal issues in greater detail later. First, let's look at the forms of business ownership that do give you protection from legal liability for your company operations.

Limited Liability Company

Partnerships and sole proprietorships can be set up as limited liability companies (LLCs). Although these are not corporations, they fall somewhere between a corporation and a sole proprietorship or partnership. LLCs are state entities, and the degree to which your legal liability is limited depends on the state in which your LLC is organized. In most states, an LLC is given the same protection from liability as a traditional corporation.

These hybrids can give you some relief from legal exposure, but they can still be run for accounting and tax purposes as a sole proprietorship or partnership. This is a huge advantage if you want to avoid the taxes your business would have to pay as a corporation but still limit your liability. While the liability limits might sound attractive, you must realize that you probably will need to put your individual assets on the line when you try to borrow money. Few financial institutions will loan money to a new business without the owners taking personal liability for repayment of the debt unless there are some significant business assets that can be put up as collateral.

In order to avoid classification as a corporation for federal tax purposes, an LLC can only have two of these four corporate characteristics:

1. Continuity of life
2. Centralized management
3. Limited liability
4. Free transferability of ownership

When you set up an LLC, you must decide which of the two you most want. To avoid a continuity-of-life issue, many LLCs are organized for a set lifespan or until some specific event occurs, such as the death of a partner. To avoid losing LLC status on the ownership transfer issue, many LLCs restrict how ownership can be transferred. For example, some law firms and accounting firms will draw up new partnership agreements each time a partner is added or leaves. This leaves the two key benefits partners want from an LLC—limited liability and centralized management of certain functions.

While there is a good deal of flexibility when it comes to management, LLCs must still operate in ways similar to a corporation to protect their legal liability. Many times a suit will be filed against both the LLC and its partners individually. Whether the partners will actually be protected from being held personally liable will depend on the determination of a court. Here are the key tests a court will consider:

- Whether the LLC has complied with basic corporate practices in the areas of records, bookkeeping, and periodic corporate meetings.
- Whether the LLC is sufficiently capitalized.
- Whether the affairs of the LLC are kept separate from personal affairs.
- Whether the corporation has been used to further personal interests.
- Whether the corporation was set up to perpetrate a fraud.

Limits of Limited Liability Companies

LLCs were a legal entity in some states beginning twenty years ago, but they became a popular alternative in the mid-1990s as more states approved the business structure. Many law firms and accounting firms quickly reorganized to take advantage of the limits for legal liability. The partners of the accounting firm Arthur Anderson could be the first members of a major LLC to test the legal liability limits in court as cases filed by shareholders, creditors, and employees hurt by the Enron scandal make their way through the court system. Whether the courts will pierce the "corporate veil" that protects LLCs is yet to be determined. This test could have a major impact on the future of LLCs for large partnerships. If the partners of Arthur Anderson lose the protection of an LLC in court, many major accounting and law firms may seek to reconsider the use of these legal entities.

If a plaintiff can prove that an LLC is actually operating as a sham for the activities of one or more of its shareholders, rather than as a separate business entity, a court could remove the protection of the "corporate veil." If you do plan to use the LLC structure for a business you are starting, here are some key steps you should take when establishing and operating your LLC:

1. Be sure your operating agreement is in writing.
2. Determine a specific management team and develop written business plans.
3. Set up a separate bank account or accounts for the LLC and never commingle LLC funds with your personal funds or with the funds of another company.
4. If you are operating as a sole proprietor, consider adding a member to your LLC board.
5. Actually schedule corporate meetings and take minutes of these meetings. Maintain these meeting minutes in a formal record for the corporation.
6. Maintain corporate records and generate reports that include information about capitalization, ownership, interests, dividends, and loans either to the company or from the company to others including the LLC owners.
7. Be sure you know the rules for operating an LLC in your specific state and follow those rules. At the very least, this is likely to include filing a certificate of formation with the secretary of state and paying state taxes.
8. Be sure you separate your personal activities from the activities of the LLC. Also, if you are running more than one business, be sure you keep both businesses separate and distinct. For example, if you are sharing personnel, office space, and equipment between two companies, have established record-keeping that shows how you divide these costs between your companies.

By following all these steps, you run a much lesser risk of a court's piercing the "corporate veil" and holding the partners personally liable. If you do plan to raise capital at some point in the future and go public, you probably are better off establishing the business as a corporation from the start.

Consult both your legal and financial advisers to determine which structure is best for you.

Corporations

Your greatest liability protection as a small business owner can be found by establishing your company as a corporation. In the courts, a corporation is treated as a separate legal entity. You cannot be sued for the corporation's actions or face collection from the corporation's creditors. If you are running a business that incurs a great risk of being sued, many legal advisers will recommend that you establish that business as a corporation. There are actually two types of corporations for tax purposes: C and S. The C corporation is seen by the IRS as a separate entity that must pay corporate taxes.

Most major corporations are C corporations. The S corporation is a designation for small companies that want to avoid corporate taxes but still want the other protections of a C corporation. The S corporation is solely an IRS designation, not a unique legal entity. To option status as an S corporation, the owners file a form with the IRS to indicate they elect that designation.

Small businesses that want to apply for status as an S corporation with the IRS must abide by the following restrictions:

- Must be organized under the laws of the United States or one of its states or territories and be taxed as a corporation under local law.
- Have the agreement of all shareholders to the S corporation election.
- Must have only one class of stock. C corporations may have more than one class, such as common stock and preferred stock.
- Must have fewer than seventy-five shareholders. If the number of shareholders for the S corporation exceeds seventy-five, its S corporation status is lost.
- Must include only residents of the United States. Shareholders in an S corporation cannot include a nonresident alien or a nonhuman entity (such as ownership by another corporation or partnership). There are some exceptions. A shareholder may be a trust or estate authorized as an S corporation under tax laws. Also, some tax-exempt organizations—including pension plans, profit-sharing plans, or stock bonus plans—may be shareholders.

> If you are running a business that incurs a great risk of being sued, many legal advisers will recommend that you establish that business as a corporation.

Why do some small business owners prefer S corporations to C corporations? These owners want the legal protections but prefer to avoid corporate taxes. S corporations are treated in a way similar to partnerships for tax purposes. Profits and losses are passed through to the owners and taxed only at individual tax rates. How an S corporation divvies up these profits and losses is a key difference between an S corporation and a partnership. S corporations must allocate their profits and losses based on actual stock ownership, while a partnership has more flexibility in determining its distributions and can consider other issues, such as day-to-day management responsibilities, when divvying up its profits and losses.

> S corporations are treated in a way similar to partnerships for tax purposes.

C corporation income is taxed twice—once at the corporate level and again at the individual level for any distributions to stockholders. This burden was greatly reduced with the new tax law passed in 2003. Prior to the 2003 law, dividends were taxed at individual income tax rates. Under the new law, dividend taxation is capped to the same rates as long-term capital gains, which are 15 percent for most people. Corporate tax rates vary based on your company's taxable income. Here is a chart that shows corporate tax rates:

$ TAXABLE INCOME	C CORP.
0–50,000	15%
50,001–75,000	25%
75,001–100,000	34%
100,001–335,000	39%
335,001–10,000,000	34%
10,000,001–15,000,000	35%
15,000,001–18,333,333	38%
Over 18,333,333	35%

The primary reason business owners choose to organize as a corporation and pay the additional legal, accounting, and tax costs involved is to gain the legal protection from personal liability. Just organizing as a corporation does not guarantee that protection. The company must also operate according to basic corporate formalities. Corporate minutes are a key proof of these operations. The following activities should be included in those minutes:

- Establishment of banking associations and any changes to those arrangements.
- Loans from either shareholders or third parties.
- Sales or redemption of stock shares.
- Payment of dividends.
- Authorization of salaries or bonuses for officers and key executives. The actual list of salaries does not have to be in the minutes but can be included as an attachment.
- Any purchases, sales, or leases of corporate assets.
- Purchase of another company.
- Merger with another company.
- Changes in the articles of incorporation or bylaws.
- Election of corporate officers and directors.

Remember these corporate minutes are the official records of the company and can be reviewed by the IRS, state taxing authorities, or the courts. These minutes should be in formal business tone. Legal obligations for a corporation are complex and fill up volumes that go far beyond the scope of this book. If you are considering setting up your company as a corporation or have already done so, be sure you are aware of your legal obligations so that you don't risk a suit being brought against you and your company in which a court decides to lift your veil of protection.

Understanding Business Law Basics

MBA programs do not include extensive legal coursework. Most MBA programs have one or possibly two business law courses, usually focused on contract law. Students who are interested in pursuing further legal studies may take courses at the university's law school or possibly even take a joint MBA/JD program, completing both law school and business school at the same time, usually in a four-year program. While this subject is not discussed in great detail, here are some of the key legal issues any business must consider.

Business Succession

Any businessperson must consider what will happen to the business after he or she retires or dies. Planning carefully for succession while still actively involved in the business will help ensure that the business continues to be viable no matter what happens to the original owner(s). Businesses with two or more owners should develop a "buy-sell agreement" at the start of the business operations to be sure it is clearly spelled out what will happen to the business if a partner wants to leave the business for some reason or if one of the partners dies. Also, the owner must determine who will take over the day-to-day operations if he or she is no longer able to do so and must train that successor. Many times, a family-owned business fails after the death of the founder because no successor was designated and trained. Family infighting or attempts at dividing up the business assets end up killing what had been a successful business.

Compliance with Environmental Laws

Too many businesspeople think the best way to comply with complicated environmental laws is to ignore them until the state or local inspectors come knocking at their door—and hope it will never happen. Depending on the type of business you are running, this can be a costly decision. Be sure you know the regulations and comply with the law related to any chemicals used in the business and the appropriate methods of disposal. Compliance with the law is usually cheaper than the penalties you can incur if caught.

Product Liability

If you produce or even sell a product, be sure you understand related product liability law and carry whatever insurance your company needs to protect itself from product liability claims. If someone is injured using your product, a lawsuit could be filed. The court will determine who is liable. If the injury was caused by a malfunction of your product, your manufacturing process could be at fault or it could be the fault of the user who did not maintain the product properly. Review your product liability exposure with your attorneys and put safeguards in place to protect you and your company.

Intellectual Property

Most businesses develop unique products, brands, or other items that are not physical, also known as *intangible property*. These can include trade secrets, trademarks, copyrights, and patents. You want to be certain this intangible property is protected from use by others. Trade secrets can include a unique formula or even a collection of information that you do not want your competition to know. When sharing confidential information with employees or other companies, be sure to draft and require others to sign confidentiality agreements before sharing key information. Trademarks or names that are unique for your company or unique products your company develops should be registered with the U.S. Patent and Trademark Office to protect your intellectual property rights.

When sharing confidential information with employees or other companies, be sure to draft and require others to sign confidentiality agreements before sharing key information.

Labor and Employment Law

Before you even hire the first person, be sure you understand the basics of labor and employment law. Even the way you hire someone can become the subject of a lawsuit. One of your best sources for understanding compliance issues is the U.S. Department of Labor. You can get a quick tutorial in labor regulations and compliance online at *www.dol.gov/compliance*.

Legal Compliance Reviews

Your best way to be sure you aren't getting into trouble legally before a suit is filed is to conduct corporate compliance reviews internally. These reviews can reduce your risk of litigation and civil or criminal sanctions. Their purpose is to be sure that you and your key staff are aware of the legal issues and potential legal problems your particular type of business faces and develop internal rules to avoid the problems. Periodic reviews with your legal team that look at issues of corporate conduct, antitrust, employment, environment, product liability, and workplace safety will save you money in the long run by minimizing your risk of a costly legal battle in the future.

Understanding Industry Types

When you want to find out how well your business is performing compared to other similar businesses, you usually turn to the myriad of business statistics developed by the U.S. Department of Commerce, U.S. Census Bureau, and many other private business sources. Most of the data are developed using what was known as the U.S. Standard Industrial Classification (SIC) system, but it will now be part of a new North American Industry Classification System (NAICS) that was developed jointly by the United States, Canada, and Mexico. This new system will give businesses a clearer view of activity within their industrial sector that includes all three countries.

These North American statistics are developed to carefully mirror similar worldwide classifications, so business owners can find statistics that are relevant internationally as well. You can get more detail about the industry designations, as well as their statistics, on the Census Bureau's Web site at *www.census.gov/epcd/www/naics.html.*

Choosing Your Business Structure

Deciding how to structure your business is a decision that crosses legal, accounting, and tax boundaries and should be made carefully with the help of both legal and financial advisers. Once you make your choice, the work of implementing that choice is in its infancy. Be certain you fully understand the implications of that choice before going full-steam ahead in starting your business.

Your careful diligence up-front will save you the hours of heartaches and considerable financial costs that will be incurred if you don't dot all your t's and cross all your i's. Proper business operation means a lot of careful thought, a lot of paper pushing to document those plans, and a lot of record-keeping to show that you are following your business plans. Not only does it help keep your business on track, but it also gives you what you will need for financial institutions, prospective partners or investors, as well as government entities. If legal issues arise, proper record-keeping gives you the ammunition you need to defend yourself and your company. Much of what you will be learning by reading this book of MBA basics will help you develop the key accounting, finance, management, and marketing tools you'll need to carry out your business plans.

> **Chapter 2**

Business Trends

Part One

Part Two

Part Three

Part Four

Part Five

Part Six

PART ONE   TODAY'S BUSINESS CULTURE

■ CHAPTER 1 Defining a Business ■ CHAPTER 2 Business Trends ■ CHAPTER 3 Business Ethics

■ CHAPTER 4 Economics

Current Developments

As the economy showed signs of life, businesses in early 2004 began to believe recovery was finally taking hold, even though job growth to replace the more than 2 million jobs lost during the 2000–01 downturn still was not showing up in the economy. Many believe some of those jobs are lost forever because companies have moved them offshore. While manufacturing jobs have been moving offshore for years, service and information systems jobs are now joining the exodus, creating a political backlash that will likely lead to new legislation at both the federal and state level.

Another global issue reaching the boiling point at the beginning of 2004 was the possibility that trade sanctions would be imposed on the United States by the World Trade Organization (WTO) if it did not change its controversial tax law that gives U.S. companies an advantage over foreign companies. If the trade sanctions are imposed, billions of dollars of U.S. goods sold overseas could be affected.

The computer industry has seen another round of consolidation, primarily in the software area as it is becoming more and more obvious that the field is overcrowded. In addition, computer software companies are looking to partner more and more with other companies, so they can offer businesses a more comprehensive solution while concentrating their efforts in their specialty areas.

The Internet is coming back to life, and the Internet companies that survived the carnage are again showing the viability of the Web for business use. Businesses are adopting the Internet in new ways, as software to facilitate its use continues to improve.

This chapter will cover these four key business trends and what they may mean to your business.

> The Internet is coming back to life, and the Internet companies that survived the carnage are again showing the viability of the Web for business use.

Outsourcing: The Controversial Staffing Trend

Outsourcing has been growing rapidly in the United States, as more and more companies are learning of its cost-saving advantages. In a survey of senior executives at more than 100 U.S. companies with revenues averaging $4.4 billion, PricewaterhouseCoopers was told by 73 percent of the executives that outsourcing of businesses' processes to external service providers is already in place. Executives told PricewaterhouseCoopers that the key advantages of outsourcing are as follows:

- The company can focus on its core competencies to increase efficiency without investing in people and technology.
- It improves company profits and leads to better service levels than internal departments can provide.
- It helps the company maintain a competitive edge.

The study also found that 84 percent of the executives were satisfied with their outsourcing of finance and accounting, which was rated as the top business process to be outsourced, along with payroll. About 70 percent of the executives interviewed agreed that finance and accounting was the best candidate for outsourcing. Real estate ranked next at 65 percent, with human resources at 59 percent.

While right now much of this outsourcing in done with other U.S. firms, more and more of it is moving overseas. India is a favorite location for many of these outsourcing opportunities because it has built a high-quality, cost-effective outsourcing industry that includes services in information technology as well as information technology–enabled services in finance and accounting, human resources, and customer service.

Gartner Research found in its study in late 2003 that "by 2004, more than 80 percent of U.S. executive boardrooms will have discussed offshore outsourcing, and more than 40 percent of U.S. enterprises will have completed some type of pilot or will be sourcing IT (information technology) services." IBM was one of the first to announce in 2004 that it will be outsourcing programming jobs offshore. Beginning in 2006, the company believes it can save $168 million by moving jobs offshore, according to the *Wall Street Journal*, which based the report on an internal IBM memo. IBM would not comment on this document but did admit that it planned to move 3,000 U.S. jobs overseas in 2004.

A study done by Forrester Research found that 88 percent of the firms that use offshore services believe they get better value for their money and 71 percent said offshore workers do better-quality work. Forrester predicted in a 2002 report that "over the next 15 years, 3.3 million U.S. service industry jobs and $136 billion in wages will move offshore to countries like India, Russia, China and the Philippines."

Minnesota Moving to Ban Offshore Outsourcing of State Jobs

Minnesota joined the ranks of the states seeking to ban offshore outsourcing of state jobs in February 2004 when two lawmakers called for legislation to bar state work from being sent offshore. Right now, several Minnesota departments have contracts with companies that sent the jobs to India. When people call about lost or stolen food stamp cards, the phones are answered in Mumbai, India, rather than Shoreview, Minnesota, which used to be the service location. This contract is one of two multimillion-dollar consulting contracts that were negotiated by Minnesota's department of human services. Another company that has a contract with the state is using Indian software programmers to build a Web-based system so the state can automate its Medicaid eligibility and other health-care aid programs.

While economists don't believe offshore outsourcing is a trend that will have a major impact on the broader U.S. economy yet, this could become a major issue especially if the more than 9.3 million people unemployed at the beginning of 2004 don't start to find work. This high level of unemployment is not only impacting the unemployed, it is also starting to slow salary growth as U.S. workers have less leverage when they ask for a raise. As wage and salary growth slows, this could impact consumer spending, which fuels more than two-thirds of the economy.

Anger among U.S. workers is growing, and it's being heard in both state and federal legislatures. New Jersey and Indiana already have laws that prevent government contractors from using cheaper offshore labor. Other states are considering similar legislation as well. The first federal bill on the subject was attached to the 2004 fiscal spending bill, which barred companies that receive federal contracts from doing some or all of the work overseas in two government agencies. Numerous bills have floated around Congress to stop offshore sourcing of jobs to satisfy government contracts. One of these measures was almost successfully added to the Defense Department bill in 2003 but was stopped because the department wanted more flexibility in negotiating its purchasing contracts. There is little doubt that these issues will surface again.

Facing Trade Sanctions

As attempts are made to protect U.S. jobs, the country faces a greater possibility that trade sanctions could be imposed. In fact, the European Union announced on February 9, 2004, that it would impose trade sanctions beginning on March 1, 2004, if the United States didn't change an export subsidy that was ruled illegal by the World Trade Organization (WTO) in January 2004. These sanctions could impact billions of dollars of U.S. goods sold in Europe.

The WTO decision was requested not only by the European Union but also by Canada, Japan, India, Brazil, Mexico, Chile, and South Korea. All these countries asked for permission to impose sanctions on the United States if the Congress failed to repeal an export subsidy known as the "extraterritorial income" deduction. This deduction gives U.S. companies a big advantage on competitors and is funded by U.S. taxpayers.

The controversial export subsidy, more commonly known as the Byrd Amendment, has been used over the past three years to protect several U.S. industries, including those involved in ball bearings, steel, candles, pasta, and seafood. The United States has paid $710 million to companies to help them fight off what is seen by some as dumping activities by foreign companies. American lumber companies are expected to receive billions of dollars annually under the program if the proposed antidumping duties are imposed on Canadian wood. The Bush administration proposed repealing the provision in 2003, but faced stiff opposition in Congress.

No matter how this immediate threat of trade sanctions is handled currently by the White House and Congress, the larger issue of offshoring U.S. jobs is just beginning to rise to the surface. One of the media leaders in the struggle to educate the public about this critical issue is CNN's Lou Dobbs *(www.cnn.com/CNN/Programs/lou.dobbs.tonight)*. He even keeps a list posted on his Web site of companies that are shipping jobs overseas. If your company is considering offshoring jobs or already does, be sure you follow the issue closely, because there is no doubt public anger will grow and your company could get caught in the crossfire.

Consolidations in the Computer Industry

CEOs in the computer industry are predicting that one of the top ten business trends for 2004 will be a continuation of the move to consolidate technology companies in order for these companies to survive. This prediction is part of an annual survey conducted by Michael Levy, chairman and partner of CEO Networking, which is an executive networking organization.

Executives believe the software industry is experiencing what will likely be acceleration of mergers and acquisitions because there are too many players to serve a marketplace with too few customers. While business process outsourcing is a growth field, as mentioned earlier, executives still

Computer Security Becomes Board Room Issue

Computer security will become an even greater concern in the immediate future as computer viruses and other security threats are growing. Lawrence Dietz, director of North American Enterprise Marketing for Symantec, has said, "Boards of directors and top management will be held accountable for business stoppages as a result of information security issues. CEOs will be replaced in the event critical systems are brought down by foreseeable security problems such as failed patch management and worms." These sentiments were echoed by Greg Bolcer, chief technical officer and founder of Endeavors Technology: "Security will get grounded in reality which includes destroying the myth that everything inside the firewall is safe (and everything outside isn't). Security vendors will uproll their products so that intrusion detection, anti-spam, anti-virus, and personal firewall policy and management will have to be included on every desktop."

expect supplier consolidation among the software companies that provide products for that outsourcing.

Executives are also expecting enterprise computing to mature and move from a position of functional competency, which were its goals in the 1990s, to one of full integration by the end of this decade. They believe the next step will be greater collaboration among software design companies so that business systems around the world will be able to interact more seamlessly with each other over the Web.

The CERT Coordination Center at Carnegie Mellon University reported 137,592 computer security incidents in 2003, which is six times the number reported in 2000. Security exports warn companies that once a hacker gets access to a computer, he or she can gain full control, with results that may include wiping out a hard drive, adding a spying program, and even shutting down a plant. Yet even with these warnings, companies do not have strong protocols in place to be certain that all available patches have been installed to fix identified software security holes. Security specialists also believe that password and other systems in place to identify computer users are still vulnerable to attack. The growth of wireless connections and the increase in notebook computers add to the problems because it makes it even harder to police internal computer systems.

The Impact of the Internet

The CEO networking survey quoted earlier also concluded that e-commerce will be back in vogue and that all enterprise software companies will have to deliver a solution that provides their software services on the Web. Companies will pay for these services as they use them. Those surveyed believe that Web-hosted services will grow as companies look for quick solutions without a great deal of up-front cost or human resource investment.

Regulation of the Internet is still an open issue with state and federal legislatures and could impact the growth of the

Internet and its use for online business transactions. Forrester Research predicts that local U.S. governments will miss about $11 billion in revenue this year because they cannot tax online transactions. The moratorium was put in place in 1992, and the restrictions were expanded in 1998 to include a ban on Internet access taxes. A major battle has ensued between federal legislators and state and local officials over this contentious issue. No one knows what will actually be passed in federal or state legislation, but whatever regulations are adopted could have a major impact on your business if it has a strong Internet base.

Patents for software that drive Internet operations are becoming a major battlefield as well. The lawsuit Microsoft lost in 2003 to Chicago-based Eolas Technologies could end up costing it over $500 million. A jury for a U.S. district court in Illinois awarded the small technology company $521 million in August 2003 because it found that Microsoft had violated a 1998 patent that protects its software invention relating to how Web browsers work with other programs.

This lawsuit could result in a requirement that Microsoft change its Internet browser, Internet Explorer, which is used by most online searchers. This could, in turn, force changes in design for companies that have Web sites. These Web sites may need to be modified so they will be able to work with any changes Microsoft makes to satisfy the concerns raised in the Chicago lawsuit.

Other patent suits making their way through the courts involve patents affecting online purchases and other systems that now populate the Internet. Rulings in any one of these suits could impact a company and its Web operations.

The Internet is also changing the way companies interact with their customers. Consumers are far more sophisticated in their use of the Internet and have much more experience with computers than they did in the past. As they become more literate with the Internet's communication capabilities, companies are being forced to change the way they use the Internet to meet customer expectations.

This ability to have more direct communication with a company, at little or no cost, makes consumers less responsive to mass market communication. Instead they are looking for more open and specific communication that directly responds to their needs and wants. The Internet is turning the tables as more consumers seek to find out what they want to know about brands, rather than learn when the marketers want them to learn. This is not all bad.

Banks and the Internet Age

As consumers became more computer and Internet savvy, banks have changed the way they do business. In the past, bank tellers were the center of the customer service operation of a bank, handling transactions and developing a personal relationship with customers. However, this is no longer the primary way people do their banking. First, the introduction of the ATM changed the way customers did business with the bank. Customers liked the convenience of being able to deposit funds and get cash at any time that was convenient for them rather than having to wait for the bank to open. Today, the Internet has taken this to a new level as customers pay bills and handle other banking transactions online. If customers aren't comfortable using the online services, they frequently turn to the twenty-four-hour telephone banking services now available as well.

Companies also gain a deeper understanding of their customers and their buying behavior, so they can develop a deeper relationship with their customers if they make proper use of the information collected.

This two-way information stream between the company and the consumer is changing the way companies must manage their brands. Consumers seek out information to determine whether they even want to have a relationship with the company and what form they want that relationship to take. Consumers can initiate a conversation or they can respond to something the company sends out. Rather than just do classical brand building, companies must find new ways to use this interactive communication format to educate consumers and build their brand's identity and personality.

The online retailer Amazon is one of the leaders in making two-way communication a critical part of its operation by using its extensive data collection system to individualize messages to its customers based on previous purchases. Customers get book ideas targeted to their order history when they log into the front page of the Web site. They can quickly assess how successful these communications techniques have been through their order-tracking software. Consumers also become part of this system by posting book reviews and by rating book listings. They can create their own favorite lists of books and post that as well. Amazon's used book offerings add to this interactive community by providing people with an outlet to sell books they no longer want. Consumers can even rate booksellers, so other consumers will feel more comfortable ordering through sources that are no more than a code on the Internet.

The Internet also poses challenges for companies when consumers are unhappy with their service or products. Web sites abound that are built by dissatisfied customers or by customers who are not happy with a company's political stance. Boycotts and protests are more easily and quickly organized on the Internet and companies can be flooded with e-mail and calls in a matter of days, when prior to the Internet organizing a protest or boycott took months or even years.

Everything in business moves more quickly thanks to the Internet. This can be both a blessing and a curse because customers expect rapid response to any question. Companies that take more than twenty-four hours to respond to an e-mail frequently find that the customer has moved on to a competitor who responded more quickly to an inquiry. E-mail, which in many companies used to be handled by someone who had some free time, is now a key responsibility frequently handled by one or more dedicated staff people to be sure their response time is swift. Where customer service operations used to be built solely around the telephone, today's companies have people assigned to respond instantly on the Web using some kind of chat program or within a certain number of hours by e-mail.

The business trends for 2004 and beyond will be greatly influenced by the ever-expanding globalization of business and the more sophisticated use of the Internet. Trade protection legislation will likely fall by the wayside, as other countries flex their muscle through the World Trade Organization. The United States will need to challenge protections in place in other countries that prevent its companies from successfully competing abroad in exchange for lifting its own protections. Watch the news for stories about trade sanctions, export legislation, and tax incentives to keep up with the shifting global trends even if you are not currently involved in international trade. You never know when an opportunity will arise that opens the world to your business and offers you new opportunities for growth and expansion.

> **Chapter 3**

Business Ethics

Part One

Part Two

Part Three

Part Four

Part Five

Part Six

PART ONE   TODAY'S BUSINESS CULTURE

▦ CHAPTER 1 Defining a Business   ▦ CHAPTER 2 Business Trends   ▪ CHAPTER 3 **Business Ethics**
▦ CHAPTER 4 Economics

The Importance of Strong Business Ethics

Each day, as you open the business section of your daily newspaper, you probably see yet another story about a major corporation caught up in an ethics scandal. While some of these scandals have resulted in the complete destruction of the company—Enron and Arthur Anderson come quickly to mind—most primarily end in fines and a loss of respect for the company.

Even the venerable home tips diva Martha Stewart found that the questioning of her stock trading ethics hurt her company—Martha Stewart Living Omnimedia. Even though the scandal involved Martha Stewart's stock trading in another company, her company stock dropped from $20 to as low as $5 in September 2002.

It takes years to build your company's reputation, and unfortunately, most of the work can be lost if an ethics scandal finds its way to your company doorstep. Your best way to prevent such an event is to develop a strong ethical business culture within your company.

Exploring Issues in Business Ethics

You may be thinking that you run your company ethically, and the types of things that happened in companies like Enron and Arthur Anderson couldn't possibly happen in your company. However, problems start small and build into bigger ones unless you set standards, make sure those standards are well known, and make sure your supervisors are following those standards even under the daily pressure of fulfilling customer orders.

You'll find it doesn't take much for ethics problems to arise in a business. Any service outlet faces these problems on almost a weekly basis.

For example, let's look at a computer repair business. There are times, especially after a storm that has fried computer systems in the area, when workers find it hard to meet customer demand. There are more computers sitting on the shelf needing repairs or upgrades than can be handled to meet pending deadlines.

A supervisor, whose main concerns are to satisfy customer demand and avoid irate customers who don't receive their computers on time, could push a technician to take some shortcuts to get the jobs done quickly. The employee is uncomfortable with that decision but fears she could risk her job rating or possibly get a poor performance evaluation if she doesn't comply. If she does comply, however, the shortcut would compromise the work for the client. Hence, she has an ethical dilemma.

These kinds of dilemmas face small companies around the country every day. In fact, the Ethics Resource Center *(www.ethics.org)*, a nonprofit education and research organization based in Washington, D.C., found in a 2000 National Business Ethics Survey (NBES) that:

- One in eight employees feels pressure to compromise their organizations' ethics standards.
- Approximately two-thirds of employees attribute this pressure to internal sources—supervisors, upper management, and coworkers.
- Long-term employees report they feel more pressure to compromise their organizations' ethics standards.
- About one in every three employees observes misconduct at work.

The Ethics Resource Center dug a little deeper into the issue of misconduct and found five types of conduct occurred most frequently.

1. Lying
2. Withholding needed information
3. Abusive or intimidating behavior toward others
4. Misreporting actual time or hours worked
5. Discrimination

Planning to Operate Ethically

You can't be around every one of your offices or stores every day, so how can you make sure employees are not compromising the ethics standards you set? Major corporations are contracting with third-party sources to provide employees with a

Company Ethics Improving

The Ethics Resource Center reported that American workers are seeing significant improvements in ethical conduct and practices within their organizations. In its 2003 survey based on interviews with 1,500 American workers, the ERC found the first drop in observed misconduct in a decade—from 31 percent in 1994 and 2000 to 22 percent in 2003. Employee reporting of misconduct actually increased to 65 percent in 2003. This trend of increasing reporting also showed in 2000 when reporting increased from 48 percent in 1994 to 57 percent in 2000. Employees also reported perceptions that management "keeps promises and commitments" increased from 77 percent in 2000 to 82 percent in 2003. In addition, the 2003 report showed that lying to employees, customers, vendors, and the public fell from 26 percent in 2000 to 19 percent in 2003. Over the same period, withholding needed information dropped from 25 percent to 18 percent, and discrimination on the basis of race, color, gender, and age declined from 17 percent to 13 percent.

completely anonymous way to report breaches of ethics. In addition, universities are getting more involved in the issue, creating interdisciplinary coursework throughout their schools as well as reaching out to local business owners.

One such program is the Jean Beer Blumenfeld Center for Ethics at Georgia State University in Atlanta *(www.gsu.edu/~wwwphl/EthicsFramesIndex.html)*. The center not only takes the responsibility for educating Georgia State students, it reaches out to the local community as well. In its mission statement, the center says, "Universities should provide moral leadership by example and through innovative programming designed to stimulate critical thinking about the ethical issues inherent in our personal, professional and civic lives. To that end, the Center sponsors conferences, lectures, research in ethics, and a variety of theoretical and practical programs tailored to specific constituencies, all designed to support students and members of the larger community who wish to construct lives of personal integrity and responsible citizenship."

Dr. Christopher Wellman, who is director of the center, says he finds ethics centers have expanded their mission on campuses to "make ethics more accessible." Textbook discussions are no longer enough, and schools instead implement applied ethics programs. Students don't just write a paper on ethics as part of a course assignment; instead they go out and work in the community and keep a journal of their experiences from an ethics perspective.

Establishing an Integrity Culture

"At the core of organizational good governance is the building of an integrity culture. The leaders of every organization must not just have a meaningful institutional code of ethics, but a plan to ensure they are seen across their organizations as ethical role models. Their pro-active stance, backed by superb ethics-directed communications and employee training, ensures that an ethical culture is built and sustained. Organizations that fail to assign the highest priority to this challenge will lose their reputations in due course. They will fail."

—Frank Vogl, president of Vogl Communications and ERC board member in a speech to the Goodwill Delegate Assembly 2003 at the annual meeting of Goodwill Industries International Inc.

Bellsouth's contractor for business ethics, who offers employees a place to call to discuss ethical dilemmas in total confidence, told Dr. Wellman that he receives about fifty calls per day from the employees at the 200 companies that contract his services. Harassment issues are the most frequent ones that come up in these calls. Other issues include equal opportunity, health and safety, environment, substance abuse, conflict of interest, fair competition, customer information, insider trading, privacy of communications, intellectual property, computer systems, and political involvement.

Ethics training at Lockheed-Martin is so important that it starts with the CEO and filters down through the corporation every year. Each employee must participate in ethics training every year. Tracy Carter Dougherty, director of ethics at Lockheed-Martin Worldwide, says, "We've taken an approach to try to create a safe environment, where employees can discuss issues that affect them in the workplace."

Lockheed runs its courses by developing a series of cases based on actual ethics dilemmas that have occurred at the company. A facilitator leads each course, picking three to five cases out of a group of thirty-five possible cases that have been developed. The choices are geared to cases most appropriate to the local work force that will be attending the classes. Training is reinforced throughout the year with a *USA Today*–type newspaper that is circulated corporate-wide.

Small companies are turning to programs like the one at Georgia State's Center for Ethics to seek help in making ethics a greater part of their office culture. Georgia State even assigned a faculty member to work directly with companies that seek help in developing their programs.

The center makes its work known through print, radio, and television appearances in both local and national media. It also runs continuing legal education courses on ethics in collaboration with Georgia State's College of Law and members of the legal community. In addition, it offers private, confidential consultation to companies that request help and runs workshops on business ethics for local businesspeople.

Company reputation is not the only reason to develop an ethics programs. The 1991 federal crime law encourages the development of corporate ethics programs as well. Under Federal Sentencing Guidelines, corporations with effective ethics programs in place to prevent and detect violations of the law can reduce their culpability for employee misdeeds.

Establishing an Ethical Business Culture

So what can you do to establish an ethical business culture that meets the federal standards for an effective program? Basically there are four steps, according to ethics professor Ann Moceyunas, who teaches at Kennesaw State in Georgia and is a practicing attorney:

1. Establish corporate standards and procedures.
2. Appoint at least one high-level individual in the business organization to oversee compliance.
3. Require participation in training or, at least, provide written materials about standards and procedures.
4. Implement regular monitoring and auditing systems.

Developing Ethics Training

Companies that want to develop an ethics-training program can break this down into five steps:

1. Assessing the company's ethical culture
2. Developing an ethics program
3. Implementing the ethics program
4. Assessing and modifying the ethics program
5. Evaluating the ethics program

Let's look at each one of these steps, so that you'll know what each step entails and how you can move forward on this critical path to an ethical business culture.

Assessing the Company's Ethical Culture

As a business owner, you know what kind of product or service you want to sell, you know your market potential, and you've carefully spelled out your business goals. But have you ever thought about the kind of company you want to have? Have you thought about the characteristics of that company and its employees?

Watching the corporate scandals parade across your television screen every night, do you think, "How can I keep something like that from happening to my company"? You certainly don't want to find your company following the path of an Enron or Tyco. The best way to avoid this is to clearly define your company's ethics and be sure your staff knows what those ethical considerations are. Here are some ways to achieve this:

- Start by meeting with your managers and determining what your greatest ethical risks could be and how to put procedures in place to minimize those risks. Have your managers meet with their staffs to discuss the initial findings and see if the staff can name additional risks based on situations they witnessed in the workplace.
- Review any past ethical problems that your company has faced and how they were handled. Then think about what you can do to avoid these problems in the future, and if they should occur, how you would prefer they be handled.
- Appoint one key executive to serve as the ethics point person who can manage the entire program and be responsible for its success. Depending on the size of the company, you may decide to establish a full- or part-time ethics department.
- Write up a statement of company values, and be sure to post those values for all employees to see.

> Start by meeting with your managers and determining what your greatest ethical risks could be and how to put procedures in place to minimize those risks.

Developing an Ethics Program

Posting the values will not make them a reality for the company. Your next step is to develop a program that will help you implement these values. The first step is to develop a "code of conduct" that clearly spells out how progress toward living by these values will be measured.

The following are the most common provisions that are addressed in a code of conduct statement, as defined by the Ethics Resource Center *(www.ethics.org)*. This is not an exhaustive list, but it should help you get started in developing your own company's code of conduct:

Employment Practices

Workplace harassment

Diversity

Work-family balance

Illegal drugs and alcohol

Equal opportunity

Fair treatment of staff

Discrimination

Use of organization property

Employee, Client, and Vendor Information

Maintaining records and information

Privacy and confidentiality

Disclosure of information

Public Information/Communications

Advertising and marketing

Clarity of information

Transparency of information

Development and fundraising

Access to information

Conflicts of Interest

Gifts and gratuities

Outside employment

Political activity

Family members

Relationships with Vendors

Procurement

Negotiating contracts

Environmental Issues

Commitment to the environment

Employee health and safety

Ethical Management Practices

Accuracy of books and records and expense reports

Proper use of organizational assets

Protecting proprietary information

Employment Practices

Proper exercise of authority

Employee volunteer activities

Conflicts of Interest
Disclosure of financial interests

Political Involvement
Political activities

The Ethics Resource Center offers consulting and training for businesses seeking help with developing their company ethical culture.

The next step after forming a code of conduct is to develop a training program that will help inform everyone about your corporate ethical values and how these values should be demonstrated daily when carrying out company business. In addition to introducing these values to your employees, you should also develop a training program for your vendors and other contracted staff to be sure they understand your company's value system as well.

Vendors and contracted staff should be trained after staff is trained. Training these outsiders separately will avoid any possibility of contract or legal difficulties later. Many companies have found role-playing to be an effective training method. By developing scenarios likely to happen in your own business, your staff not only learns your ethical values but also practices how to handle problems if they should arise.

Implementing the Ethics Program

Communication is the key to successfully implementing the ethics program. It's not only a matter of posting the statement of values and running ethics classes, but it's also a matter of demonstrating management's adherence to these values.

> Communication is the key to successfully implementing the ethics program.

You and your managers are the first line of defense in a successful ethics program. Employees will follow the lead set by their managers and supervisors. Establishing a good ethical values program must start with actions at the top. Also, be certain you have some anonymous method for employees to report ethics violations. Take any reports of ethics violations seriously and establish a method for investigating violations.

Investigating violations will establish the credibility of the program. Even if the report seems frivolous at first, the investigation could uncover a more serious problem. The big advantage of internal investigations is that they give you and your executives the ability to deal with a problem before it is splashed across your local newspaper or finds its way to a regulatory agency.

Assessing and Modifying the Ethics Program

Once the program has been in place for a month or two, take the time to assess how well it has done in conveying the message and developing an ethical culture in your company. Some of the aspects of the program will prove successful, while others will be a total failure.

Take the time to determine what works and what doesn't. Fix the problems and expand on what is working. New ethics issues that may not have been apparent when the program was first developed may now be more visible. Develop new value statements and a code of ethics if needed to fortify your ethics program.

You also may want to develop a program for recognizing those who have been most effective in implementing the program or even start an awards program for employees who have made the right ethical decision in a difficult situation. Rewarding employees is a great way to get the word out about how serious you are about your ethics program.

Also, never publicly reprimand an employee who has made an ethics mistake. Part of a good ethical program is to maintain each employee's dignity. This gives the program credibility and ensures its success. You'll find you will have more success in implementing the program if those who do the right thing are rewarded and those who do the wrong thing are quietly counseled about what they did wrong and what changes should be made in their behavior in the future.

> Rewarding employees is a great way to get the word out about how serious you are about your ethics program.

Evaluating the Ethics Program

Complete a comprehensive review of the program on an annual basis. Many companies will do this by asking employees to complete a confidential questionnaire that explores the company's values and how well these values are followed every day in the workplace.

If you find your values are not well defined after evaluating these questionnaires, you may want to call in outside help to review and evaluate your program and give suggestions about how it can be improved. Many universities have ethics centers that will provide individual assistance to companies that are trying to develop a strong, ethical culture.

The key to keeping an ethics program going is strong commitment of the company's leadership with visible acts that prove this commitment to the values set. By keeping people involved and keeping the focus on the positive, you can develop a corporate culture that matches the values you have set for your company.

In addition to improving your company's ethics, you will also meet the standards set by the U.S. Sentencing Guidelines, which, as mentioned earlier, can protect your company from the misdeeds of your employees.

> **Chapter 4**

Economics

Part One

Part Two

Part Three

Part Four

Part Five

Part Six

PART ONE   TODAY'S BUSINESS CULTURE

■ CHAPTER 1 Defining a Business ■ CHAPTER 2 Business Trends ■ CHAPTER 3 Business Ethics ■ CHAPTER 4 Economics

Economics Defined

Each day you open up your newspaper, you look for economic news. Are interest rates going to rise or fall? Is consumer sentiment on the rise or is it looking bleak? Obviously what happens economically is going to impact your business. But do you understand what is behind those numbers?

Learning what various forces impact the economy helps you to understand what those numbers mean and what is likely driving those numbers. Improving your understanding of economics will help you do better business forecasting and planning. There are many definitions for the word *economics,* but the one generally accepted by economists is that economics is the study of how people and society choose to employ scarce resources that could have alternative uses in order to produce various commodities and to distribute them for consumption, now or in the future, among various persons and groups in society.

Basic Economic Concepts

You can translate this definition into three basic concepts that drive our economy every day: demand, supply, and equilibrium.

Demand encompasses the behavior of buyers. Buyers' demand for a product is based on price. As the price for a product rises, demand for that product will likely fall. For example, when gas prices are relatively cheap (about $1.30 per gallon, for example), demand for gas increases; but when prices approach $2 per gallon, demand drops off considerably.

Supply encompasses the other side of the market—the behavior of sellers and producers. The quantity of a product produced and offered for sale will depend on the price that buyers are willing to pay for that product. The more buyers are willing to pay for the product, the more incentive there is to increase the supply. For example, looking at the price of oil from the producers' perspective, if a barrel of oil sells for only $10, not many producers are going to seek out new sources of oil; when the price of a barrel rises to $30, many more producers are willing to take the risks of looking for more oil supplies.

Equilibrium encompasses the outcome of supply and demand in the market. When there is a lack of demand because buyers see the price of the product or service as too high, the quantity that is supplied will exceed the quantity that is demanded. This will create a surplus of the product. Sellers will respond by lowering the price to get rid of the product. At some point, the price will drop too low, and producers will no longer want to make the product. Supplies will then dry up, and there will likely be a shortage of the product. This shortage allows sellers to raise prices. When the price is just right with no surplus and no shortage, that particular product is considered to be in equilibrium—the quantity demanded equals the quantity supplied. As you can imagine, this rarely actually happens in the marketplace.

As a businessperson, your key concern is to track the economic trends and to try to anticipate whether demand for your product is going to increase or decrease. Knowing this is essential for pricing your product correctly to maximize both sales and profits.

This is what economists use to look at the supply and demand for a product. In the example shown in the following chart **(FIGURE 4-1)**, the product is at equilibrium with a market price of $30 and a product supply and demand of 9 million units. Reading this chart, you can see that if the market price for this product drops to $10, the supply will drop to about 6 million units, but consumer demand will jump to 12 million units. Demand will exceed supply, and prices will rise. If the market price increases to $60, supply will increase to 12 million units and demand will decrease to 6 million units. Supply will exceed demand, and prices will drop.

Northeast Blackout Increases Gas Prices

The 2003 electricity blackout in the Northeast is a classic example of how the supply/demand curve can be tossed out of equilibrium by a shock to the market. The blackout, which cost businesses millions, could end up costing consumers even more in long-term increases in gasoline prices. The director of the Federal Energy Information Administration expects this blackout to add several cents to the price of a gallon of gasoline. In this case, seven gasoline refineries were forced to go offline and many could not go back online for as much as two days. Gas supplies were already tight because the blackout happened at the end of a period of usually high demand. The *Wall Street Journal* reported on August 18, 2003, that the New York Mercantile Exchange found gasoline prices for September delivery already increased five cents on its exchange and anticipated a steady increase over time.

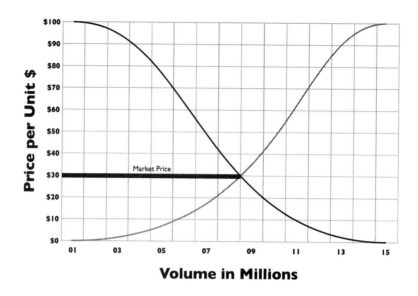

FIGURE 4-1

Price per Unit $

$100
$90
$80
$70
$60
$50
$40
$30
$20
$10
$0

Market Price

01 03 05 07 09 11 13 15

Volume in Millions

Demand Curve ——
Supply Curve ——

Developing a similar chart for your product is a good marketing tool. You can do this by looking at the historical sales for your product. You can quickly see at what points a set price either resulted in increased demand or reduced sales. Finding the equilibrium for your product can put you at a great advantage against your competitors.

The study of economics is broken up into two distinct disciplines: micro-economics and macroeconomics. *Microeconomics* tracks the behavior of individual entities, such as people or businesses. This branch of economics seeks to understand how individual households will respond to changes in prices or wages. Microeconomists also want to understand how individual businesses make decisions regarding product production and pricing. *Macro-economics* looks at the big picture. Macroeconomists seek to learn why the economy is growing and more about what impacts economic cycles. This chapter looks at what is being studied in each of these disciplines.

Understanding Microeconomics

Microeconomics is primarily concerned with supply and demand. Microecono-mists study factors that impact the output and price of products and how individual consumers or businesses respond to various economic forces. They also study the impact that competition or lack of competition has on supply and demand.

Why is this study important for you as a businessperson? Basically, you want to find the highest price you can charge without losing too many sales.

How Economics Impacts Your Product Demand

Microeconomics actually studies the shifts in demand based on income and other consumer factors. Historically, an increase in income normally leads to an increase in the amount individuals are willing to pay for any good. Goods that are necessities tend to be less responsive to income changes, while luxuries are more responsive. There are four key factors that drive supply and demand:

1. Consumers' income level.
2. The availability and price of substitutes for the products or services you are selling.
3. The availability and price of complementary products or services you are selling.
4. Prevailing consumer tastes, styles, and fashion.

The importance of the first factor is obvious. Consumers must be earning enough to be able to buy your product. If you are producing a product that is intended to sell to the middle class, it must be priced at a level the middle class can afford and will want to spend their money on. If incomes are rising, consumers will have more money to spend and are more likely to buy your product, but if incomes are dropping, consumers will have less money to spend and will cut back on how many products they buy.

In addition to income factors, competing pressures for those sales will be products or services that can substitute for your product. The more substitutes on the market, the greater pressure there will be for you to lower your price. Also, having products or services that are complementary to others on the market can greatly impact your sales. For example, if you are producing and selling games for a particular product like Gameboy, there have to be enough Gameboys on the market to increase the demand for your product.

Sales on most products depend on prevailing trends and consumer tastes. The key exceptions to that are the staples of life, such as basic foods and health care. Many of the decisions about what to sell and how much to produce are marketing decisions, which are covered in Part Five, but understanding microeconomics can improve your decision-making. Microeconomists collect information on the various aspects that impact consumer demand and produce reports for their clients.

> Historically, an increase in income normally leads to an increase in the amount individuals are willing to pay for any good.

Microsoft Declared Monopoly

In November 1999, Judge Thomas Penfield Jackson wrote, "Microsoft enjoys so much power in the market for Intel-compatible PC operating systems that if it wished to exercise this power solely in terms of price, it could charge a price for Windows substantially above that which could be charged in a competitive market. Moreover, it could do so for a significant period of time without losing an unacceptable amount of business to competitors. In other words, Microsoft enjoys monopoly power in the relevant market." This is a classic case of imperfect market competition where one company controls a key product and can control the market. Although minimal sanctions were imposed in the United States, more severe sanctions were expected from the European Union at the time this book was written. On August 6, 2003, the European Commission issued a statement finding that "Microsoft's abuses are still ongoing" and indicated they may consider fines up to 10 percent of worldwide sales, which, in Microsoft's case, could mean billions of dollars.

How Economics Impacts Your Supply of Goods

The other side of the microeconomic equation is how business decisions impact the supply/demand curve. In a perfect business world with perfect competition where no producer can affect the market price, there would be no forces at work that unfairly influence competition. In this scenario, a large number of small firms would each produce an identical product and each firm would be too small to affect market price.

In reality, the business world is rarely perfect. Large competitors can beat out smaller competitors by setting lower prices at first. This price war will drive the smaller competitors out of the market because they cannot afford to sell their products at the lower price. Once the smaller competitors are out of the marketplace, the large competitor has more control on pricing because there are few substitutes for the product being produced.

For businesses, the decision of how much to supply is based first on a review of their marginal costs, which means calculating the total cost of producing each additional unit of product. This will include the fixed and variable costs for producing that product. How to calculate those costs is discussed in Chapter 6. When setting a price for a product, a company wants to sell that product at some price above its marginal costs, but that price must also consider what the competition is doing. So a firm's pricing decisions are not based solely on their costs, but also on their competition's pricing decisions. To get a view of the larger picture, microeconomists collect data about each firm's supply curves and then calculate a supply curve for the market.

Pricing becomes difficult whenever there is a situation of imperfect competition. Two key factors that create situations of imperfect competition are barriers to entry and cost conditions. Common barriers to entry include patents that protect a company's right to produce that product and trademarks that protect the company in control. Government regulation can also be a factor in creating barriers to entry.

Whenever there are significant savings caused by a firm's ability to do large-scale production, which drives down the cost of producing a product, small firms will have a hard time competing with larger firms. In such cases, smaller firms simply cannot produce a product that can be sold at a competitive price without the advantages of economies of scale.

Most imperfect markets are created because of factors relating to economies of scale. For example, success in selling beer and cigarettes is highly dependent on creating a national brand image and advertising, something that only large corporations can afford to do. Can you imaging trying to compete with your own new brand of cigarettes or beer? While some companies have successfully marketed beer locally, when is the last time you can remember a new beer being adding to the national scene?

The days of new entrants to the oil industry are gone. Not only are costs a major barrier to entry, there aren't many places left under U.S. control to even look for new oil potential. The risks of searching for oil are so great that few firms have the capital even to consider trying to explore.

Legal restrictions can also be a major barrier to entry. We've already mentioned patents, but other considerations include government restrictions, such as those that control local utilities for water, electricity, natural gas, or telephones. Trade tariffs are another legal restriction that can dampen entry into foreign markets and contribute to imperfect market competition.

The U.S. government does try to prevent imperfect competition from driving consumer prices too high by imposing antitrust laws. The first major breakup of a corporate monopoly was the breakup of Standard Oil in 1911 using the Sherman Antitrust Act of 1890, which outlawed monopolist trade and any combination or conspiracy that results in the restraint of trade. This law was refined with the Clayton Antitrust Act of 1914, which added provisions related to price competition and lease and sales contracts that were not covered sufficiently in the Sherman Antitrust Act. The Clayton Antitrust Act also makes it illegal to acquire a company if the acquisition could substantially lessen competition.

When major companies want to merge, the federal government can act to block the merger if it believes the transaction could lessen competition. Most companies will negotiate privately with government agencies and even offer to sell off certain parts of the business to get federal approval for the merger. The company's only other alternative would be to fight the government in

Breaking Up a Phone Monopoly

From 1915 to 1985, the United States actually permitted a monopoly—the American Telephone and Telegraph Company—to control our telephone services. AT&T was organized by local telephone companies, usually one per state, and also included a long-distance division and an equipment-manufacturing division called Western Electric. The local telephone companies were regulated by state authorities, which limited rates that could be charged to customers. These rates were based on documented costs plus a modest guaranteed profit. As pressure for permitting additional competition mounted, AT&T agreed to split itself into eight new companies, including seven regional holding companies to run local telephone divisions and a new corporation to absorb the long-distance services and manufacturing divisions. The regional companies remained regulated monopolies, but the breakup allowed competition for long distance and equipment.

court if the government agency rules that the merger is a violation of U.S. antitrust law, which could delay a merger for years.

Primarily, what the government is trying to prevent with its antitrust laws is the establishment of a monopoly (in which only one company controls the market for a particular product). Even oligopolies (in which a few companies control a particular product) tend to control prices. The aluminum and oil industries are good examples of oligopolies where the product is fairly similar. The automobile industry is a second kind of oligopoly in which the number of companies offering products is small, but they do sell differentiated products.

Understanding Macroeconomics

Now that we've reviewed the basics of microeconomics, let's turn our attention to the big picture—macroeconomics. As a businessperson, the aspects of this branch of economics that will concern you the most are the impact on money supply, interest rates, and government deficits. You may wonder why government deficits are a factor. The main reason is that if the government is running large deficits, you as a businessperson must compete for the same money supply and your costs of borrowing will increase.

Let's start with a discussion of aggregate supply and demand. While microeconomists look at the details of supply and demand for individual consumers and businesses, macroeconomists look at the larger picture by measuring aggregate supply and demand, which encompasses the general business climate. Aggregate supply looks at the amount of output businesses will produce and sell, given the prevailing prices, production capacity, and costs. When the economy is in balance, most businesses will produce to their potential output. If prices and spending are too low, businesses may produce less than their full potential output, which can lead to shortages in supply. If prices and demand are high, businesses may push the envelope and produce at more than their potential output until there is a situation of oversupply and product surpluses, which leads to falling prices and demand and, ultimately, a readjustment to lower production.

Aggregate demand looks at the amount that consumers, firms, and governments will spend considering the variables of prices, income, and other economic conditions. While microeconomics looks at specific types of products, macroeconomics considers the larger picture. A macroeconomic analysis, for example, might combine cars bought by consumers, tanks bought by the government, and trucks bought by businesses to gauge the health of that sector of the economy.

Macroeconomists also consider the larger picture by looking at policy instruments that impact the economy, such as fiscal policy (government expenditure and taxes), monetary policy (control of money supply that affects interest rates), income policy (both voluntary wage-price guidelines and mandatory controls), and foreign economic policy (trade policies and exchange rate interventions). Macroeconomists also consider variables outside the control of the country, including weather conditions, wars, and output by foreign companies.

When setting these policies, governments seek to encourage a high level of output, a rapid growth rate, a high level of employment, price-level stability, and foreign trade balance. Yes, these are lofty goals for a perfect economic environment, which rarely exists. In the United States, the Federal Reserve, the central bank that controls the supply of money and interest rates, makes most decisions impacting monetary policy. While the Federal Reserve does not directly control interest rates charged to consumers and businesses, it does control the interest rates at which banks can borrow funds. Changes made to those rates also impact rates for consumers and businesses.

Policies relating to fiscal and income issues are controlled by the legislative and executive branches of government, usually in a process of give-and-take. Foreign trade policies can be influenced by decisions made at the Federal Reserve regarding exchange rate policies in conjunction with the Treasury Department. The legislative branch gets involved when a trade agreement must be signed. But there is much less control of foreign policy within any one country because it depends on governmental actions by other countries.

By measuring aggregate supply and demand, macroeconomists track one of the key yardsticks of national production—the gross national product (GNP), which represents the total value of output for the nation. Watching

A Valuable White House Source

The White House Economic Statistics Briefing Room *(www. whitehouse.gov/fsbr/esbr.html)* is an excellent place to find the most current statistics on employment, income, money, prices, production, output, and transportation. On employment, you can find information about the civilian labor force, unemployment levels, average wages, and productivity. The Income page has statistics for disposable income, per capita income, household income, and household wealth. In addition to interest rates, the Money page tracks bond yields and money supply data. The Output page has information on corporate profit levels and quarterly reports on retail trade and manufacturing, mining, and trade. You'll also find data on personal consumption and on national expenditures for research and development by sector and by the federal government.

the ups and downs of GNP helps economists to understand and tackle issues such as employment, inflation, and economic growth. While GNP is not the only key measurement, it is the granddaddy of them all. GNP includes the sum of the money values of all consumption and investment goods, along with government purchases.

Gross national product can be measured in two ways—as a flow of final product, or as the total costs or earnings of these products. Under the total cost approach, profits are defined as residual costs; so in the end, either method yields the same GNP. Today, GNP is measured using the flow of final product approach, which means that only final goods and services are included in the calculation. Goods or services bought for the production of the final goods are not included separately, because in reality they are part of the price of the final goods.

As a businessperson, GNP may give you a quick overview of the general economy, but you certainly want more detail about economic indicators that impact your business directly.

Luckily, as a businessperson, you are not required to do all the statistical work to develop basic economic models for your business. Many business schools around the country have Economic Forecasting Centers, such as the one at Georgia State University *(http://robinson.gsu.edu/efc/index.html)*. You can get local data from these forecasting centers as well as macroeconomic data from economics researchers at the Federal Reserve *(www.federalreserve.gov/rnd.htm)*.

The Prices page has key price indexes, including the Consumer Price Index, the Producer Price Index, and Gross Domestic Purchases Prices. The Production page monitors key indexes including housing starts and manufacturer's data relating to durable goods, industrial production, and capacity utilization. The Transportation page has information critical for anyone in the travel industry.

In December 1991, the Bureau of Economic Analysis began using the gross domestic product (GDP) as the primary measure of United States production. The GDP measures output generated through production by labor and property that is physically located within the borders of a particular country. The index does not exclude factors such as income earned by a country's citizens working overseas, and it includes data about rental property income. This figure makes it easier for the United States to compare its production to other countries because its method of calculation is a standard in international guidelines for economic accounting. A good location on the Internet to track both current and past GDP data is the Federal Reserve Bank of St. Louis *(http://research.stlouisfed.org/fred2/categories/18)*.

As you can see, macroeconomics will become a critical part of your business day. Locating additional sources for economic statistics gathered specifically for your industry will also help you make better-informed business decisions. While you don't need to become an economist, you certainly do need to understand the information they collect and how you can use it effectively.

> **Chapter 5**

Financial Accounting

Part One

Part Two

Part Three

Part Four

Part Five

Part Six

Understanding Financial Accounting

When you think of financial accounting, the two words that probably pop quickly into mind are *debits* and *credits*. You probably know that sometimes debits increase an account's total value and sometimes they decrease its value. That's also true for credits. So how do you make sense of these numbers? Does it all really matter if you never intend to be an accountant anyway? The answer to the second question is a resounding yes.

Financial accounting does matter to all managers, even those who decide to concentrate in marketing, finance, or other management areas. No matter what area of a business you plan to work in, being able to understand the numbers on a report from the financial accounting department is critical to your success as a manager. As you are undoubtedly aware, information is power. Think of accounting as a key to getting information about the financial status of your operation and the power that comes from knowing and understanding that information.

Yes, you do need to learn an entirely new language to fully understand accounting, and, yes, sometimes the processes seem to defy your understanding of how numbers should work. But, once you understand the basics of "double-entry" accounting, you will understand how important this sometimes-tedious task is to keeping your books in balance and understanding how your business is doing. Financial accounting is driven by the rules of double-entry accounting. Every transaction has two sides.

Basically, double-entry accounting involves always being certain that both sides of a transaction are entered in your books and that every entry is balanced in this double-sided equation. For example, if you purchase new equipment for your department, two financial activities must occur. The new equipment becomes an asset for your department, but the cost of adding that asset requires spending money or incurring debt. In recording that transaction in the financial accounting records, you have to record an increase to assets and a decrease to either cash or an increase to debt.

To help you understand double-entry accounting, you need to consider what it is you are tracking and how you will use the information. In addition to recording the financial activity of the business, the financial accounting department is also responsible for preparing the reports that will be used internally by department managers and externally by financial institutions, investors, and others with whom you want to do business. Two key financial statements that are produced are called the balance sheet and the profit and loss statement (or income statement).

The *balance sheet* includes all company assets, liabilities, and equity. Assets (cash or other items of value) are in the left column of the sheet and are offset by either liabilities (debts owed) or equity (money invested in the company by shareholders, if a corporation, or owners plus any retained earnings from profits that are reinvested in the company). You can think of the balance sheet as an equation:

$$ASSETS = LIABILITIES + EQUITY$$

The *profit and loss statement* includes income and expenses. After calculating all income and expenses for the year, the bottom line can either be a profit or loss for the company. Any profit would be added to the retained earnings account on the balance sheet and any loss would be subtracted. In the end, the balance sheet must be in balance. Dual-entry accounting, if done accurately, helps to keep the accounting records in balance. Debits and credits are what make this possible even in the most complex business structure. The key is to know how to record each of the four critical types of accounts: assets, liabilities, income, and expenses. Here is a chart that summarizes how debits and credits impact each of these accounts:

ACCOUNT	DEBIT	CREDIT
Assets	Increases	Decreases
Liabilities	Decreases	Increases
Income	Decreases	Increases
Expenses	Increases	Decreases

Just to show you how you would make an entry into the accounting system using the dual-entry accounting method, let's look at the purchase of equipment for a business. A desk is bought for a new employee costing $1,000; the purchase is made with cash. This is how the entry would appear in the financial records:

	DEBIT	CREDIT
Office Furniture	$1,000	
Cash		$1,000

In this scenario, two asset accounts are affected by the transaction. The office furniture account is increased in value and the cash account is decreased in value. Note that the entry is balanced. There is no change to the bottom line of the asset column on the balance sheet, because you are both adding and subtracting the same amount from two different accounts on the same side of the sheet.

Now let's assume the desk was bought using credit. Here is how that entry would appear in the financial records:

	DEBIT	CREDIT
Office Furniture	$1,000	
Accounts payable		$1,000

In this scenario one asset account and one liability account are affected. The asset account, office furniture, is increased, and the liability account, accounts payable, is increased. Again the entry is balanced, but this time both accounts are increased. In this case, you are increasing the asset side of the balance sheet by buying new furniture and increasing the liability side of the sheet by adding new debt.

If you've had no exposure to accounting, this may also sound overwhelming. However, as we work through how to set up accounting records for the company, learn to track your financial activities, and then close out your books so you can generate financial reports, you'll get a better handle on the process and it will become easier.

Setting Up Your Books

The first step in developing an accounting system for any company is to make up a chart of accounts. This serves as a guide for entering all transactions into your accounting records. By following this guide consistently, your financial transactions will be entered in a logical way, and it will make it easy to extract usable bits of information about your business activities.

The primary purpose for your financial accounting system is to be able to develop the needed financial statements at the end of the month, quarter, or year, so the chart of accounts is ordered based on those statements. First, you list your balance sheet accounts starting with assets, then liabilities, and finally equity accounts. Next, you add the accounts for the profit and loss statement—income accounts, and then expense accounts.

Most companies work with computerized accounting systems that include charts of accounts for common business operations. Your first step in using one of those systems will be to choose a chart of accounts for a similar business and then edit that list based on accounts you expect to need in your business. Your list doesn't have to be perfect. The chart of accounts is not cast in stone, so you can add accounts throughout the life of your business. Generally, it is not a good idea to subtract an account in the middle of an accounting year, but you can retire accounts at the end of the year if you find that they are no longer useful for your business needs.

Just to give you an idea of the types of accounts common to each category, here are some of most common account types:

Asset Accounts

Cash in Checking—This is always the first account. It is the account that will most likely handle the majority of your transactions through the year. All revenue and expenses will at some point during the year point pass through this account.

Cash in Savings—This account will be used for any surplus cash until you decide how you want to use it. Savings accounts generally generate interest income for the business until a better alternative for the cash is found.

Cash on Hand—This account is usually used for petty cash or other cash you keep on hand at your business rather than in the bank.

Accounts Receivable—This account is used if you sell any of your products or services on credit. You only need this account if you are operating your business on an accrual basis. If you are planning a cash operation, you only record receipts when the cash is actually received, so there would be no need for this account.

Inventory—This account is used to record and track the products you purchase to sell.

Vehicles—This account is used to record and track any vehicles you purchase for your business.

Furniture and Fixtures—This account is used to record and track any furniture or fixtures you purchase for the business.

Other Assets—This account tracks any assets that don't specifically have their own separate account.

In addition to these basic accounts, you would add accounts that are specific to your asset holdings, such as land, buildings, and other assets. Many businesses also have an asset account called organization costs where they track their initial start-up costs. Start-up costs cannot be written off entirely during the first year of the business but must be amortized over time. The amount of time will depend on the type of expense. Your tax adviser would help you determine those write-offs based on IRS rules.

> Many businesses also have an asset account called organization costs where they track their initial start-up costs.

Liability Accounts

Accounts Payable—This account tracks all the money a business owes to vendors, contractors, suppliers, and consultants, provided the debt must be paid within one year.

Sales Tax Collected—When you sell your product, you are usually obligated to collect sales taxes. These taxes are actually a liability that must be tracked until you actually pay them to the local, state, or federal government entities.

Accrued Payroll Taxes—This account is used to track any payroll taxes you withhold from employees' paychecks until they are due to local, state, or federal government entities.

Credit Card Payable—This account is used to track business credit card accounts. Many businesses will set up a separate account for each of its major cards, such as Credit Cards Payable—Citicorp Visa and Credits Cards Payable—American Express.

Loans Payable—This account tracks any loans that are payable over more than a one-year basis. Many businesses will establish a separate payable account for each major loan. For example, a mortgage on a building would be Loans Payable—State Bank, and a car loan would be Loans Payable—Citizens Bank.

Other Liabilities—This account tracks any liabilities that do not have their own separate account.

Equity Accounts

Common Stock—This account tracks the value of all outstanding shares of stock.

Retained Earnings—This account tracks profits and losses each year.

Capital—This account tracks the initial investment in the business by the owners. This type of account will be found in a sole proprietorship or partnership but not in a corporation. Capital invested in corporations is shown in Common Stock or possibly Preferred Stock accounts.

Drawing—This account tracks any withdrawals by the owners. This type of account would only be found in a sole proprietorship or partnership but not in a corporation.

Here's how this chart of accounts would be used to develop a balance sheet at the end of an accounting period:

Assets	Liabilities
Cash in Checking	Accounts Payable
Cash in Savings	Sales Tax Collected
Cash on Hand	Accrued Payroll Taxes
Accounts Receivable	Credit Card Payable
Inventory	Loans Payable
Vehicles	Other Liabilities
Furniture and Fixtures	
Other Assets	**Equity**
	Common Stock
	Retained Earnings
	Capital
	Drawing
Total Assets	**Total Liabilities and Equity**

As a manager in a non-accounting department, your primary responsibilities for the balance sheet will be to monitor any asset or liability accounts that involve your department's activities. For example, if you are in sales, you'll want to track the accounts receivable accounts for customers to be certain they are paying the bills. You certainly don't want to sell product to customers who don't pay. If you are in advertising, you want to be certain that bills are paid on time for advertisements you have placed or you may have a hard time placing the next set of ads. You probably would get a report from accounting regarding bills in the accounts payable accounts related to your advertising activities.

Every department likely gets reports periodically about accounts for which they are responsible. Understanding how to read these reports and knowing what they mean for your department's activities are critical skills for all managers. The reports related to income and expense accounts can be even more crucial to your department's success at generating profits for the company. Let's look at the key accounts in the chart of accounts that impact those numbers.

Income Accounts

Sales of Goods or Services—This is the account used to book the revenue from sales or services or both.

Sales Discounts—This account is used to track any discounts you offer to your customers. You should always enter full price in Sales of Goods or Services and track discounts using this account so you have a good idea of the level of discounts you offered to generate sales.

Sales Returns and Allowances—This account is used to track any returns or allowances you offered customers who were unhappy with their purchases. You want to carefully monitor this account and how frequently these adjustments need to be offered.

Other Income—This account is used to track any income earned that is not part of your normal business operations.

Interest Income—This account is used to track any interest earnings from your company's savings account.

Sales of Fixed Assets—This account is used to track any profits you may receive if you sell any of the company's assets.

Sales Costs

Even if you don't sell products, you will still have a cost of sales for offering your services. Developing a list of accounts that helps you carefully track your costs is critical to understanding your profit margin. Looking at these costs and finding ways to minimize them is a good way to increase that profit margin. These costs are tracked separately from other company expenses, so you can calculate gross sales and subtract your cost of sales to determine your gross profit.

> Developing a list of accounts that helps you carefully track your costs is critical to understanding your profit margin.

- **Purchases**—This account is used to track purchases of goods you plan to sell.
- **Purchase Discounts**—This account is used to track any discounts you get from vendors.
- **Purchase Returns and Allowances**—This account tracks any returns or allowances you got from a vendor for goods or services that were not satisfactory.
- **Freight Charges**—This account is used to track the cost of shipping the goods you sell.

These income accounts are then used to determine cost of goods sold and your gross profit. Here is how you calculate sales and cost of goods sold using these accounts.

Sales

	Goods Sold
Minus:	Sales Discounts
Minus:	Sales Returns and Allowances
Equals:	Total Sales

Cost of Goods Sold

	Purchases
Minus:	Purchase Discounts
Minus:	Purchase Returns and Allowances
Minus:	Freight Charges
Equals:	Total Cost of Goods Sold

On the profit and loss statement, these numbers would be used at the top of the statement to calculate gross profit. Here is how they would appear on the profit and loss statement:

Sales	$
Cost of Goods Sold	$( )*
Gross Profit	$

*On a financial report, numbers enclosed in parentheses are an indication of a negative number.

Expense Accounts

Advertising tracks anything that involves promoting the product, not just paid ads in the media. Flyers and direct mail expenses would also be recorded in this account.

Amortization Expense is used to track any expenses for items that are amortized. This is similar to depreciation but is used for intangible (anything that you cannot physically touch) items. We'll discus amortization and depreciation in greater detail later.

Bank Service Charges is the account used to track any fees you must pay to the bank to service your business accounts.

Depreciation Expense is used to track any expenses for items that are depreciated. This includes vehicles, equipment, and other tangible (physical) items owned by the business that have a useful life of more than one year.

Dues and Subscriptions tracks any expenses for membership in business or professional organizations as well as subscriptions for publications related to your business.

Equipment Rental tracks any expenses related to renting equipment for your business.

Insurance tracks all expenses for insurance for business assets, as well as life insurance on key business personnel.

Interest Expense is used to track any interest expenses related to running your business, such as interest on a car loan or mortgage payment.

Income Taxes is used to track any income tax expenses paid by the business.

Legal and Accounting is used for recording all business expenses related to legal and accounting fees.

Meals and Entertainment tracks any expenses for meals or events related to your business activities.

Miscellaneous Expense is a catchall term for any business expenses that do not fall into a specific account.

Office Expense is used to track expenses related to running your business's offices.

Payroll Taxes is used to track any taxes paid by the employer, such as the employer's share of Social Security and Medicare.

Postage is used to track any shipping expenses including items shipped by the U.S. Postal Service as well as by private services such as Federal Express and UPS.

Rent Expense is used to track any rental expenses for business offices, warehouses, or retail space needed to operate the business.

Repairs and Maintenance tracks all repairs and maintenance on business assets.

Salaries and Wages tracks money paid to your employees.

Supplies tracks supplies needed for your business.

Travel is used to track any expenses related to business travel.

Telephone Expense is used to track all expenses related to your office phones and cell phones.

Utilities is used to track the payments you make to utility companies, such as gas, electric, and water.

Vehicle Expenses is used to track expenses related to operating the company's vehicles.

As you can see, expense accounts tend to be the most numerous class of accounts. Keeping a close watch on expenses is one of the best ways for a business to improve its profit margins. Breaking down the key elements into separate accounts helps managers carefully monitor the expenses related to each aspect of business operations.

Here is what a profit and loss statement would look like for a business using these accounts.

Sales	$
Cost of Goods Sold	$( )
Gross Profits	$
Advertising	$( )
Amortization Expense	$( )
Bank Service Charges	$( )
Depreciation Expense	$( )
Dues and Subscriptions	$( )
Equipment Rental	$( )
Insurance	$( )
Interest Expense	$( )
Income Taxes	$( )
Legal and Accounting	$( )
Meals and Entertainment	$( )
Miscellaneous Expense	$( )
Office Expense	$( )
Payroll Taxes	$( )
Postage	$( )
Rent Expense	$( )
Repairs and Maintenance	$( )
Salaries and Wages	$( )
Supplies	$( )
Travel	$( )
Telephone Expense	$( )
Utilities	$( )
Vehicle Expenses	$( )
Net Income	$

Tracking Your Operations

Once the chart of accounts is developed, you now have the elements you need to develop the general ledger, which summarizes all your business financial transactions. The entries that detail your transactions are all posted in the general ledger or its sub ledgers or journals. Some accounts are so large, such as accounts receivable or sales, that most businesses will have a separate ledger or journal to track these accounts and only post to the general ledger at the end of the month. The general ledger is the tool used to develop all your financial statements.

Now that we have the building blocks in place, let's look at how these financial accounting tools are used to track your day-to-day operations. Before even opening the doors, you need to be certain your controls are in place to track transactions and document them. Without good controls in place, you risk:

- Assets being used without proper authorization.
- Transactions that are not included in your books.
- Loss or theft of assets or key documents.
- Entries made in your accounting system to hide instances of theft, fraud, or embezzlement.

Everyone, including the owner, must adhere strictly to the accounting controls you put in place. Just as with ethics rules, employees follow the lead of management. If management is lax about how carefully it follows the accounting procedures, staff will tend to be lax as well. The more serious you, as the owner, and your managers are about maintaining strict accounting procedures, the greater the chance is that your accounting rules will be followed. Here are ways to avoid accounting errors caused by poor accounting controls.

Just as with ethics rules, employees follow the lead of management.

Loss of business assets can be avoided with controls in place that prevent these common mistakes:

- Invoices might be paid more than once if you don't have a system that accurately tracks payments and documents all payments that have been made.
- Unpaid accounts can go undetected if you don't have a clear process for recording sales and carefully tracking the payment of any credit given to customers.
- Loss of goods you sell could escalate out of control if you don't carefully monitor inventory levels. Losses could be from theft or breakage.
- Cash could disappear if there is not a concrete process in place for monitoring all employees who handle cash.

The most important step you can take when setting up internal accounting controls is to practice careful separation of duties. For example, any time cash is expected to change hands, the task should be separated between at least two employees. When paying bills, one employee should be responsible for researching invoices and writing out the checks. A second employee should have responsibility for reviewing the payments, signing the checks, and sending them out. The employee you assign to the preparation of the payroll should be separate from the one who actually has the right to sign and give out the checks. Here are three basic rules to follow when setting up internal accounting controls:

1. Any person handling assets (cash, credit, or checks) should be separate from the person recording the transactions.
2. Authorization of transactions should be separated from the people or persons who will actually disperse the cash.
3. Do not assign duties related to operational responsibilities to someone who handles record-keeping responsibilities.

When designing your internal accounting controls, remember that they too have a cost. You should never design a system so cumbersome that the costs of implementing it outweigh the potential savings from avoiding error, theft, or embezzlement. For example, in keeping strict controls on inventory, you must be careful not to design a system so restrictive that your salespeople are not able to satisfy the needs of customers. Plan to meet with staff affected by any significant internal control change after it is implemented to be certain you understand the full impact and costs of its implementation.

Tracking Sales

Once you have controls in place for handling cash, the tracking of cash sales can be fairly well automated using cash registers and proper close-out procedures at the end of the day. Credit sales are more complicated because not only do the day's activities need to be tracked, but proper record-keeping must be in place to be certain that credit accounts are paid on time. Customers who do not pay on time must be quickly detected and cut off from future purchases until their accounts are paid in full.

Credit sales are monitored in the accounts receivable account. Periodic reports should be generated that track accounts that are paid on time, sixty days late, ninety days late, and others more than ninety days late. Policies should be in place to determine how late payers will be handled and when late payers will be cut off from future purchases.

Monitoring Costs

For the costs side of the sales equation, there are two key areas that management must carefully monitor. One is inventory control and the other is cost control. There are actually two methods for managing inventory. One is called the periodic inventory method and the second is the perpetual inventory method.

Under the periodic method, a physical count of inventory is done periodically—usually daily, monthly, or yearly, whichever makes sense for the type of business you operate. Changes to the inventory account in the assets section of the general ledger are made only after the physical count.

Perpetual inventory methods adjust the Inventory account with each transaction. Computerized inventory control is definitely a necessity for perpetual inventory. In fact, many major retailers link their cash registers to their inventory control system. Even using this method, it is still a good idea to do periodic physical checks to be sure what is on your shelves or in your warehouse matches what is in your computer. When you go into a store and the clerk cannot complete the sale without a stock number, this is usually a sign that the store is using the perpetual inventory control method. Yes, it can be frustrating when you're stuck at the cash register as the clerk scrambles to find the right code.

Not only must you track how much inventory you have on hand, but you also must know which inventory was bought first and which last. The value of inventory must be calculated to determine costs. There are actually five ways

Accounts Receivable Prime Target for Abuse

Clerks who record transactions in accounts receivable payments can take advantage of their position to pocket cash that comes in. One common scheme is called lapping or kiting. In this scheme, the clerk takes the money received by Jane Doe. When payment is received from John Doe, his payment is credited to Jane Doe. The next payment received from Michael Doe is used to credit John Doe. Periodic checks on records for which you know payments have been received will help catch a clerk implementing this scheme, but you certainly don't have the time to check every payment. Many companies send out periodic notices to customers asking them to verify their account balance. This helps find any errors or deliberate schemes impacting your accounts receivable accounts. A good cash control in place for many companies is a lock-box system where payments are send directly to the bank, money is deposited into the company account, and a report of payments is then sent to accounts receivable.

from which to choose your costing methods: last in, first out (LIFO); first in, first out (FIFO); average costing; specific identification costing; and lower of cost or market (LCM). The costing method you choose can greatly impact your bottom line.

Last in, first out (LIFO) assumes that the last items put on the shelf are the first items to be sold. *First in, first out* (FIFO) assumes that the first items put on the shelf are the first items to be sold. *Average costing* is the simplest method. It doesn't track which items are sold but just maintains a running average of costs per unit sold. In reality, no one from the accounting department actually goes out to the shelves to identify which item was sold; instead, these are just assumptions used to calculate inventory costs.

> Last in, first out (LIFO) assumes that the last items put on the shelf are the first items to be sold.

Specific identification is the only inventory method that actually tracks each unit of inventory individually. This is used primarily for big-ticket items, such as a car or major appliance.

The *lower of cost or market* (LCM) system is rarely used. The costs are calculated by whichever amount is lower—the actual cost of the inventory or the current market value. Companies whose inventory costs are rapidly changing in the marketplace may use this.

FIFO is used most often by businesses whose goods spoil quickly or frequently become obsolete. As prices go up, the FIFO method gives you the lower cost of goods sold because goods bought at the lower prices are the first to be used. A company using this system will have a better bottom line or net profit because cost of goods sold is lower and therefore gross sales are higher. Higher profits also mean a higher tax bite.

Companies whose inventory does not quickly spoil or become obsolete use LIFO. When the cost of goods rises, they first sell the more costly items. Cost of goods sold will be higher, and therefore gross sales will be lower. The net profit, of course, will be lower as well, so the tax bite will be lower.

Companies whose cost of goods sold fluctuates frequently throughout the year usually use the average costing method. This tends to even out the peaks and valleys and minimize the impact on the bottom line. As a manager, it's important to understand which method of inventory costing is being used and how that method impacts the bottom line for your department's activities.

Adjusting Your Accounts

Adjustments are also made to company profits either once a month or once a year to account for expenses such as depreciation and amortization. Both have two roles to play in an organization—one for business statements and a second for tax returns. Some businesses actually use two different methods of calculating depreciation because the government allows faster depreciation write-offs as tax incentives to buy new equipment. While businesses generally take advantage of any incentive that lowers their taxes, the faster write-off may not make sense when reporting their bottom line to investors and also when determining what equipment or other assets are ready for replacement.

While keeping net profits as low as possible for the tax man might make sense, most businesses want to give investors the rosiest outlook possible within financial reporting rules. For this reason, many businesses keep two sets of books for purposes of calculating depreciation, one based on tax schedules and one based on normal life span for the asset. Normal life spans could differ depending on the type of business. For example, a trucking company may believe their trucks need to be replaced more frequently than a small business that uses a truck occasionally for business purposes.

The IRS has official tables that specify the life span for various types of business equipment. Here is the official IRS table:

IRS DEPRECIATION TABLE FOR BUSINESS EQUIPMENT

Property Class Recovery Period	Business Equipment
3-year property over two years old	Tractor units and horses
5-year property	Cars, taxis, buses, trucks, computers, office machines, research equipment, and cattle
7-year property	Office furniture and fixtures
10-year property	Water transportation equipment, single-purpose agricultural or horticultural structures, and fruit- or nut-bearing vines and trees

IRS DEPRECIATION TABLE FOR BUSINESS EQUIPMENT (CONTINUED)

Property Class Recovery Period	Business Equipment
15-year property	Land improvements, such as shrubbery, fences, roads, and bridges
20-year property	Farm buildings that are not agricultural or horticultural structures
27.5-year property	Residential rental property
39-year property	Nonresidential real estate, including a home office but not including the value of land

Tax incentives to write off equipment vary depending on types of businesses. Consult a tax adviser when trying to determine which method to use for depreciation to get the best tax advantage.

Major corporations frequently handle depreciation for the management of assets and reporting requirements differently. For accounting purposes, only one type of depreciation can be used—straight-line depreciation. This method allocates costs over the expected lifetime of the asset. Using the Property Class Recovery Chart, depreciation is calculated by dividing the cost basis of the asset by the number of years to determine the depreciation expense. These expenses are usually recorded in the accounting system at the end of the year when doing final adjustments before preparing the financial statements. If a business decides that their assets' life spans are different than those listed as standard IRS recovery periods, the business can develop its own recovery periods for its property classes. The business would then need to document the recovery periods chosen and use those periods consistently.

In addition to using depreciation to report expenses, the accumulated depreciation numbers also help businesses monitor when an asset is nearing the end of its useful life and plan for replacement. Monitoring accumulated depreciation numbers for assets is a very useful tool for future business planning.

Keeping Accounting and Financial Records

Your business will generate lots of paper, and you need to make plans to keep most of it in order to have the necessary documentation for the IRS as well as for your investors and the banks with which you deal. At some point, the paper can overwhelm you, and it's critical to know what you must keep and what can be thrown away.

When deciding what to keep, there are a number of things to consider:

- Keep any records you need to back up your financial statements in case you are questioned by the government or your investors.
- Keep any receipts or other materials to prove tax deductions you expect to take in case the IRS audits you.
- Keep cash sales records so you have what you need to report and pay sales taxes.
- Keep records that will help you prove to a contractor or vendor that you have paid any money due them.
- Keep employee records regarding compensation and benefits.
- Keep any correspondence regarding legal disputes that arise from your business activities.

How long must you keep all this paperwork? The answer varies depending on the type of paperwork. Records you are keeping solely for the purposes of supporting your tax returns can be destroyed once they are four years old. The IRS does not audit returns that are more than three years old.

If questions of fraud or embezzlement arise, however, financial records could be needed beyond that date. In that case, the statute of limitations for the state in which your business in based will determine how far back the records should be kept. To be safe, many businesses retain records

Tax Advantages of Depreciation

Businesses can use numerous types of depreciation methods to gain tax advantages by depreciating their assets. The quickest way to write off an asset for tax purposes is called Section 179, which allows a business to deduct up to 100 percent of what it spends on equipment each year. The maximum dollar amount a business can deduct is $100,000. This is a dramatic increase over the $25,000 that was permitted prior to the passage of the 2003 tax bill. Other methods for accelerating depreciation are also used to reduce a business's tax bill by writing off the assets as quickly as possible using what the IRS calls Modified Accelerated Cost Recovery System (MACRS). For more details on MACRS and depreciation for tax purposes, read IRS Publication 946, "How to Depreciate Property," at *www.irs.gov/pub/irs-pdf/p946.pdf*.

Record-Keeping in a Digital World

Many businesses are moving to digital storage for their records. With the widespread availability of scanners, this task has become much simpler and less costly. Even small companies can buy a copier that can be used as a scanner, printer, and fax machine, making digital storage an easy option for any business. Besides taking up a lot less space than paper records, digital storage offers another key benefit. The records are easier to retrieve and search. Once found, they can even be e-mailed to the person who needs them. Many companies, banks, newspapers, and libraries are still using microfilm to store their records, which certainly is another method to consider. Either method will likely be cheaper than paying for storage space for all the paper you must keep on a long-term basis.

for a minimum of six or seven years. Some records, such as board meeting minutes, are kept indefinitely.

Personnel records must be kept throughout the entire time an employee works for the company. After that, records can be destroyed once the employee has left the company for more than three years unless the employee has rights to a retirement plan. Then you'll need to save those records and any records of compensation that could be used to calculate retirement benefits.

Hiring and Paying Your Employees

You may think that hiring employees is primarily the venue of human resources, but hiring policies must be carefully integrated between the human resources and the accounting departments. As a manager, you must adhere to the rules set up by accounting as well as human resources when hiring and firing employees.

Even before a company can begin hiring, it must apply for an Employer Identification Number (EIN). A corporation will be given this number when it incorporates. A small business that has not incorporated will have to apply for an EIN before it can start hiring.

On the accounting side, the department usually gets involved with information collection starting with the Social Security number. Also, a company must get proof of U.S. citizenship or proof that the employee has the right to work in the United States.

As you set up procedures for your employees and contractors, you need to be sure that you understand the differences between the two in the eyes of the IRS. If you try to avoid paying Medicare and Social Security taxes plus other benefits by hiring all your employees as independent contractors, it could come back to haunt you later if the IRS determines these contractors were actually employees. Companies must pay the employer's half of Medicare and Social Security taxes for all its employees but are not required to pay them for independent contractors. The IRS has a 20-point test for determining whether a person can be considered an employee or contractor. Here are the key questions you must consider:

1. *Is the individual's work vital to the company's core business?* A person is considered an employee if the answer is yes. Contractors usually provide services for nonessential business activities.
2. *Did you train the individual to perform tasks in a specific way?* Employees are usually trained. Contractors are usually skilled professionals who do not need training to perform the services you require.
3. *Do you (or can you) instruct the individual as to when, where, and how the work is performed?* For employees, you can control these aspects of performance. Contractors must be given flexibility into how, when, and where the work is performed, provided they meet contract requirements.
4. *Do you (or can you) control the sequence or order of the work performed?* Again, you can control the way the work is performed by employees. Contractors instead are measured by contract-specified outcomes and not by the way they do the work.
5. *Do you (or can you) set the hours of work for the individual?* You can set work schedules for employees, but not for contractors. Contractors instead are given deadlines to meet and set their own hours.
6. *Do you (or can you) require the individual to perform work personally?* An employee must do the work personally, but a contractor can hire others to do the work either on their own staff or with subcontractors.
7. *Do you (or can you) prohibit the individual from hiring, supervising, and paying assistants?* Employers can forbid employees from hiring assistants, but contractors must be able to make this decision. If contractors do hire others, the contractor pays the assistants. Usually a contractor will bid for the work and include in the bid funds for paying others.
8. *Does the individual perform regular and continuous service for you?* Employees, whether full-time or part-time, do work on a regular

and continuous basis. Contractors are hired on a project-by-project basis. New contracts are drawn up for each project

9. *Does the individual provide services on a substantially full-time basis to your company?* You can put limitations on whether a full-time employee can work for others, but a contractor must have the freedom to work for others provided they accomplish the contracted tasks on time.

10. *Is your company the sole or major source of income for the individual?* This will be true for employees. Contractors usually work for more than one company at a time.

11. *Is the work performed on your premises?* Employees usually work on-site unless they have been granted permission to work elsewhere. Contractors can choose to work on-site (if space is available) or at a location of their choosing.

12. *Do you (or can you) require the individual to submit regular reports either written or oral?* Employees can be asked to provide regular status or activity reports. Contractors are obligated to complete work on time. Many contractors will give regular reports either orally or verbally as part of their customer service, but these reports cannot be required unless they are part of the original contract.

13. *Do you pay the individual by the hour, week, or month?* Employees are paid at fixed times. Contractors are paid based on contract specifications, usually when the work is completed or on a particular scale based on percentage of work completed. Payment schedules are negotiated at the time of contract.

14. *Do you pay the individual's travel and business expenses?* Employees are usually compensated for their travel and business expenses. Contractors usually include anticipated travel and business expenses in the contract as part of the initial bid.

15. *Do you furnish tools and equipment for the individual?* Employees usually are given all the tools and equipment they need. Contractors usually provide their tools and equipment.

16. *Does the individual have a significant investment in facilities, tools, or equipment?* Employees usually use the facilities, tools, and equipment provided by the employer. Contractors usually provide these items themselves.

17. *Can the individual realize a profit or loss from his or her services to your company?* Your employees don't expect to realize a profit or loss; instead they expect a steady paycheck. Contractors do risk nonpayment if they do not fulfill contract obligations and usually expect to make a profit from their work.

18. *Does the individual make his or her services available to the general public?* Employees don't sell their services to the public; contractors do.

19. *Can the individual terminate the relationship without liability?* Employees can quit at any time. Contractors must complete their contract stipulations or risk penalties for nonperformance of contract.

20. *Do you have the right to discharge the individual at any time?* Employees can usually be fired at any time, provided labor laws are followed. Contractors can only be discharged for failing to perform contracted services.

Microsoft "Temps" Sue for Benefits

Microsoft faced a lawsuit brought by people who were not hired as full-time employees and not paid benefits but essentially performed their duties that way. The employees were labeled "temporary employees," "freelancers," or "independent contractors." Some were employees of "staffing" firms. The lawsuit was filed to recover benefits, including participation in the Microsoft Employee Stock Purchase Plan, because these workers believed they should have been hired as employees.

The suit was filed in 1992, and the workers won the case in court with a final appeal decided by the Ninth Circuit Court of Appeals ruling that the employees were entitled to participate in Microsoft's stock purchase plan, which cost Microsoft millions. As a result of this landmark case, many companies realized they must change their policies relating to contract labor and temporary staff. Companies became more careful about controlling the length of time someone could be a "contractor" and could be "on assignment" at the corporate site. They also set up payroll differentiations and stricter policies for use of temporary agencies.

As you plan your staff, be certain you review these key questions and know whether you are designing the work for an employee or contractor. If you want the person to work under the controls of an employee, but you try to save money by hiring them as a contractor, your company could face IRS scrutiny. Review your plans with the accounting and human resources departments to be certain you are following company policy on employee hiring.

When an employee is hired, they fill out two forms, one for the IRS—the W-4, which indicates tax withholding information, and is given to accounting so they can prepare salary or wage payments—and I-9, which is required by the 1986 Immigration Reform and Control Act and is used to prove U.S. citizenship or prove the right to work in the United States if a person is a resident alien.

Each employee is hired with a specific status and pay period in mind: weekly (52 times a year), biweekly (26 times per year), semimonthly (24 times per year), or monthly (12 times per year). A business has a lot of flexibility on setting pay periods, but once determined they should be clearly stated. The accounting department has primary responsibility for paying employees on time and deducting all necessary tax payments. At the end of each quarter and the end of the year, the accounting department also completes all required local, state, and federal tax forms related to employee hiring.

> A business has a lot of flexibility on setting pay periods, but once determined they should be clearly stated.

Closing Out Your Books

As you operate the business throughout the year, you will be making journal entries for each business transaction. At the end of each month, the accounting department closes the books and reports on the company's financial status. The process of closing the books can be tedious, but it is critical to get a snapshot of how the business is doing.

The first books to be closed are the cash journals. This includes the cash receipts journal (which tracks all incoming cash transactions) and the cash disbursements journal (which tracks all outgoing cash transactions). The information in these journals is reconciled with the bank statements. If any differences are found, they must be researched and corrected before any accounts can be closed. Changes that need to be made in the cash journals can impact any account and must be found before closing the other accounts so corrections can be posted. The most common errors will be sales or returns that were not properly recorded or bills paid without a proper entry.

Sometimes, these can be innocent mistakes; at other times, they are an indication of a serious internal control problem.

The next accounts to be closed out will be accounts receivable (which tracks all items sold on credit) and accounts payable (which tracks all bills paid for obligations of less than one year). Bills will be sent to customers for any outstanding balances. The accounting department will prepare a report on the status of each customer's account to determine who is paying on time and who is late. The report is organized by columns labeled Customer Name, Balance Due, Current Month, 60 Days, 90 Days+. Accounting staff usually start more aggressive collections once an account is more than 60 days overdue and likely cut off a customer at 90 or 120 days.

When the accounts payable account is closed, any outstanding bills not yet paid will be entered as accruals. This will allow the business to recognize costs for the month that have not yet been paid. Accrual entries will be posted to their proper expense accounts. As the accruals are paid the next month, the accrual account will diminish in value.

Once all corrections are made to the accounts receivable and accounts payable accounts, their final totals are posted to the general ledger. This process of closing accounts, reviewing for errors, and posting to the general ledger will be carried out for all open accounts.

The balances in asset and liability accounts are carried over to the next month, while income and expense accounts are zeroed out at month end. Any profit or loss is then posted to the retained earnings account. When the total of all assets accounts is equal to the total of all liability and equity accounts, then the books are in balance. This is tested using a procedure called the *trial balance*, which is a calculation that tests the accuracy of the entries for the month. If the trial balance shows that the books are not in balance, then accounting must go back and find the reason for the differences. Sometimes the books balance on the first try, but more often than not accounting will have to run a series of trial balances before all errors are found. Once the books are in balance, the accounting department can prepare the month-end, quarter-end, or year-end financial statements.

> **Chapter 6**

Managerial Accounting

New Manufacturing Methods Change the Face of Managerial Accounting

Managerial accounting has changed in recent years to respond to changes in manufacturing processes and information technology. Just-in-time manufacturing, which focuses on reducing inventories and the lead time needed to produce goods while still meeting the needs of the customer and maintaining or improving customer satisfaction, has increased the need for accurate numbers on a daily basis. Managerial accounting is a crucial function to fulfill this need in the manufacturing environment. Also, a technique called flexible manufacturing systems has dramatically impacted the role of managerial accounting. Dell is probably the best-known company using flexible manufacturing, which means the company has short setup times to quickly respond to customer orders. Customers call in and work with Dell computer specialists to design a computer that meets their needs. Dell then builds it, usually in about a two- to three-week turnaround time.

Understanding Managerial Accounting

As discussed in the last chapter, financial accounting is primarily concerned with providing information to external organizations, such as investors and creditors; managerial accounting focuses on the needs of internal operations. Managerial accounting uses the information collected by financial accounting to make key decisions, plan operations, and control activities by manipulating the data in various ways to calculate costing, plan for profit-making, prepare budgets, and decide on investments. In this chapter, methods for making use of financial accounting information to direct and control business operations will be discussed.

Managerial accountants provide a series of reports to assist managers with planning effectively, directing day-to-day operations, and solving problems through analyzing data and developing alternative methods. By helping managers stay on target and providing alternative solutions when problems arise, managerial accountants can become a critical element in the success of all departments.

At the beginning of each year, top executives determine the company's goals and formalize those plans using budgeting. Tracking success in meeting those plans is critical for managers. If they are off target on spending or income generation, profit goals will not be met. Managers need accurate and timely information about their actual results versus their budgets to be certain they are on track. Managerial accountants prepare performance reports that detail the comparison of budgeted data with actual data for a specific time period, most commonly on a monthly basis. If these performance reports indicate the department is off budget, the manager must find out why and correct the problem. If the performance report indicates all is going as planned, he or she can concentrate on something else. The performance reports are a critical aid that helps a manager determine the problem spots and plan his or her time effectively to keep the department on track.

While monthly performance reports aid in overall management, accounting details are needed more regularly for managing direct operations. Changes in cost data is a critical piece of information that can't be put off until the end of the month. For example, managers of the sales floor must know as quickly as possible if there has been a significant increase in the cost of products, because pricing may need to be adjusted quickly to keep profit margins on track. Store managers and marketing departments rely on managerial accountants for up-to-date information that could impact the cost-price relationship. Store managers also need daily reports on sales volumes and inventory levels to effectively manage their stores. Purchasing needs the same information to be certain that orders are placed on time so products will be on the shelves to satisfy customers. If you think about it, accurate and timely information from accounting is critical to almost all functions of a business.

When a manager finds his numbers are off-track, he will work with managerial accounting to find solutions to get the department back on track. The managerial accountants will target problem areas and recommend alternative solutions. Each alternative will have different costs and benefits, and the manager will need to decide which alternative best meets his department's needs. For example, when executives are trying to decide whether reducing prices, increasing advertising, or both can maintain or increase market, it is up to the managerial accounts to come up with the numbers to support this decision-making.

Changing the Way Managerial Accounting Information Is Distributed

Before the age of databases and the Internet, managerial accountants circulated lots of paper to supply the reports that managers needed. Today, managerial accountants post their reports on the company intranet, and managers access these reports on their desktops. Employees can check inventory levels on their computers rather than having to contact the person responsible for inventory control each time they have a question. Databases and the Internet have made it possible to reduce staff time spent on gathering and dispersing needed information.

The Watchdog for Financial Reporting

Financial reporting standards are set by the Financial Accounting Standards Board (FASB), which has been the designated organization in the private sector since 1973. These financial and accounting standards govern the preparation of financial reports. FASB is recognized as the authoritative source for this information by the Securities and Exchange Commission (SEC) and the American Institute of Certified Public Accountants (AICPA). As the FASB acknowledges, these standards are critical to our economy because they provide investors, creditors, auditors, and others with credible, transparent, and comparable financial information. Cracks in this credibility were certainly evident as scandals such as Enron and Tyco broke. Rebuilding this credibility is a critical task for the future of the U.S. economy. While these standards are mandatory for financial reporting done by the financial accounting department, managerial accounting is not required to abide by the same rigid rules when developing its reports for internal use.

The primary role of the managerial accountant is to gather the information needed and to present it in a way that is most useful to department managers. The ability to summarize the accounting information into a format that aids decision-making is crucial. Managers do not need, nor do they have the time to sort through, all the detail; instead they need summaries that help them target the problem areas and then focus on the detail in only those areas.

Managerial accounting focuses on the future rather than reporting on the past, which is the primary role of financial accounting. While financial accounting has formal methods of reporting its data, such as the Financial Accounting Standards Board rules for producing the balance sheet or profit and loss statement, managerial accounting is more flexible and puts its emphasis on the data that are relevant to a specific decision or task. While financial accounting seeks to report on the company as a whole, managerial accounting focuses on segments of the organization to aid in decision-making.

Costing

The first critical element any business needs to understand before it can plan for the future is the cost of the products it plans to manufacture and sell. Even if manufacturing a product is not part of the business plan, knowing the costs of goods to be sold is critical. First, let's look at the elements that go into determining manufacturing costs:

- Direct materials
- Direct labor
- Manufacturing overhead

Direct materials or *raw materials* include any materials that become an integral part of a finished product, such as the wood used to build a table. A finished product for one company could be a raw material for another company. For example, the logging company that cut down and processed the wood considers the wood sold to the furniture company finished product, but the furniture manufacturer considers it raw material.

Direct labor costs are the labor costs that can be physically traced to the actual production of a product. For example, assembly line workers would be considered direct labor costs. If labor costs are not directly traceable, they are considered indirect labor. As an example, people designated to the operation of the plant, such as janitors or security personnel, would be indirect labor. While one might be able to calculate some fraction of indirect labor to the production of each individual unit produced, it would not make sense to take the time to calculate and monitor these costs as direct labor. When calculating direct labor costs, a company must consider idle time (time the direct laborers could not work because of machine breakdowns, materials shortages, power failures, etc.), overtime premiums (overtime paid to get a product out on time), and fringe benefits (including insurance, retirement programs, and other employee benefits).

Manufacturing overhead encompasses all the costs that go into manufacturing a product that are not designated as direct materials or direct labor. These costs can include items such as indirect labor, indirect materials, utilities, property taxes, insurance, depreciation on factory facilities, maintenance, repairs, and administrative functions.

In order to price its goods properly, a company must determine non-manufacturing costs, which include marketing or selling costs and administrative costs. Marketing or selling costs include all costs necessary to secure customer orders and get the finished product or service into the hands of customers. Examples of these costs include advertising, shipping, travel by sales staff, sales commissions, sales salaries, and warehousing costs. Administrative costs include all executive, organization, and clerical costs that are not included as direct costs in either the production or marketing of a product. Examples of administrative costs include executive compensation, general accounting, secretarial, public relations, and other costs that are attributed to the general administration of the company as a whole.

Managerial accounting breaks down these costs into six categories to help managers control day-to-day operations, as well as plan for the future. These categories include:

- Variable costs
- Fixed costs
- Direct costs
- Indirect costs
- Controllable costs
- Uncontrollable costs

We've already discussed direct and indirect costs. Now we'll take a closer look at these other cost factors.

When trying to determine whether a cost is a fixed cost or a variable cost, consider how the cost will be affected when there is a change in business activity. When looking at total costs, a *variable cost* will increase or decrease as business activity increases and decreases. For example, direct material costs will increase as more of the product is made, but they will decrease if there is a cutback in production. A *fixed cost*, such as the amount paid to lease a piece of machinery each month, will be the same even if the plant is shut down for a period of time.

When you look at fixed versus variable costs per unit, the impact is opposite that of total costs. A variable cost will remain constant per unit. For example, if a part that is put into every unit costs $5, that $5 cost will remain constant for each unit made. A fixed cost will change per unit based on the level of activity. For example, if it costs $50,000 a month to rent a piece of equipment used in manufacturing, the cost per unit will vary depending on the number of units produced. Here is a chart showing that relationship:

MONTHLY RENTAL COST	NUMBER OF UNITS PRODUCED	AVERAGE COST PER UNIT
$50,000	100	$500
$50,000	1,000	$50
$50,000	10,000	$5

As you can see, the fixed cost per unit drops dramatically as the volume of production increases.

Controllable versus *uncontrollable costs* relate to how much control a manager has in the authorization of that cost. For example, a sales manager may have control over how much is spent toward entertainment and sales awards, but she may not have any control over how much is allocated to her budget for warehousing of products to be sold. The entertainment and awards costs would be controllable costs, and the warehouse costs would be uncontrollable costs.

When making managerial decisions, there are three additional costs managers must consider:

- Differential costs
- Opportunity costs
- Sunk costs

Differential costs are similar to the economic concept of marginal costs and revenues. As with marginal costs, differential costs relate to the cost involved in producing one more unit of goods. Differential revenue, like marginal revenue, relates to the increase in revenue that can be attained with the sale of one more item of goods. Managerial accounting uses the differential concept to help managers make decisions about future plans. For example, let's look at a situation where marketing is trying to determine whether to continue selling its product using the current retailer distribution system or to move to a direct sales operation. Here is a chart that lays out the variable costs using differential analysis:

	RETAILER DISTRIBUTION	DIRECT SALES	DIFFERENTIAL COSTS AND REVENUES
Revenues	$900,000	$1,200,000	$300,000
Costs of goods sold	550,000	650,000	100,000
Advertising	90,000	120,000	30,000
Commissions	0	50,000	50,000
Warehouse depreciation	60,000	100,000	40,000
Other expenses	70,000	70,000	0
Total	$770,000	$990,000	$220,000
Net income	$120,000	$210,000	$90,000

Looking at the differential analysis, you can see that the marketing plan shows a $300,000 potential increase in sales with a move to a direct sales operation, as well as an increase in costs of $120,000. The potential

Inventing the Concept of Opportunity Costs

Austrian economist Friedrich von Wieser, whose contributions to economics were made in the late 1800s and early 1900s, is credited with developing the theory of opportunity costs. He named his theory the alternative cost theory, which analyzed costs in terms of the foregone use of the product. His theory is credited wtih turning economics toward the study of scarcity and resource allocation by focusing on factors related to a fixed quantity of resources and unlimited wants. His classic 1889 book, *Natural Value*, details the alternative cost theory today known as opportunity costs.

increase in net income would be $90,000. Managerial accounting would be directly involved in producing the numbers needed to make these calculations and support the plans of the marketing department. If the plan to move to direct sales is implemented, managerial accounting would then take the responsibility to produce performance reports to ensure the plan is performing as expected. If actual numbers vary from planning, marketing managers will need to work with managerial accounting to find and fix the problems.

Opportunity costs are the costs involved when a company must decide among various options. By deciding to spend the money on one option, the opportunity costs will be the cost of not being able to spend on another option. This can be a much larger cost than anticipated if, by having money tied up related to the first decision, management then must pass on the newer and possibly better opportunity. Each time a company spends money on a project, it risks the possibility of missing a future opportunity.

Sunk costs are costs already incurred that cannot be changed. For example, the construction of a facility or purchase of equipment is a sunk cost. Even if the decision is later determined to have been a mistake, the cost of the equipment or facility has been made and cannot be part of differential analysis to correct that mistake in the future. Differential analysis only looks at the costs that can be changed.

Using Data for Decision-Making

Most decision-making based on managerial accounting falls under the umbrella of cost-volume-profit (CVP) analysis. Key decisions made using CVP look at the interplay among these factors:

- Product pricing
- Activity levels or volume of activity
- Variable costs per unit
- Total fixed costs
- Mix of products sold

Using CVP, managers can make decisions related to issues such as product pricing, marketing strategies, choice of product lines, and the efficient and productive use of facilities. Many managers consider CVP analysis to be the best way to unlock the doors to untapped profit potential in an organization. While a traditional income statement uses sales less the cost of goods sold to calculate gross margin, CVP uses a statement based on a contribution approach to find the contribution margin. This margin separates out fixed and variable costs to determine the contribution margin. Here is how the two types of statements vary:

Many managers consider CVP analysis to be the best way to unlock the doors to untapped profit potential in an organization.

Traditional Approach	Contribution Approach
Sales:	*Sales:*
Less cost of goods sold	Less variable expenses
Gross margin	Variable production
	Variable selling
Less operating expenses	Variable administrative
Selling	
Administrative	Contribution margin
=Net income	Less fixed expenses
	Fixed production
	Fixed selling
	Fixed administrative
	=Net income

While the contribution approach cannot be used for external reporting, it is an essential tool for internal reporting purposes. By separating the variable expenses, a company can more easily analyze alternatives for changing operations and determine how these changes will impact variable expenses and ultimately profit margin. Since fixed expenses cannot be changed, only changes in variable expenses can help improve the profit picture.

The *contribution margin* is essentially what is left from sales revenues after calculating variable expenses. Once the contribution margin is known, the fixed expenses are subtracted to find net income. Since fixed expenses can't be changed, only those relating to the contribution margin are significant for decision-making. Whenever the contribution margin is not high enough to cover the fixed expenses, the company will show a loss.

Companies use the data generated by CVP to find their break-even point, which is the point at which the company will generate enough in revenues to cover fixed expenses. For example, if a company's fixed expenses total $50,000, then it must sell enough units to generate a $50,000 contribution margin to break even. Here is an income statement using the contribution approach to calculate the contribution margin for a product that sells for $100 and has fixed costs of $50,000. The variable expenses per unit total $50:

	TOTAL	PER UNIT
Sales (500 units)	$50,000	$100
Less variable costs	$25,000	$50
Contribution margin	$25,000	$50
Less fixed expenses	$50,000	
Net loss	($25,000)	

There are two options to turn the loss around. One is to increase sales and the second is to decrease variable costs. If the company determines the variable costs factors can't be changed, then they need to determine the break-even level of sales in order to cover fixed expenses. In this scenario, to generate the needed $50,000 to cover fixed expenses, sales must increase to 1,000 units to break even.

> Since fixed expenses can't be changed, only those relating to the contribution margin are significant for decision-making.

	TOTAL	PER UNIT
Sales (1,000 units)	$100,000	$100
Less variable costs	$50,000	$50
Contribution margin	$50,000	$50
Less fixed expenses	$50,000	
Net income	0	

Once the company knows its break-even point, it then knows that every sale above 1,000 units will generate $50 in profit per unit sold. The known contribution margin can be used for all future profit planning. To plan future profits goals, a manager can use the per-unit contribution margin without having to prepare an income statement each time he wants to consider different planning scenarios. Let's look at the calculation one more time, with the goal of increasing sales by 100 units:

	TOTAL	PER UNIT
Sales (1,100 units)	$110,000	$100
Less variable costs	$55,000	$50
Contribution margin	$55,000	$50
Less fixed expenses	$50,000	
Net income	$5,000	

Without even doing this statement, the manager could easily do the same calculation by multiplying the per-unit contribution margin of $50 by the increased sales goal of 100 units to get the same answer—a net income increase of $5,000.

Another common tool developed after knowing the contribution margin is the *contribution margin ratio (C/M ratio)*, which is also known as the *profit-volume ratio*. This ratio shows how the contribution ratio is affected by a change in total sales. In looking at the example, you see that variable costs are 50 percent of sales and that the contribution margin is also 50 percent of sales. So in this scenario, the C/M ratio is 50 percent; for each additional $1 of sales, the company will make a 50-cent profit provided there are no changes to fixed costs.

By using the C/M ratio, management can do long-term planning without breaking calculations into per-unit sales. For example, suppose management wants to improve set sales goals to increase sales by $40,000. Using the C/M ratio, this would mean an increase of $20,000 in the contribution margin and—provided fixed costs don't change—an increase of $20,000 in net profit. Let's look at how this works:

	PRESENT	GOAL	PER UNIT	PERCENT
Sales	$110,000	$150,000	$100	100%
Less variable costs	$55,000	$75,000	$50	50%
Contribution margin	$55,000	$75,000	$50	50%
Less fixed expenses	$50,000	$50,000		
Net income	$5,000	$25,000		

Companies that have more than one product line tend to prefer to use the C/M ratio because it is easier to compare the impact of increasing volume of sales among products. If all else is equal, managers will seek to increase the sale of products with the highest C/M ratios because increases in sales of these products will have the greatest impact on covering fixed expenses and increasing net income.

Another key factor to consider when planning a company's production facilities is to look at the proportion of fixed versus variable costs. Companies do have some control of these variables. For example, a company could decide to automate production and reduce its labor pool. Automation will likely increase the initial construction of the facility and its fixed costs, but could lower its variable costs because fewer employees would be needed and therefore variable direct labor costs would be lower. Let's compare two companies, one with higher fixed expenses and one with higher variable expenses.

	COMPANY A Sales volume	Percent	COMPANY B Sales volume	Percent
Sales	$200,000	100%	$200,000	100%
Less variable expenses	120,000	60%	60,000	30%
Contribution margin	80,000	40%	140,000	70%
Less fixed expenses	60,000		120,000	
Net income	$20,000		$20,000	

In this scenario, both companies have the same net income. Company A chose to reduce its initial costs and pay more in variable costs, which we'll assume in this case is direct labor costs. Company B paid more to build its facilities because it automated a part of its assembly line; so its fixed costs are higher, but its variable costs are lower, which we'll assume is primarily because of lower direct labor costs. Which structure is best? That depends on several factors including long-term trends for your product, fluctuation of sales levels year-to-year, and the company's attitude toward risk. If you anticipate a rapid increase in sales volume, then Company B has the better cost structure because for each unit of sale the increase to contribution margin will be higher—70%, which ultimately will increase net income by that amount provided fixed costs stay the same. But if sales volume is not expected to increase dramatically or possibly even to drop in future years, carrying those fixed costs could be a drain on the company's profits.

First, let's look at what happens if both companies experience a sales increase of 10 percent. The new contribution income statement would look like this:

	COMPANY A Sales volume	Percent	COMPANY B Sales volume	Percent
Sales	$220,000	100%	$220,000	100%
Less variable expenses	132,000	60%	66,000	30%
Contribution margin	88,000	40%	154,000	70%
Less fixed expenses	60,000		120,000	
Net income	$28,000		$34,000	

As expected, with increasing sales volume, Company B saw a greater increase in net income because it has the higher contribution margin. Now let's look at what happens if instead the companies faced a drop of 10 percent in sales.

| | COMPANY A | | COMPANY B | |
	Sales volume	Percent	Sales volume	Percent
Sales	$180,000	100%	$180,000	100%
Less variable expenses	108,000	60%	54,000	30%
Contribution margin	72,000	40%	126,000	70%
Less fixed expenses	60,000		120,000	
Net income	$12,000		$6,000	

Company A is in better position because it had more variable expenses and it could reduce its labor levels to offset the reduced sales volume, while Company B didn't have the same option since a greater percentage of its costs were tied up in fixed expenses. This risk factor is gauged by using a measurement called *operating leverage*, which looks at the degree to which fixed costs are used by an organization. The degree of operating leverage is calculated by:

$$\frac{\text{Contribution Margin}}{\text{Net Income}} = \text{Degree of Operating Leverage}$$

Calculating the degree of operating leverage for Companies A and B, we find:

$$\text{Company A:} \quad \frac{80,000}{20,000} = 4$$

$$\text{Company B:} \quad \frac{140,000}{20,000} = 7$$

What this measurement means is that for a given percentage change in sales, Company A can be expected to change its net income by four times, and net income changes for Company B would be expected at the level of seven times. Therefore, a 10 percent increase in sales for Company A would be a 40 percent increase in net income, while the 10 percent increase would mean Company B would see a 70 percent increase in net income.

Let's take another look at these figures. Company A's net income increased from $20,000 to $28,000, which was a 40 percent increase in income or $8,000. Company B's income increased from $20,000 to $34,000, which was a 70 percent increase in income or $14,000. When sales dropped, the impact of operating leverage in that direction was obvious as well. Company A's income dropped from $20,000 to $12,000, also a 40 percent drop or $8,000, while Company B's income dropped from $20,000 to $6,000, also a 70 percent drop in income or $14,000. So you can see that the higher the fixed costs, the greater the risk taken if sales do not continue to increase; however, by taking those risks, net profit could increase dramatically for the company with lower variable costs but higher fixed costs.

Using these CVP concepts, companies can test the impact on the bottom line of making changes to fixed and variable costs. Managers can test whether increasing advertising costs would add to the bottom line or using less costly components would increase profit margins.

First, let's look at a change in fixed costs and sales volume. Suppose the marketing manager decides that increasing advertising by $20,000 each month would increase sales volume by a total of $50,000. Going back to our initial example of the units selling for $100, let's look at what that will do to the sales volume and net income.

> Using these CVP concepts, companies can test the impact on the bottom line of making changes to fixed and variable costs.

	TOTAL		PERCENT
	Current	*Proposed*	
Sales	$100,000	$150,000	100%
Less variable costs	50,000	75,000	50%
Contribution margin	$50,000	$75,000	50%
Less fixed expenses	$50,000	$70,000	
Net income	$0	$5,000	

In this scenario, spending $20,000 on advertising would increase fixed costs by $20,000 and increase net income by $5,000. Rather than use the contribution income statement method, you could even come to this conclusion more quickly using the C/M ratio to find the incremental contribution margin:

$50,000 x 50% C/M Ratio	=	$25,000
Less advertising expenses	=	20,000
Increased net income		$5,000

When you are using the C/M Ratio, you do not have to go back and find the original sales numbers or prepare an income statement. Instead, you can quickly look at the incremental analysis and determine the proposal's expected effect. You can see how much simpler it is to use this incremental approach.

Let's use the incremental method to calculate a change in variable costs and sales volume. For example, the manufacturing manager located a part that is less costly and could reduce the costs of producing its units by $25 per unit. The sales manager counters this plan and warns that the new part could lower the overall quality of the unit and risk reducing sales by 20 units. The contribution margin would increase from $50 to $75 with a decrease of $25 in variable costs. The number of units sold would decrease to 80 with this change.

In that case, here is the calculation to find the incremental contribution margin.

Expected total contribution margin:	
80 units x $75	$6,000
Present total contribution margin:	
100 units x $50	$5,000
Increase in total contribution margin	$1,000

In this scenario, net income would increase by $1,000, so using the cheaper parts would make sense from a financial viewpoint. Of course, in a real-world situation, the company would also be concerned about any potential long-range impact on its brand and may not make the decision purely on the numbers.

These types of analysis can be made when looking at multiple changes as well as when considering changes that could impact areas such as manufacturing, sales volume, and pricing. Basically, what a company is seeking when it uses CVP analysis is the most profitable combination of variable costs, fixed costs, selling price, and sales volume. There are some limitations to the assumptions used in CVP analysis, as follow:

- Economists question the CVP assumption that the impact on revenues and costs is linear throughout the entire range of decision possibilities. They believe that changes will not remain linear because certain changes in volume will trigger changes in both revenues and costs in such a way that will not be linear.
- CVP assumes costs can accurately be divided into fixed and variable elements, which is not always the case.
- CVP assumes the sales mix is always constant, which is rare in most businesses.
- CVP assumes worker productivity and efficiency do not change throughout the range, which is rarely true as pressures to produce more and more units may impact both in a negative way.
- CVP does not consider the time value of money, which means the value of a dollar today will not be the same as the value of a dollar at some future time.

CVP is a way of thinking, not a concrete set of problem-solving procedures. While CVP can be used to find the optimum combination of costs, selling price, and volume, managers must still use their experience in the business to look at other less concrete factors, such as the changing dynamics that will be triggered in the true world once the proposed changes are implemented. They must consider the reaction of employees, customers, and suppliers to the change. Many times these factors are more a question of instinct than any concrete numbers that can be put on a piece of paper.

> CVP is a way of thinking, not a concrete set of problem-solving procedures.

Profit Planning and Budgeting

When businesses do profit planning, they are looking for ways to achieve a desired level of profits. The primary way to successfully meet profit goals is through the budgeting process. A business actually develops a series of different kinds of budgets, which are combined to form an integrated business plan known as the master budget.

The first step in budgeting is to determine the budget period. That will differ depending on what is being budgeted. Capital budgets for the acquisition of land, buildings, and major equipment usually are planned over a long period, such as twenty or thirty years. Operating budgets, on the other hand, usually are planned over a twelve-month period. For operating purposes, some companies operate on quarterly budgets, while others break things down to monthly budgeting. Some companies are now using continuous or perpetual budgeting. In this process, the budget in place always covers a twelve-month period with a new month constantly being added as one month is completed.

The success of the budgeting process will depend on how the budgets were developed in the first place. For the following reasons, the most successful budgeting programs are those that fit the self-imposed budget design:

1. The people who are in the most direct contact with the activity develop the budget estimates. Budgets prepared at that level are the most accurate and reliable.
2. People are more apt to meet budget guidelines if they have a role in developing that budget rather than have a budget imposed by management.
3. Allowing people a role in developing budgets for their section or department makes the budget easier to enforce. If a section or department is unable to stay within the budget guidelines, the employees have only themselves to blame. This differs from imposing a budget developed by upper management, which lower level managers can say was unreasonable or unrealistic, so therefore budget levels could not be met.
4. By including people in the budget-planning process, top management clearly shows they recognize everyone's views and value their judgments, creating a stronger team atmosphere to meet the goals and objectives set for the business.

Usually a budget committee oversees the budgeting process. This committee is responsible for overall budgeting policy and for coordinating the preparation of the budgets. It is usually made up of the president, chief financial officer, controller, and vice presidents of various functions, such as marketing, sales, production, purchasing. The budget committee resolves any disputes that might arise among various functions during the budgeting process (such as a plan to reduce manufacturing costs by lowering quality standards, which sales considers a problem in maintaining customer satisfaction).

Even though budgets are developed at section or departmental levels, the budget committee gives final approval for all budgets. Usually before the budgeting process even begins, the committee develops guidelines that include some general rules, such as a request to hold all budgets to a certain percentage increase in costs or possibly even a reduction. By setting the rules upfront, departments and sections know what to expect and can plan accordingly rather than face automatic rejection if they do not meet company-wide mandates and needs.

A critical first step in the budgeting process is sales forecasting. This step must be completed in order to know what resources will be available to the company as a whole. Factors used to develop an accurate sales forecast include:

- Past sales volume experience
- Potential pricing policy
- Unfilled orders and backlogs
- Market research that includes potential sales and competitive data for the entire industry as well as forecasts for the individual company
- General economic conditions
- Industry economic conditions
- Advertising and product promotions
- Industry competition
- Market share

Once this information is collected, forecasts can be developed about future business potential. After the key data are developed, top management should then encourage staff at all levels of the organization to share their input based on actual day-to-day experiences within the business operation. This knowledge can put a real-world spin on the information collected and assess how useful and accurate the data are to decisions that directly affect

> A critical first step in the budgeting process is sales forecasting.

the company's plans. Once potential revenues are determined, a more accurate estimate can be made of the resources that will be available and the overall budget objectives can be set.

The next step in the process of developing a master budget is for each department to develop its own budget. This includes the following:

- Sales budget
- Production budget
- Inventory purchases budget
- Direct materials budget
- Direct labor budget
- Manufacturing overhead budget
- Finished goods inventory budget
- Selling and administrative expense budget
- Cash budget
- Budgeted income statement
- Budgeted balance sheet

Let's take a closer look at the variety of budgets that are developed in order to arrive at the master budget.

Sales Budget

Usually this is the first budget developed, because nearly all other budgets depend on its numbers, including production, purchases, inventories, and overall expenses. Sales managers forecast their expected sales levels and gross revenues. Typically, this will include a forecast by month or quarter, so cash-flow estimates can be developed for use by other departments in planning their budgets

Production Budget

For manufacturing companies, once the sales budget has been prepared, the production budget can then be developed based on these forecasts. Production will consider what it already has on hand in beginning inventory for the period and then plan what needs to be produced to meet the sales forecast numbers. Careful planning of these inventories is critical to avoid a backlog of unnecessary resources that are tied up in unneeded inventory at the end of the year. But it is also important to be certain that enough product is available to meet customer demand and to avoid either crash production efforts that require a lot of overtime or the risk of not being able to meet shipping schedules and thus losing sales.

Inventory Purchases Budget

For nonmanufacturing companies, the budgeting process looks at inventory purchase planning rather than production. Similar issues of having the inventory on hand when needed to meet customer demands also drive this part of the inventory budget–planning process. To be sure, suppliers will have the needed product available throughout the year; it is important for the purchasing department to be able to give suppliers an accurate schedule for the next budget year or quarter.

> For nonmanufacturing companies, the budgeting process looks at inventory purchase planning rather than production.

Direct Materials Budget

For manufacturing operations, once the production budget is known, the next step is to plan the direct materials budget, to be certain the right amount of raw materials will be available to meet the production schedule. Again, the key is to have the materials available when needed so there is no risk of production interruptions, while also avoiding having too many materials on hand, which can increase warehousing expenses.

Direct Labor Budget

The direct labor budget can also be developed once the production budget is in place. Direct labor requirements can be calculated based on the planned production schedule. This will ensure that certain labor needs are met throughout the budget year without incurring the extra costs of overtime because of poor planning or risking the possibility that a labor shortage could result in insufficient amounts of product to meet customers' needs.

Manufacturing Overhead Budget

The manufacturing overhead budget is another budget that depends on the production budget. Manufacturing overhead is usually planned based on past experience, which calculates overhead determined by its relationship to direct labor and direct materials needs.

Finished Goods Inventory Budget

Once the budgets for direct labor, direct materials, and manufacturing overhead are known, a budget estimate for finished goods can be developed. Using the numbers from these three budgets, a cost per unit of production can be calculated. Then using information from the sales and production forecasts, a finished-goods inventory budget can be developed.

Selling and Administrative Expense Budget

The selling and administrative expense budget is a compilation of numerous smaller sections or departments that involve areas other than manufacturing. Usually the manager for each section or department develops her own budget and submits it to the person responsible for developing the overall selling and administrative budget.

Cash Budget

Once the needs of all the departments are translated into budgets, data about the cash that will be needed by each department is then used to prepare a cash budget. This budget will map out the cash that must be on hand to meet the demands of each department. Based on this budget, the finance department will determine whether cash needs can be met by operations or whether outside financing will be needed at certain times of the year. If outside financing will be needed, the finance department will add interest expenses in this budget. Many companies develop a cash budget on a weekly basis. Some larger companies even prepare daily cash budgets.

Budgeted Income Statement

With all the budgeted data collected, a budgeted income statement can be developed to be certain this budgeting process has actually created a budget that meets profit-planning objectives. If it does not, the budget committee, working with the department managers involved, will then have to decide where to make changes in the budget to meet those goals.

Budgeted Balance Sheet

Once profit planning is complete, a budgeted balance sheet can be developed using the information from the various departments, as well as the cash budget and the budgeted income statement.

With all these budgets in place, a master budget for the company can be developed. Throughout the budget period, managerial accounting will prepare progress reports for each of the managers to be sure they are staying within budgeted targets or work with them to find the problems and fix them.

> With all these budgets in place, a master budget for the company can be developed.

Flexible Budgeting

The type of budgeting just discussed is called *static budgeting*. In other words, there is a set level of expected activity and budgets were developed for that set level. Another type of budgeting being used by more and more companies is flexible budgeting. Flexible budgeting differs by using these four steps to develop budget goals:

1. Management determines an expected range of activity that is possible during the next budget period.
2. Costs are analyzed based on this relevant range to determine cost behavior patterns for fixed and variable costs, as well as for costs that are a mix of the two.
3. Mixed costs are separated to pull out the variable components.
4. A variable costs formula is developed that shows what these variable costs are expected to be based on various points within the expected range.

Managers can then use these variable cost factors to determine whether they are meeting budget goals based on the actual level of activity.

Investment Decision-Making

One type of budgeting we left out of the mix is *capital budgeting*. That's because this budgeting actually involves long-term investment concepts. Capital expenditures never impact only one period of the accounting cycle; instead they usually impact a company's decision-making for a much longer period. Many times when companies consider a capital budget expenditure, they are weighing key decisions such as:

- Should new equipment be purchased to reduce costs?
- Should new facilities be purchased to increase capacity or sales?
- When selecting new equipment, which option will best meet future needs?
- Should new facilities be purchased or leased?
- Should older equipment or facilities be replaced now or can the decision be put off for a year or two?

All of these decisions will be based on analysis done by finance, which we will cover in much greater detail in Part Three on finance. Before moving on to the key factors in capital budget decision-making, we'll first take a closer look at the development of financial statements, which are used both internally and externally, in the next chapter.

> **Chapter 7**

Preparing Financial Statements

Part One

Part Two

Part Three

Part Four

Part Five

Part Six

PART TWO ACCOUNTING

▪ CHAPTER 5 Financial Accounting ▪ CHAPTER 6 Managerial Accounting
▪ CHAPTER 7 **Preparing Financial Statements**

Financial Reporting Standards

At the end of each accounting period, a series of financial statements are prepared to report results to external entities, such as bankers, investors, and governmental entities. These statements have required formats established in guidelines set by the Financial Accounting Standards Board (FASB, pronounced "faz-bee"), which is recognized by both the Securities and Exchange Commission and the American Institute of Certified Public Accountants as the guiding force in developing rules for financial statements.

These guidelines are called "Generally Accepted Accounting Principles," or GAAP. When reviewing financial statements, be sure they are prepared using GAAP. If not, be very wary of the numbers. GAAP has many loopholes, but not using GAAP is usually an even greater sign of problems.

In its mission statement, FASB says it seeks "to establish and improve standards of financial accounting and reporting for the guidance and education of the public, including issuers, auditors and users of financial information. Accounting standards are essential to the efficient functioning of the economy because decisions about the allocation of resources rely heavily on credible, concise, transparent and understandable financial information. Financial information about the operations and financial position of individual entities also is used by the public in making various other kinds of decisions."

In order to accomplish its mission, FASB set these goals:

- "Improve the usefulness of financial reporting by focusing on the primary characteristics of relevance and reliability and on the qualities of comparability and consistency;
- "Keep standards current to reflect changes in methods of doing business and changes in the economic environment;
- "Consider promptly any significant areas of deficiency in financial reporting that might be improved through the standard-setting process;
- "Promote the international convergence of accounting standards concurrent with improving the quality of financial reporting; and
- "Improve the common understanding of the nature and purposes of information contained in financial reports."

> When reviewing financial statements, be sure they are prepared using GAAP.

FASB develops what it calls "broad accounting concepts." Then using this conceptual framework, it sets standards for financial reporting. The concepts and standards are based on research by staff and others, including foreign national and international accounting standard-setting bodies. Once in place, the concepts and standards give accountants and others who prepare financial statements "reasonable bounds for judgment" in preparing financial information with the goal of increasing "understanding of, and confidence in, financial information on the part of users of financial reports." FASB also seeks to educate the public on the "nature and limitations supplied by financial reporting." Some would say success at meeting these goals showed there are severe limitations when the scandals regarding Enron, WorldCom, Tyco, and others hit the front pages. Even so, the guidelines are in place and must be followed by companies in order to meet the SEC requirements for corporate reporting. Even non-corporate entities follow these guidelines in order to satisfy their investors and banks.

Just to give you an idea of what a FASB summary mandates, here is a portion of one issued in September 1979 called "Financial Reporting and Changing Prices," which required that supplementary information be added to annual reports. FASB changed requirements as of December 25, 1979. Financial statements issued by companies with inventories and property, plant, and equipment of more than $125 million (before deducting accumulated depreciation) or total assets amounting to more than $1 billion (after deducting accumulated depreciation) were required to comply with these changes. The changes specified were as follows:

"For fiscal years ended on or after December 25, 1979, enterprises are required to report:
–Income from continuing operations adjusted for the effects of general inflation
–The purchasing power gain or loss on net monetary items

"For fiscal years ended on or after December 25, 1979, enterprises are also required to report:
–Income from continuing operations on a current cost basis
–The current cost amounts of inventory and property, plant, and equipment at the end of the fiscal year

–Increases or decreases in current cost amounts of inventory and property, plant, and equipment, net of inflation."

The primary difference in these two requirements is that annual reports before December 25, 1979, could state the value of continuing operations after adjusting for the effects of inflation and their gain or loss in purchasing power could be stated on net monetary items. For statements after that date, income from continuing operations, inventory, and property plant and equipment had to be stated based on current cost amounts. Increases or decreases in current cost amounts of inventory and property, plant, and equipment had to be stated net of inflation.

As you can see, FASB guidelines are highly technical. Just by reviewing a portion of the summary data of one element of financial reporting, you can see why corporations seek major accounting firms to help prepare their financial statements. Most small businesses that want their financial statements to be accepted by investors and financial institutions will seek the help of an accounting firm to prepare them. Since that is the case, we won't delve into the details of accounting requirements for these statements. Instead, we'll just review the components that should be included in each type of statement and how that statement would be formatted.

So what are the statements required? There are actually two statements produced by every company—the *balance sheet* (or *statement of financial position*) and the *income statement* (or *profit and loss statement* or *statement of earnings*). Many companies also prepare a *statement of cash flows* and a simpler form of all these statements called *pro forma statements*. Let's take a closer look at each.

> Most small businesses that want their financial statements to be accepted by investors and financial institutions will seek the help of an accounting firm to prepare them.

Balance Sheet (Statement of Financial Position)

A balance sheet details items the company owns, commonly called assets, and claims that are made against the company, which include liabilities (claims made by debtors) and owners' equity (claims made by owners or investors). It is actually a snapshot of a business's financial position at some set point in time. As we discussed in Chapter 5, the balance sheet is based on the equation:

ASSETS = LIABILITIES + EQUITY

Assets will always appear on the left side of the balance sheet and liabilities and equity will always appear on the right side of the balance sheet. How each of these components is valued is mandated in guidelines set by FASB. If you have questions about how to present the value of an asset, liability, or equity on the balance sheet, you can search FASB rulings on the topic at *www.fasb.org/st,* where you can find the full text of a ruling, a summary of that ruling, and the status of a pending ruling. This holds true for a search of FASB on all required financial statements.

Balance sheets have a number of requirements for how to order each listing, as well as how to value and define each item. First and foremost is the idea that the left side (assets) must be in balance with the right side (liabilities and equity).

The next consideration is how to order the balance sheet. Items are listed in their order of liquidity, which means you list cash assets first, which are followed by items closest to cash. Assets are usually broken down into two categories: current assets and long-term assets.

Assets that will be used up in less than twelve months are current assets; all others fall into the category of long-term assets. Examples of current assets include cash, marketable securities (which you can convert to cash easily by selling them), accounts receivable, and inventories. Long-term assets include assets that take a longer time to convert to cash and are usually held for more than twelve months. These include assets such as buildings, land, and equipment.

Liabilities are ordered in a similar way with short-term or current liabilities listed in order based on how quickly the claim against the company matures or comes due. Current liabilities include any claim that matures in twelve months or less. Long-term liabilities include any claims that mature in more than twelve months. Current liabilities include *accounts payable, credit card payable,* and *notes payable,* while long-term liabilities include claims such as *mortgage payable* or *lease payable.*

Equity accounts are listed according to the claims against the company as well. Preferred stock accounts are listed first because their claim to dividends comes before common stockholders. The last item on the equity list is *retained earnings,* which is the final balancing item and includes dates from over the years related to profits and losses from the income statement.

Playing the Numbers Game

Companies sometimes find ways to hide falling profits within accepted FASB accounting principles by altering their reports. Some go as far as using fraud in their deception, but more commonly other tricks are used to hide poor results. Charles Mulford and Eugene Comiskey, accounting professors at the Georgia Institute of Technology in Atlanta, have written a ground-breaking book titled *The Financial Numbers Game* (Wiley & Sons, 2002) that will help you learn how these tricks work. Bob Acker, editor/publisher of the *Acker Letter,* says, *"The Financial Numbers Game* identifies the steps businesses may take to misstate financial performance and helps its readers to identify those situations where reported results may not be what they seem. Authors Mulford and Comiskey also describe the flexibility built into the GAAP principles and discuss ways companies can take advantage of that flexibility while remaining within the rules of proper reporting."

Items on the balance sheet are usually valued at cost with two exceptions: marketable securities and inventories. Both are valued at whichever is lower—cost or market value. For example, if the current value of marketable securities is lower than its original cost, it would be listed on the balance sheet at market value. A share of stock that was originally purchased for $100 several years ago but has since fallen in value to $75 would appear on the balance sheet at $75.

Assets that are depreciated are listed at their cost value and then adjusted using an accounting practice called *accumulated depreciation,* which shows the long-term reduction in value. For example, a building purchased for $1,000,000 with accumulated depreciation of $300,000 would be listed like this on the balance sheet:

Building	$1,000,000
Accumulated depreciation	($300,000)
Net building	$700,000

Here is an example of a balance sheet:

BALANCE SHEET

Company Name
Company Address   *As of December 31, 2003*

Assets   ### Liabilities

Current Assets   *Current Liabilities*
Cash   Accounts Payable
Marketable Securities   Notes Payable
Accounts Receivable   Taxes Payable
Notes Receivable   Accrued Expenses
Inventories   Other Current Liabilities

Total Current Assets   *Total Current Liabilities*

Long-Term Assets   *Long-Term Liabilities*
Land   Notes Payable
Buildings   Bonds Payable
(Accumulated Depreciation   Pension Obligations
– Buildings)   Deferred Taxes
Equipment
(Accumulated Depreciation   *Total Long-Term Liabilities*
 – Equipment)
Goodwill   *Total Liabilities*
Patents
Trademarks   *Owner's Equity*
Organizational Costs   Preferred Stock
Other Assets   Common Stock
                                                         Retained Earnings

Total Long-Term Assets

Total Assets   *Total Owner's Equity*
                                                         Total Liabilities and Owner's Equity

The total assets should equal the total liabilities and owner's equity. The balance sheet is the last to be prepared, since its numbers depend on the net profit or loss calculation on the profit and loss statement or income statement.

Income Statement (Statement of Earnings)

The income statement provides information about a company's revenues and expenses and any taxes associated with those expenses for a given financial period, whether the report is for a month, a quarter, a year, or some other accounting period that makes business sense. The income statement does not have a left-right orientation, as the balance sheet, but instead uses a top-down approach starting with gross income and working its way down to net profit or loss.

Here is a basic format for an income statement:

INCOME STATEMENT

Company Name
Company Address   *For the Period January 1, 2003, to December 31, 2003*

Sales
Less: Cost of Goods Sold
Gross Profit

Operating Expenses
  Advertising
  Bank Service Charges
  Dues and Subscriptions
  Equipment Rental
  Insurance
  Legal and Accounting Expenses
  Meals and Entertainment Expenses
  Miscellaneous Expense
  Office Expense
  Payroll Taxes
  Postage Expenses

Rent Expense
Repairs and Maintenance Expenses
Salaries and Wages
Supplies
Travel
Telephone Expense
Utilities
Vehicle Expenses

Operating Income Before Depreciation
Amortization Expense
Depreciation Expense

Operating Profit
Less: Interest Expense

Pretax Accounting Income
Less: Income Tax Expense

Income Before Extraordinary Items
Less: Any Extraordinary Items

Net Income

Earnings Per Share

As you can see, a company separates out its operating income and determines its operating profit before it includes information about depreciation and amortization expenses, interest expense, income tax expenses, and any extraordinary items, such as the discontinued operations or other activities not carried out each business year.

Statement of Cash Flows

The income statement is based on accrual accounting. To give external sources a view of a company's cash position, however, most companies also provide a statement of cash flows. This statement has three parts: operating activities, investment activities, and financial activities.

The operating activities section is the most critical because it gives outsiders a view of the cash available for the company's core business operations. Usually a company will include information for the current period and for at least one previous period. This section includes the following:

	Previous Year	Current Year
Operations		
Net income		
Depreciation and amortization		
Gain on sales		
Unearned revenue		
Other current liabilities		
Accounts receivable		
Other current assets		
Net cash from operations		

Essentially, all the included elements are used to make adjustments in net income so an outside person can get a quick view of the actual cash available by adding back items that were not cash expenditures (but were required for financial reporting purposes) and subtracting out accrued items, which reflect actual cash on hand, such as accounts receivable. After all the adjustments are made, this will show the company's actual cash (net cash) from operations.

The next section summarizes the financing activity and will include any new common stock issued or repurchased, as well as any new loan activity. Here is how that section will look:

	Previous Year	Current Year

Financing
   Bonds issued
   Mortgage obligation
   Stock issucd
   Stock repurchased
   Preferred stock dividends

Net cash from financing

This section will tell you how much cash is being drawn from borrowing and other financing activities. It is a good indicator of whether the company is having trouble meeting its daily operating cash needs.

The final section is investments. Here is how that section would look:

	Previous Year	Current Year

Investments

Additions to property and equipment
Acquisition or merger activity
Sale of assets
Equity investments
Short-term investments

This section shows how much is being spent on capital expenses, which are used to build the business for the future. This section gives investors an idea of what major long-term planning activities have taken place during the period.

The final section is a summary of the cash-flow activities:

	Previous Year	Current Year

Net change in cash and equivalents
Effect of exchange rates on cash and equivalents
Cash and equivalents, beginning of period
Cash and equivalents, end of period
Short-term investments, end of period
Cash and short-term investments, end of period

We'll take a closer look at how this information is used to gauge a company's financial position in Chapter 8 when we discuss analyzing financial statements.

Pro Forma Statements

Companies sometimes use pro forma statements to emphasize their results using either current or projected figures. These statements do not necessarily meet standards set by FASB and typically should not be used when making decisions about whether to invest in a company.

These statements are commonly used to summarize how a proposed change, such as a merger or acquisition, might impact a company's earnings picture. Pro forma statements can vary greatly from the numbers that would be presented using generally accepted accounting principles required by FASB and the SEC.

> **Chapter 8**

Understanding Financial Management

Part One

Part Two

Part Three

Part Four

Part Five

Part Six

PART THREE   FINANCE

■ **CHAPTER 8 Understanding Financial Management** ■ CHAPTER 9 Valuation and Cost of Capital ■ CHAPTER 10 Capital Budgeting ■ CHAPTER 11 Long-Term Financial Funding ■ CHAPTER 12 Managing Working Capital

What Is Financial Management?

Financial management's main goal is to provide analysis to top executives so they can plan for, acquire, and use a business's assets to maximize its efficiency and value. This is very different from the role of accounting, which seeks to provide quantitative financial information so both internal and external forces can make economic decisions.

A key part of this decision-making is how a business will finance its activities, whether it is best to take on additional debt or to raise capital by selling additional shares of stock. We'll be exploring all these issues in this section of the book. Valuation and cost of capital will be covered in Chapter 9. Capital budgeting issues will be covered in Chapter 10.

Many companies have failed because their debt levels were just too high to sustain during times of rising interest rates. Finding the right mix of debt and equity is a key role for financial managers. While avoiding debt might sound good if a company can avoid rising interest charges, selling additional shares does water down the value of ownership. We'll be talking more about this relationship in Chapter 11. Finally, we'll explore how to manage working capital in Chapter 12.

Financial managers must keep a close eye on the following:

- Inflation and its possible impact on the company's operations.
- Changes in the structure of financial institutions and how these changes could impact the business's ability to get capital when needed.
- Investors' perceptions of how the business is doing and how this might impact the company's stock price and ultimately the company's ability to raise capital, if needed, in the equity markets by issuing new stock or possibly deciding to buy back stock.
- Expansion plans and whether those plans make good economic sense given market conditions.

Financial managers are a crucial part of long-range strategic planning for corporations today. As corporations have shifted to global enterprises, expertise in financial management has become even more important to weigh the impact of not only interest rates and inflation, but also the effect foreign exchange rates could have on the use of capital.

> Finding the right mix of debt and equity is a key role for financial managers.

Within a corporate structure, the chief financial officer (CFO) usually reports directly to the president or chief executive officer. In many companies, the controller (who is responsible for the accounting and tax departments) and the treasurer (who manages the credit departments, inventory control, and capital budgeting) are also under the CFO's command. Although these functions all fall under the direction of the CFO, structures and titles vary company by company. Whatever the structure, the CFO always keeps track of maximizing stockholder wealth and ultimately maximizing the price of common stock.

Analyzing Financial Statements

As was discussed in the accounting section, the primary tools the outside world uses to evaluate a company are its financial statements. Maintaining a positive image is critical to financial managers when they seek to raise capital, whether they are applying for credit with a vendor so needed supplies can be bought on credit, borrowing from a financial institution, or selling additional shares of stock. The financial statements are snapshots of the company that these potential sources of cash will review before making a decision about whether to supply that cash.

When looking at the statements, stockholders are concerned about whether the company's growth or cash-flow potential (from dividends) warrants holding on to the stock and creditors are concerned about whether the company can pay its interest obligations and debts. They will also consider whether the debt levels are too high, making it risky to loan the company additional money. When looking at these statements, managers are concerned about profitability, availability of funds, and the financial picture for generating additional capital for future growth. Each entity essentially looks at the financial picture for the future that matches its individual concerns and potential involvement with the company.

Financial statements are static, historical documents that give a snapshot of one period in the history of the company. For these statements to be of any value, statement users must look for trends. They review current financial statements as well as statements of prior periods looking for trends such as:

1. Are debt levels rising or falling?
2. Is retained earnings increasing or decreasing?

Researching Ratios

Most of the ratios we'll be discussing mean very little without knowing how the company's ratios compare to other similar companies, as well as to industry averages. Numerous sites on the Internet offer these statistics. One excellent site for getting all types of company and stock market statistics is Yahoo Finance *(http://biz.yahoo.com)*. It is one of the few sites where the information is entirely free. Other excellent sites that are partially free, with much of the analysis only available to subscribers, include Morningstar *(www.morningstar.com)*, Standard and Poor's *(www.standardandpoors.com)*, and Value Line *(www.valueline.com)*.

3. Is the company depending on long- or short-term debt, and what are the interest obligations of each type of debt?
4. Is accounts receivable rising or falling? Does the company have good controls in place to collect on the credit given to customers?
5. Is accounts payable rising or falling? Is the company falling behind in its short-term debt obligations?
6. Are inventory levels rising, indicating a possible slowdown in sales?

These are just a few examples of the kinds of questions investors and financial institutions will consider when being approached for new capital investment in a company. Let's take a look at some of the key ratios investors or financial institutions calculate when they consider the health of a business based on its financial statements.

Earnings Per Share (EPS)

One of the simplest and most common ratios you will see is earnings per share. This ratio is calculated by dividing the net income remaining for stockholders by the number of common shares outstanding. For example, let's assume ABC Company's net income for common stockholders is $200,000 and there are 100,000 shares outstanding. The EPS would be calculated as follows:

$$\frac{\$200,000}{100,000} \quad = \quad \$2.00$$

Sometimes these net earnings can be impacted by an extraordinary gain or loss. For example, a company can sell off a major asset or experience a major loss. For this reason, when looking at a company's financial statements, many analysts will calculate earnings per share from operations and earnings per share after extraordinary items. Remember in Chapter 7 when the format for the income statement was discussed; there is always a separate section on that statement for extraordinary items.

Price-Earnings Ratio (PE)

Investors use the price-earnings ratio (PE) as an indicator for stock value. This ratio looks at the relationship between market value and earnings per share. It is calculated by dividing market price by earnings per share. For example, let's assume the ABC Company is selling at $20 per share. The PE ratio would be calculated as follows:

$$\frac{\$20}{\$2} \quad = \quad 10$$

This means that the PE ratio is 10 and that the stock is selling for about 10 times its currents earnings per share. Is this good or bad for investors? It depends. Investors will accept a much higher price-earnings ratio if the company has strong growth potential. When considering this ratio, investors will compare one company's ratio to other similar companies, as well as to the industry average to determine whether to invest. If the ABC Company's stock is viewed favorably, its market price could rise, increasing the PE ratio. For example, let's say investors were pleased with the last quarter's financial reports and the stock was in great demand. The price for the stock increased to $30. The PE ratio would then be 15.

Dividend Payout Ratio

Another key ratio investors consider is the dividend payout ratio, which measures what portion of current earnings is paid in dividends. Many growth companies don't pay dividends at all, because they reinvest earnings in future operations. Investors, who are looking primarily for capital gains, seek companies with low dividend payouts, while investors who want a regular cash flow in dividends seek a high payout ratio. Let's assume ABC Company is reinvesting for growth and pays just a small dividend of 10 cents per share. This ratio is calculated by dividing dividends per share by earnings per share. The dividend payout ratio for the ABC Company is calculated as follows:

$$\frac{\$0.10}{\$2.00} = 5\%$$

Whether this is a good ratio will depend on investor expectations. Also, investors will compare this company's dividend payout ratio to similar companies to gauge how well the company is doing and where the company puts its priorities on use of operating capital.

Dividend Yield Ratio

Another key ratio for investor decision-making is the dividend yield ratio, which looks at how much the investor will make on her investment based on dividend payout. This ratio is calculated by dividing dividends per share by current market price. ABC is selling for $20 per share and pays a dividend of 10 cents per share. Its dividend yield ratio is then:

$$\frac{\$0.10}{\$20} = .5\%$$

Although this may please investors seeking capital gains, the stock would not be attractive for investors seeking regular cash payouts.

Return on Total Assets

Internal company managers and analysts, investors, and creditors will all want to see how well the company is using the assets in hand. Return on total assets is a common ratio for testing this question. The ratio is calculated by:

$$\frac{\text{Net income} + [\text{Interest expense x } (1-\text{Tax rate})]}{\text{Average total assets}} = \text{Return on total assets}$$

Interest expense is added back to calculate the return before any money is paid out to stockholders or creditors. This ratio eliminates the question of how assets were financed and how that financing impacted how they were employed.

Let's assume ABC Company has average total assets of $2 million, with an interest expense of $50,000 and a tax rate of 35 percent. Its return on total assets would be calculated as follows:

$$\frac{\$200,000 + [50,000 \text{ x } (1-0.35)]}{\$2,000,000} = 11.625\%$$

This means that ABC Company had a return on average total assets for the past year of 11.625 percent. As with all other ratios, ABC Company's results would need to be compared to other similar companies within the industry to determine how well it has done.

Return on Common Stockholders' Equity

Generating income or growth for the stockholders is the primary objective of any company. One way to measure a company's success is the return on common stockholders' equity. The formula for this ratio is as follows:

$$\frac{\text{Net income} - \text{Preferred dividends}}{\text{Average common stockholders' equity}} = \text{Return on stockholders' equity}$$

One way to measure a company's success is the return on common stockholders' equity.

Preferred stockholders have first dibs on dividends, but they do not have voting rights. If the company were to go bankrupt, preferred stockholders get their portion of what's left before common stockholders. This ratio looks at the return for common stockholders. In this example, we'll assume ABC Company has no preferred stockholders. Its average common stockholders' equity is $1.5 million, so its return on stockholders' equity would be as follows:

$$\frac{\$200,000}{\$1,500,000} = 13.3\%$$

As you can see, the return on common shareholders' equity is higher than the return on total assets computed earlier. This relates to the level of leverage or amount of funds received from creditors or preferred stockholders. Since ABC Company has no preferred stock, its level of leverage from credit is the key difference. Now let's look at some of the common ratios used by creditors when determining whether to loan the company money.

Short-term creditors are most interested in the company's cash flows and how much working capital the company has or generates to gauge how much risk is being taken when loaning it additional money. Creditors are not as interested in the net income being reported by the company. One of the first things creditors will consider is a company's working capital, which shows how much of the company's assets are financed with long-term capital that doesn't need to be paid in the next year. By having more working capital, a company is in a stronger position to meet its short-term debts when payment is due. There are four key ratios that will be tested: current ratio, acid-test ratio, accounts receivable turnover, and inventory turnover.

> By having more working capital, a company is in a stronger position to meet its short-term debts when payment is due.

Current Ratio

The current ratio is widely regarded as the ratio used to test a company's ability to pay its short-term debt. This ratio is calculated by dividing current assets by its current liabilities:

$$\frac{\text{Current assets}}{\text{Current liabilities}} = \text{Current ratio}$$

Creditors are looking for a trend with this ratio, so they will want to see both the current period statements as well as the same period a year earlier. Let's assume for ABC Company, the past two years' balance sheet looked like this:

	2003	*2002*
Current assets		
Cash	200,000	100,000
Accounts receivable	445,000	320,000
Inventory	100,000	75,000
Prepaid expenses	5,000	5,000
Total current assets	750,000	500,000
Current liabilities	325,000	300,000
Working capital	425,000	200,000

Testing ABC's current ratio for 2003 and 2002:

2003   **2002**

$$\frac{750,000}{325,000} \quad = \quad 2.3 \text{ to } 1 \qquad\qquad \frac{500,000}{300,000} \quad = \quad 1.67 \text{ to } 1$$

In this case, it appears as though the working capital situation is improving because the ratio is increasing. Generally, short-term creditors seek a current ratio of at least 2:1.

Acid-Test Ratio (Quick Ratio)

In some cases, the situation for ABC may not be improving. If the increase in current assets is primarily because of an increase in inventory, this ratio can be deceiving, so the more commonly used ratio is the acid-test ratio. This ratio only looks at the most liquid assets—cash, marketable securities, and current receivables (accounts receivable and notes receivable). Inventory and prepaid expenses are not included in this calculation. This ratio tests how liquid a company's assets are and whether that company depends too heavily on its inventory for immediate cash needs. Since the economy can take a downturn, most short-term debtors look for an acid-test ratio of at least 1:1 to be sure a company can meet its obligations even in an economic downturn. So the formula for the acid-test ratio (also known as the quick ratio) is as follows:

$$\frac{\text{Cash + Marketable securities + Current receivables}}{\text{Current liabilities}} = \text{Acid-test ratio}$$

Let's assume that for ABC Company the inventory totals 100,000 in 2003 and 75,000 in 2002 and prepaid expenses in both years total $5,000. Therefore, for the purpose of the acid-test ratio, current assets would be $645,000 for 2003 and 420,000 for 2002. Calculating the acid-test ratio:

$$\frac{645,000}{325,000} = 1.98 \text{ to } 1 \qquad \frac{420,000}{300,000} = 1.4 \text{ to } 1$$

Again, ABC Company is looking like a good credit risk, and it appears that the credit risk situation is actually improving. However, the improving situation could still be based on possible problems. For example, the increase in current assets could be related to an increase in accounts receivables, which may mean sales have improved, but that improvement is because the company is allowing more flexibility to customers who want to pay on credit. Although the sales figures may look good, the actual cash available may not show the same improvement if most of the new cash is tied up in money to be collected on customers' accounts.

Making the Acid Test

The quick ratio or acid-test ratio is a tougher measure of a company's liquidity, since it does not include inventory or prepaid expenses in the calculation. Only the most liquid assets are included in this test. Businesses will find this is an important planning tool, especially when it is crucial to monitor the amount of assets tied up in inventory. By using this tool to track your asset flow monthly, you can keep an eye out for negative trends that could hamper your company's ability to meet its obligations. A quick ratio of 1 or higher is considered a good indication of a healthy financial position. If your company's ratio is sliding closer to that number or below it, the quicker you find the problem and fix it, the healthier your company will be financially. You can also use this quick test to test the financial health of any potential customers.

Accounts Receivable Turnover Ratio

To test the effectiveness of a company's ability to collect on its accounts, creditors, as part of their analysis on working assets, will use the accounts receivable ratio, which measures how quickly a company is turning its accounts receivables into cash. This ratio is computed by dividing sales on account by the average accounts receivable balance. We'll assume ABC Company's sales on account are $2,000,000. The average accounts receivable balance is $382,500 (($445,000 (2003) + $320,000 (2002))/2). So the accounts receivable turnover is as follows:

$$\frac{\text{Sales on account}}{\text{Average accounts receivable balance}} = \frac{\$2,000,000}{\$382,500} = 5.2 \text{ times}$$

You then divide 365 by this turnover figure to find out the average number of days being taken to collect an account (also known as the average collection period):

$$\frac{365 \text{ days}}{\text{Accounts receivable turnover}} \qquad \frac{365}{5.2} = 70.2 \text{ days}$$

This shows that ABC Company is taking a little more than two months to collect on accounts, which would probably indicate a problem in collecting, if thirty days is the standard credit term for customers. A creditor would likely take a closer look at the collection history before making a substantial loan to the company. Managers should also take note of an average collection period that is so high and implement improvement to its collections effort.

Inventory Turnover Ratio

Another good indicator of how well a business is doing is its inventory turnover. This ratio measures how many times a company's inventory has been sold during the year. The ratio is computed by dividing the cost of goods sold by the average level of inventory on hand. ABC's beginning inventory was $75,000 (ending inventory for 2002) and its ending inventory was $100,000, which means its average inventory balance was $87,500. Its cost of goods sold was $1,000,000. ABC's inventory turnover would be as follows:

$$\frac{\text{Cost of goods sold}}{\text{Average inventory balance}} = \frac{\$500,000}{\$87,500} = 5.7 \text{ times}$$

Using the inventory turnover number, you can then calculate the number of days it takes to sell the entire inventory, which is called the average sale period, by dividing 365 by the inventory turnover figure:

$$\frac{365 \text{ days}}{\text{Inventory turnover}} = \frac{365}{5.7} = 64 \text{ days}$$

ABC Company takes about sixty-four days to turn over its inventory. Whether this is a good figure would depend on the type of business. For example, if ABC Company were a food store, this would be very slow. If it were an electronics store, however, this might be considered good for the industry. Again, you would need to research the type of business and find out what the norms are in the area in which the business is operating.

Creditors who plan to loan money to a company for the long term would look at other calculations as well. While short-term creditors are concerned with the company's ability to pay its debts in the next twelve months, long-term creditors are looking at a much longer period for repayment. Long-term creditors look at the short-term indicators, because they want to be sure the company will be able to make ongoing interest payments, and at the company's ability to pay off the debt in full at some time in the future. Two common ratios they consider are times interest earned and debt-to-equity ratio.

Times Interest Earned

Times interest earned measures whether a company will have the ability to continue to make interest payments. This ratio is calculated by dividing earnings before interest expense and income taxes (for many income statements, this is the operating income figure) by interest expense. ABC Company had an interest expense of $50,000 and net income of $200,000. We'll assume its taxes were $70,000, so its income before interest expense and income taxes was $325,000. ABC's times interest earned is as follows:

Income before interest expenses
and income taxes

$$\frac{\text{Income before interest expenses and income taxes}}{\text{Interest expenses}} \quad = \quad \frac{\$325,000}{\$50,000} \quad = \quad 7.04 \text{ times}$$

In most cases, long-term creditors will consider a times interest earned ratio of 2 or more to be sufficient. But before making a final decision about whether to make the loan, a long-term creditor will look at the firm's earnings trend to gauge how cyclical its earnings may be and the risk an economic downturn could negatively affect its earnings.

Debt-to-Equity Ratio

In addition to looking at earnings, a long-term creditor will consider the balance between assets being provided by creditors and assets being provided by stockholders. This debt-to-equity ratio is calculated by dividing total liabilities by stockholders' equity. Stockholders' equity is $1,500,000 and current liabilities total $325,000. Let's assume ABC Company has another $500,000 in long-term liabilities for total liabilities of $825,000. You calculate ABC Company's debt-to-equity ratio by the following formula:

$$\frac{\text{Total liabilities}}{\text{Stockholders' equity}} \quad = \quad \frac{\$825,000}{\$1,500,000} \quad = \quad .55 \text{ to } 1$$

ABC's creditors are providing 55 cents for each dollar provided by the stockholders. In this case, ABC's stockholders are providing considerably more of the capital than its creditors. This would look very attractive to a lender. Creditors like the debt-to-equity ratio to be as low as possible, while stockholders usually prefer it to be as high as possible. In that way, stockholders can benefit from the assets being provided by creditors. We'll take a closer look at how to determine the balance in Chapter 11.

> Creditors like the debt-to-equity ratio to be as low as possible, while stockholders usually prefer it to be as high as possible.

Taxes

Finding ways to avoid or minimize your tax bill is a favorite game for individuals and businesses alike. If your business is a sole proprietorship or partnership that has not incorporated, you pay only one tax bill. But if you have

Microsoft's Cash Stash

Microsoft's cash stash is the largest of any U.S. corporation—$49 billion—and until March 2003, after passage of the new tax bill, Microsoft had never paid a dividend. Microsoft announced a second dividend payout for its fiscal 2004 year of 16 cents a share, which was paid in November. For investors, this was a 0.6 percent yield on their per-share investment, which places Microsoft near the bottom of the other twenty-nine companies on the Dow Jones Industrial Average. Only Intel Corporation's 0.3 percent yield is lower. The best-yielding Dow stock is the 6.7 percent yield of the Altria Group, which includes Philip Morris and Kraft Foods. While 16 cents a share is small for many Microsoft investors, the total payout for the company will be $1.7 billion, with Microsoft chairman Bill Gates getting $186 million of that. Investors are still screaming for a larger payout, now that dividends are taxed in the same way as capital gains.

incorporated, you pay both corporate taxes and individual taxes on the money your company earns.

Prior to the 2003 tax bill, many stockholders in a corporation preferred that their share of earnings be in long-term capital gains rather than dividends, since dividends were taxed at current income tax rates while capital gains were taxed at considerably lower rates for most individual taxpayers. Now both are taxed at the same rate, so companies may be changing their strategies about whether to pay dividends. Prior to 2003, companies were more likely to hold retained earnings to reinvest in the company, rather than pay out dividends. Now that there isn't as big an advantage to capital gains versus dividends, shareholders may push for higher dividend payouts.

We discussed the various tax benefits and disadvantages tied to business structures in Chapter 1 and the tax effects of depreciation in Chapter 5. Corporate taxes are too complicated for the purposes of this book. Two good books on the subject are *Strategic Corporate Tax Planning* (Wiley & Sons, 2002) by John E. Karayan, Charles W. Swenson, and Joseph W. Neff, and *Corporate Taxation: Examples and Explanations* (Aspen, 2001) by Cheryl D. Block.

Cash Flows

Monitoring cash flow is another key role of the finance department. While accounting must track income and expenses using the accrual method, those methods don't give an accurate view of how much cash is actually on hand or due to come in. Sales can be on credit with no cash exchanged. Expenses or other costs may be deducted from sales to determine profit, but no cash actually exchanges hands for those deductions. For example, depreciation of assets is an expense, but no cash is actually paid out.

Taxes are another area where expenses may be calculated but no cash is paid. In some instances, the tax expenses deducted to report net income do not match the cash actually paid out. Operating cash flows could be larger or smaller than accounting profits reported in any given year.

The two biggest potential areas where actual operating cash can be most greatly impacted are credit sales and depreciation. Cash that is held to pay quarterly or annual taxes may also make the company's cash situation look better than it actually is. Since finance is where cash will be raised when a company has a cash-flow problem, it also has the responsibility to track actual cash flows and be certain cash will be there when needed for ongoing operations.

Finance must also analyze the future cash flows from various company assets or assess the best use of cash currently available. We'll take a closer look at discounted cash-flow analysis in Chapter 9.

Financial Markets

Tracking what is happening in the financial markets is another critical role for finance. Keeping up-to-date on these factors is crucial to assist management with long- and short-range planning decisions. Key markets include:

1. **Money Markets**—markets for debt securities with a maturity date of less than one year.
2. **Physical Assets Markets**—markets for tangible assets, such as grains, autos, real estate, electronics equipment, machinery, etc.
3. **Capital Markets**—markets for long-term debt and corporate stocks.
4. **Mortgage Markets**—markets for loans on residential, commercial, and industrial real estate, as well as farmland.
5. **Consumer Credit**—markets for loans for consumers including items such as autos, appliances, vacations, and education.
6. **International, Regional, and Local Markets**—depending on the scope of a business, the finance department may need to watch markets internationally or focus more intently on regional or local markets.
7. **Primary Markets**—markets for new securities.
8. **Secondary Markets**—markets where existing securities are bought and sold.

Changes in each of these markets can help the finance department determine the general health of the economy and how these changes may impact the future success of the company's operations. Finance may want to raise a red flag on plans for expansion, if the indications from the markets seem to point toward a downturn. If the finance department sees a potential upswing in the markets, it would want to alert the company's executives to the potential for a growth spurt, so planning can be adjusted.

Interest Rates

Watching interest rate trends is of course the most important external market trend that could have an immediate and direct impact on any business. Rising interest rates will certainly mean increasing costs of capital for short-term debt and could also signal a slowdown in purchases by customers. Dropping interest rates may signal an opportunity to reduce interest expenses both in the long- and short-term. They could also signal a possible increase in consumer spending.

Unless you are operating a business that loans money and profits from a rise in interest rates, you probably will find rising interest rates a negative sign for your business and dropping interest rates a positive sign. Federal Reserve policy and federal deficits are two key factors that impact interest rates.

Federal Reserve Policy—Financial markets can move dramatically in one direction or the other if Alan Greenspan or another key member of the Federal Reserve Board even hints at an interest rate change. The Federal Reserve does not actually change the interest rates you pay for consumer or business credit, it changes the rate that is charged to member banks. The member banks then usually adjust other interest rates to reflect any change by the Fed.

Federal Deficits—Federal government deficits can have a major impact on the supply of cash available for the financial markets. As federal borrowing increases, more and more pressure is put on the money supply. As the money supply tightens, demand can exceed supply and interest rates will rise.

We've introduced you to the basics of financial management. In the rest of this section, we'll delve into the critical functions carried out by finance managers—valuation and cost of capital, capital budgeting, long-term financial planning, and managing working capital.

> **Chapter 9**

Valuation and Cost of Capital

PART THREE   FINANCE

■ CHAPTER 8 Understanding Financial Management ■ CHAPTER 9 Valuation and Cost of Capital ■ CHAPTER 10 Capital Budgeting ■ CHAPTER 11 Long-Term Financial Funding ■ CHAPTER 12 Managing Working Capital

Using Valuation Tools

Determining the value of potential investments and the cash flows these investments could generate is one of the primary roles of the finance department. Using methods of discounted cash-flow analysis and valuation models, as well as considering risk and rates of return are major tasks that fall to the financial manager.

Once a company decides what capital it needs for future expansion, finance must then find ways to maximize the value of that capital while minimizing its costs. This chapter will explain discounted cash-flow analysis, and then look at ways to use that analytical tool to value investments, as well as to understand how investors view a company's offering of stocks and bonds.

> Once a company decides what capital it needs for future expansion, finance must then find ways to maximize the value of that capital while minimizing its costs.

Discounted Cash-Flow Analysis

Before you can even consider valuation models, rates of return, and costs of capital, you first must learn the principle of discounted cash-flow analysis. This involves learning how to calculate future value and present value; these two concepts impact all capital spending decisions.

Luckily, financial calculators can now do these calculations for you, so you won't need to learn how to do these calculations manually. Each calculator is slightly different, so we'll only discuss the actual key you must find on your particular calculator. The two most popular, relatively inexpensive, financial calculators are the Hewlett-Packard 12C and the Texas Instruments BA-II Plus. More advanced financial calculators are available. If you plan to specialize in finance, you'll probably want a more advanced calculator; otherwise, one of these two should serve your purposes.

Future Value

Future value looks at how a dollar in your hand today is worth more than a dollar you will receive next year, because if you have that dollar in your hand to invest you can earn money on that investment and next year you will have more than that one dollar to invest. For example, if you have $100 to put into the bank today in an account paying 3 percent interest, how much money would you have in the future if the money is compounded (principal plus accumulated interest is used to calculate future interest payments) annually? To make this calculation, you would need to input on the calculator:

PV = Present Value = $100

I = Interest rate = 3%

N = Number of Years (or Payments if more than one payment per year) = 1

FV = Future Value—which in this case is unknown and the variable you are seeking to find. After inputting the first three values, you can push the FV key to get the answer.

Since the first year is a relatively simple calculation, you can probably do that quickly in your head. An interest payment of 3 percent at the end of the year would mean that the account's total value is $103 or 100 x 1.03. Calculating this manually for twenty years would be very time-consuming. Instead, by inputting the required data into a financial calculator, you can quickly determine these compound interest calculations for that investment over twenty years:

COMPOUND INTEREST CALCULATIONS

Year	Balance at Beginning of Year (PV)	Interest Rate	Balance at Year End (FV)
1	$100	3%	$103
2	$103	3%	$106.09
3	$106.09	3%	$109.27
4	$109.27	3%	$112.55
5	$112.55	3%	$115.93
10	$115.93	3%	$134.39
15	$134.39	3%	$155.80
20	$155.80	3%	$180.61

Of course, most discounted cost analysis problems will be much more complicated, but the basics of what variables are being calculated are more easily shown with this example.

Going Beyond the Simplest Calculations

Present and future value calculations become much more complex once you factor in inflation and interest streams. To include inflation considerations in a calculation, you must adjust your interest rate or rate of return on an investment by the expected inflation rate. Of course, you can never be certain of inflation rates in the future, but you can take your best guess based on recent history and economic predictions. Another factor is the cash stream you can expect from an investment. For example, if you are considering the potential value of rental property, you must factor in the payments as part of the future and present value calculations. Financial calculators have the key PMT for payments, so it is not difficult to add the consideration of a payment stream. Also, the payment key is used to determine payments you will need to make if you decide to finance a major purchase using a loan or lease arrangement.

Present Value

A decision you may need to make as manager may involve some known future values and you will have to try to determine the actual present-day value of the alternatives under consideration. For example, suppose you are offered a future payment of $150 in ten years or $100 today. To make this calculation easy, assume you have no current need for the money and would deposit the $100 in an account earning 5 percent interest compounded annually. Which alternative is better?

In this problem you have these variables:

FV	=	Future Value	=	$150
I	=	Interest Rate	=	5%
N	=	Number of Payments	=	10
PV	=	Present Value	=	Unknown

First, input FV, I, and N; then, press PV to find the present value of the $150. The present value is $92.09. So you would be better off taking the $100 today, if you can find a use for the money that would generate interest or profits of 5 percent or more.

These types of calculations are carried out daily in corporations to determine the best investments or capital expenditures for available funds. Whether the company is seeking to find the best investment alternatives among various investment vehicles or evaluating various ways to raise capital, present value and future value calculations are carried out before making each decision.

Valuation Models

First, let's look at how financial managers evaluate the potential for raising capital using stocks or bonds. When making decisions about whether to issue new debt (bonds) or new equity (stocks), managers must not only consider the costs and new cash potential of the options, they must also determine which option will maximize shareholder value.

Bonds

A bond is essentially an IOU. The company borrows money from bond investors and agrees to pay interest on that money, as well as repay the principal at some future date. There are five key bond terms you must understand:

1. **Par value** is the face value of the bond, which is the amount of money the investor pays to buy the bond and the amount of money the company will repay at the end of the bond period. When valuing a bond, this would be input in your financial calculator as the future value (FV).

2. **Maturity date** is the date at which the bond's face value will be paid to investors. Most bonds are issued for periods of ten to forty years, but any maturity date is legal. If a bond is issued on January 1, 2004, and matures in fifteen years, the maturity date would be December 31, 2019. If an investor bought the bond in 2004 and then sold it to another investor in 2010, the maturity date would not change. The bond would still mature on December 31, 2019. When valuing a bond, this would be input as your number (n) and should match the number of payments. For example a bond that matures in ten years and pays interest twice a year would be input as $N = 20$.

3. **Call provisions** relate to provisions set by the company to pay off the bond early. Many companies will include call provisions, especially when interest rates are high, so they can pay off the bond early (also known as retiring the debt). For example, if a bond was issued at 10 percent ten years ago and today a new bond could be issued at 4 percent, a company may issue new bonds at the 4 percent rate and then use the money to pay off the old debt by calling the bonds. This is similar to a homeowner refinancing a home mortgage when interest rates fall.

4. **Coupon interest rate** is the amount of interest a bond issuer will pay to the bondholder each year, or each payment period if more than one payment will be made in a year. Many bonds are issued with interest payments promised every six months. When bonds were first issued many years ago, investors actually had to send in coupons to collect their interest payments. Today, interest payments are sent automatically, but the interest on bonds is still called "coupon interest rate." The interest rate on bonds is not variable. It stays the same throughout the life of the bond. This rate is used to calculate the payment stream. An interest rate of 5 percent on a $1,000 bond would have a payment

stream of $50, so PMT = $50. The interest rate put into I would equal the appropriate market rate. For example, if the current market rate on bonds is 4 percent, when evaluating this bond, you would input I = 4% to evaluate this bond versus another alternative at current interest rates. That would add a premium to the value of this bond because it is paying a higher interest than other current investments. The bond would likely sell at a price higher than its par value.

5. **New issues versus outstanding bonds**—A bond is considered a new issue by the *Wall Street Journal* during the first two weeks of its being issued. After that, it is an outstanding bond. New issues sell close to their par value. Outstanding issues will vary in price depending on the interest rate paid on the bond. If interest rates are rising, a bond issued at lower rates will sell for below par value. If interest rates are falling, a bond issued at a higher rate will likely sell above its par value. In addition to interest rates, bond investors will also consider risk factors and bond rating services.

Bonds that are considered investment-grade receive Aaa or AAA ratings to Baa or BBB ratings from Moody's or S&P. Speculative or junk bond ratings vary from Ba or BB to D. When a company issues new bonds and increases debt, its bonds ratings could fall. Companies with lower ratings must then pay higher interest rates to attract investors, because investors want higher interest payments on riskier bonds. So while issuing debt may be more attractive for maintaining shareholder value and leveraging assets, at some point too much debt could greatly increase the cost of carrying debt and the overall cost of company operations.

Bond Rating Services

Bond rating services help investors assess the risk of various bonds. Top rating agencies include Standard & Poor's, Moody's Investor Services, and Fitch Ratings. Bonds are rated by various letter designations, and the safest bonds are those issued by the U.S. Treasury or a U.S. government agency or backed by the U.S. government. The Bond Market Association *(www.investinginbonds.com)* is an excellent site for learning more about the rating services.

Corporate bonds are traded primarily in the over-the-counter market and bought primarily by large financial institutions, such as life insurance companies, pension funds, and mutual funds. Individual investors do trade in bonds. One excellent site for learning more about trading in bonds is Bonds Online (*www.bondsonline.com*).

When investors consider the value of a bond, they look at the yield to maturity. To do this using a financial calculator, you would input:

N   = Number of Years to Maturity (or number of payments if more than one payment per year)
PMT   = Amount of Interest Paid with Each Payment
FV   = Par Value of the Bond at Maturity
PV   = Present Value (purchase price of the bond)

You would then hit I (Interest) to find the unknown, which is the yield to maturity. This would be the actual yield you get from the bond after the price is discounted to adjust for interest being paid.

While a corporation's decision to offer the bond is concerned with the expenses involved in long-term interest payout and eventual retirement of the debt, an investor is only concerned with the yield he or she can expect from that bond after factoring the risks of buying that particular bond. We'll talk more about risks and rates of return later.

Investors should also research the call provisions of a bond, especially if current interest rates are considerably lower than the interest being paid on the bond. A company will likely call the bond if they can retire the debt and issue new bonds at a lower interest rate. In the call provisions, the company will indicate the price they will pay for the callable bond based on how early in its life span the bond is called. Companies often state a bond will be called at par value plus one year's interest; that call price declines as the bond nears its maturity.

Stocks

When a company needs to raise a new influx of cash beyond what it is generating from operations, the only alternative to new debt is issuing new stock. There are two types of stock: preferred stock and common stock.

Preferred Stock

Preferred stock falls somewhere between a bond and common stock. While a preferred stockholder has an ownership share, he or she does not have voting rights. In exchange for the loss of voting rights, the preferred stockholders are paid dividends before common stockholders. If the company goes bankrupt, preferred stockholders will be paid their share of the remains before common stockholders.

For this reason, when companies consider issuing preferred stock, the dividends paid are similar to interest payments on bonds. If a company has a bad year, preferred stock dividends may not be paid, but the obligation to pay these dividends supersedes any future dividends for common stockholders, so essentially they are like an unpaid debt on the balance sheet. When the company again pays dividends, the unpaid dividends to preferred stockholders must be paid before common stockholders receive anything.

When valuing preferred stock, an investor uses this formula:

$$\text{Value of Preferred Stock} = \frac{\text{Dividends}}{\text{Required Rate of Return}}$$

The required rate of return is the rate the investor seeks in order to take the risk of buying the stock. We'll talk more about required rate of return later.

Common Stock

Common stock represents a partial ownership in a company with full voting rights and the right to share in the profits of the company, through dividends, if the company chooses to pay dividends rather than retain earnings. Many growth companies pay no dividends at all. Instead they reinvest profits in the business's continuing expansion.

For corporations, issuing common stock does not obligate the company to annual payments (as bonds do) or guaranteed dividends (as preferred stock does), but it does spread out the ownership of the company and the sharing of future profits. When a company is privately owned, the owners share the profits. When a company goes public and sells stock, the original owners no longer have sole rights to the company's profits.

The key then becomes who has the controlling ownership of the company. As long as the original owners still control 51 percent of the outstanding stock, they maintain control. Once their ownership falls below that level, they could lose control.

Investors who have already bought into the company will have their investment diluted when additional shares of common stock are issued. Before a company issues new stock, it must consider the issues of future control, as well as the dilution of value to current stockholders.

When valuing stock, investors consider different factors depending on expectations. If a continuing cash flow is a major concern, stockholders will look at expected dividends to determine the value of the stock purchase. If growth of capital is the primary concern, investors will look at the expected rate of return based on capital gains potential. Most investors will consider expected dividend yield and expected capital gains to determine the expected rate of return and, therefore, the price they will pay for a share of stock. Valuing stocks is a course on its own. A good place to learn the basics online is SmartMoney University *(http://university.smartmoney.com)* or Fool.com *(www.fool.com*—a free registration is required). Many of the ratios discussed earlier are part of the arsenal for determining a stock's value and whether the investment makes sense.

Risk and Rates of Return

When trying to determine the appropriate rate of return on a stock or bond, the risks involved in that investment decision must be measured. Financial managers must factor in the risks when they try to determine the rates of return for investment of a company's assets.

If a company is considering parking funds in a U.S. government bond paying 5 percent, then the possibility of getting 100 percent of that interest as well as principal returned is 100 percent, since government bonds are considered the least risky investment. Alternatively, the financial manager could decide to invest those funds in a start-up company that is developing a new product. Whether that product will ever

Giving Up Control of a Family Business

One display of what happens when a family finally gives up all control of a business happened in 2002 when Hewlett-Packard merged with Compaq against the wishes of the Hewlett family. Even though Walter B. Hewlett, Eleanor Hewlett Gimon, and Mary Hewlett Jaffe (children of HP cofounder William R. Hewlett) had more than 100 million shares of HP stock (about a 5 percent share in the company) they were not able to stop the merger. Walter Hewlett's public battle with HP CEO Carly Fiorino showed what happens to a family's interest when the family no longer holds enough common stock to control corporate decisions. Statistics for the survival of family businesses are not strong. Only 30 percent of family businesses make it to the second generation, 10 to 15 percent make it to the third generation, and only 3 to 5 percent make it to the fourth generation.

come to market and whether there will ever be a profit potential is unknown. While the potential for the investment could be a 100 percent return or more if the product is successful, the manager must also consider that the start-up could fail and the investment in the company could be worthless.

In measuring these two investments, the financial manager will consider the probability of a certain event happening. If the stock under consideration is for a company highly dependent on business cycles and in a competitive business environment, the risk of that investment is much greater than a company in a less competitive environment and less dependent on business cycles. For example, a computer hardware company is very dependent on business cycles and in a highly competitive business environment, so it is a much riskier investment then stock in a small food chain with a strong grip on a regional market. While the sale of computers is highly competitive and dependent on a strong economic environment, the sale of food is less impacted by the strength of the environment. The computer firm may offer greater profit potential, but there is also greater risk that sales could tumble if the economy takes a nosedive.

When weighing these two investments, a finance manager could set up a probability distribution chart to aid in making the decision. The chart could look like this:

PROBABILITY DISTRIBUTIONS FOR COMPUTER FIRM AND FOOD CHAIN

Economic State	Probability of Economic State	Expected Rate of Return in Each State Computer Firm	Food Chain
Boom	30%	100%	25%
Normal	40%	15%	15%
Recession	30%	−50%	10%

While the computer firm has a 50 percent possibility of a loss in a recession, the food chain has no possibility of a loss. This distribution can be used to calculate the expected rate of return as a weighted average:

Computer Firm = (0.3(100%)) + (0.4(15%)) + (0.3(−50%)) = 21%
Food Chain   = (0.3(25%)) + (0.4(15%)) + (0.3(10%)) = 16.5%

In this comparison, you can see that while the computer firm may have greater risk, its possibility of a higher return is also greater. This, of course, is a simple picture. A booming economy can have different levels. In some booms, growth is minimal; while in others, growth exceeds all expectations. Some recessions are short and shallow, while others can go on for years or even turn deeper into a long-term depression.

Most investors are risk averse and will purchase the less risky investment unless the rate of return is determined to be worth the risk. In order to buy the riskier investment, an investor will either expect a lower price for the investment or a higher return. Therefore, to sell lower-rated bonds, bond issuers will have to offer higher interest rates to entice investors. To sell riskier stocks, stock issuers will have to offer the stock at lower prices to entice investors.

When making investment decisions, investors are usually not looking solely at the risk level of an individual stock or bond, but instead how that stock will impact the risk level of a portfolio of investments. By holding a portfolio of investments, individuals or companies can minimize the risk of an individual stock by diversifying their holdings. There are two types of risks to be considered in portfolio management: market risks and company-specific risks. Market risks are caused by changes in the broad stock market and cannot be eliminated by diversification. On the other hand, holding a well-diversified portfolio can eliminate company-specific risks. Therefore, the relevant risk to most investors is market risk, which is measured by the beta coefficient.

Beta is a measurement that looks at the tendency of stocks to move up and down with the market. A stock with a low beta will be less volatile than the average stock, while one with a high beta will be more volatile. An average-risk stock is one that will move up and down with the general markets based on a particular index—such as the Standard and Poor's 500 index. For example, a stock with a beta of 1.0 to the S&P 500 will increase 10 percent in value when the S&P 500 increases 10 percent. Using a weighted average calculation of betas for each of your stock holdings, you can calculate how volatile your portfolio is to the general market. If your portfolio's beta is 0.5, then it is half as volatile as the market, while a beta of 2 would be twice as volatile as the market.

> Beta is a measurement that looks at the tendency of stocks to move up and down with the market.

Exploring the Capital Asset Pricing Theory

The capital asset pricing model (CAPM) is one model that gives investors a tool for evaluating risks. This model assumes two types of risks: diversifiable risks (known as nonsystemic risk) and nondiversifiable risk (systemic risk). Diversifiable risks can be avoided, so investors are not compensated for these risks. Systemic risks are not avoidable, so investors are rewarded for assuming those risks. These risks are measured using beta. In reality, this theory does not always mirror what you will see in the markets because beta as an indicator drawn from historical data may not reflect future results. The CAPM is recommended for use only by long-term investors.

So how do you use beta to determine the required rate of return? You can use a theory called the capital asset pricing model (CAPM). To do this, you need to know these factors:

Risk Free Rate of Return (RFR)	=	Assume that's 5%
Beta	=	1.5
Expected Return for Market (M)	=	Assume that's 10%

Using these numbers and this formula, you can find the expected rate of return as follows:

RFR + Beta (M–RFR)	=	Expected Rate of Return
5% + 1.5 (10%–5%)	=	12.5%

In order for you to consider a stock with a beta of 1.5 when risk-free investments are earning 5 percent and general market investments are earning 10 percent, you would need to expect a rate of return of 12.5 percent to take on this additional risk.

Luckily, you don't have to go through the extensive process of calculating beta for each of your holdings. The sites mentioned in the sidebar for researching ratios in Chapter 8 also include the beta on each stock. Beta is not a perfect measure. Since it is based on a stock's history, it does not give a perfect picture of a stock's future. Market conditions can change that could make the stock more or less volatile. Other influences on a stock's risk level can include its sensitivity to inflation, business cycle, interest rates, and changes in competitive forces.

You can see why trying to gauge the rate of return for a stock is much harder to do. Risks can be considered but not absolutely measured. While probabilities can be assigned, there are no guarantees that can be used to calculate rate of return.

Cost of Capital

When a firm is considering whether to issue bonds or stocks, it must try to determine its costs of new capital. While that may be easy to do for bonds and preferred stock, it is much harder to estimate the costs of equity. Before talking about how a firm decides whether to issue stock or bonds, we'll first review the reason for doing so—needs determined by capital budgeting—in the next chapter. Chapter 11 will review long-term financial planning and how a company decides on the methods it will use for raising capital.

Chapter 10

Capital Budgeting

Part One

Part Two

Part Three

Part Four

Part Five

Part Six

PART THREE   FINANCE

■ CHAPTER 8 Understanding Financial Management ■ CHAPTER 9 Valuation and Cost of Capital ■ CHAPTER 10 Capital Budgeting ■ CHAPTER 11 Long-Term Financial Funding ■ CHAPTER 12 Managing Working Capital

Understanding Capital Budgeting Basics

Stocks and bonds are not the only investment decisions analyzed by finance. Decisions to increase a company's fixed assets also fall under the realm of finance during the process of capital budgeting. In this chapter, we'll review the overall rules of capital budgeting, and then review how cash flows figure into the equation, and finally discuss how risk fits into the picture before summarizing the capital planning process.

When planning capital budgets, companies must analyze proposed projects and decide which projects should be included during the next fixed year. Capital budgeting involves large ticket items that could affect the success or failure of a company for many years.

First, a company will break down proposals offered by its departments into six categories:

1. **Maintenance of business assets**—Projects proposed to replace worn-out or damaged equipment used to produce profits fit in this category. The two key issues that must be determined before including these types of projects in the capital budget are whether the company plans to continue producing the products and whether repairing or maintaining existing plant and equipment is worth the expense.

2. **Reducing costs**—Projects in this category involve planned expenditures to replace working equipment with equipment that is more efficient and would lower the costs of labor, materials, or other budget items, such as utilities. A detailed analysis is needed to determine the long-range savings possibilities and whether the expenditure is worth it to get that savings.

3. **Expansion of existing products or markets**—Projects in this category include expansion of production facilities, outlets, or distribution facilities in order to increase market saturation in current markets. Not only must the analysis for these projects include a costs analysis, it must also determine whether there is pent-up market demand for the product in existing markets. Finance managers will be involved in developing the complex analysis for proposed capital budget items for expansion projects, but final approval for these projects will be made at a higher executive level.

4. **Expansion into new products or markets**—Projects in this category include plans to produce a new product or to enter a new geographic area. In addition to costs and market research, these types of projects require a look at the strategic goals of the company. Major moves such as these could require considerable long-term investment and could dramatically shift the future of the company. Complex analysis is needed before the project can even be considered for approval. While the finance managers will certainly be heavily involved in the capital budget decision-making process for these types of expansions, the final decision to develop new products or enter new markets is usually made at the board of directors' level.

5. **Safe and/or environmental projects**—Projects in this category are those necessary to meet governmental regulations regarding employee safety or environmental compliance or they are required to meet insurance policy terms. Usually these projects are mandatory investments that do not produce revenue. The amount of analysis needed to approve these projects and the level of approval required depends on the cost of the project.

6. **Other projects**—Any project that doesn't fall into one of the categories above becomes part of this catchall category. Projects could include decisions involving office buildings, parking lots, and other major capital needs that are not directly tied to profit generation. The amount of analysis needed and the level of approval needed will depend on the impact of the capital item on the budget.

A turning point for the project occurred in 1983, when the Suffolk County government declared that the county could not be safely evacuated and the state refused to approve any LILCO-sponsored evacuation plan. In 1984, questions were raised whether the additional electricity that would be generated by the plant would ever be needed. Even

Poor Project Projections Destroy Power Company

One of the classic cases that show how a company can destroy itself with poor capital budget planning is that of the Long Island Lighting Company (LILCO) and its Shoreham Nuclear Power Plant. The company's initial projections set the plant's construction costs at an unrealistically low half a billion dollars. By the time the plant was closed down on October 12, 1994, cost overruns had run up the cost to $6 billion. The plant never generated even one kilowatt of electric power. The error cost both LILCO and the people of Long Island dearly. Long Island customers are still paying for a plant that was never used; and LILCO was partially taken over by the state of New York in 1995.

as public opposition grew, LILCO ignored all these danger signs and continued spending the money.

Capital Budget Evaluation Methods

When deciding whether to include an item in the capital budget, there are four methods used to determine the viability of the project: payback, net present value (NPV), regular internal rate of return (IRR), and profitability index. Here is a summary of each method:

Payback period relates to the number of years expected before the company can recover its original investment. This is a type of breakeven calculation. The disadvantage of this method is that it does not take into account the ongoing costs of capital, such as the costs of carrying debt or issuing new equity. This method has been modified to consider the cost of capital used to pay for the project; this modification is known as the discounted cash-flow method. Projects with a short payback period are considered more liquid projects with lower risk. Projects with a long payback period that will require cash inflows into the distant review are less liquid and carry higher risks.

Net present value (NPV) is a variation on the payback period calculation that improves its effectiveness by finding the net present value for all cash inflows and outflows discounted by the cost of capital. Then the discounted cash flows are totaled to find the project's NPV. If the NPV is positive, the project is accepted. If it's negative, the project is rejected unless management can prove the project is needed for other reasons, such as employee safety. If all projects can't be included in a budget year, a company will usually prioritize them, using NPV to fund those projects with the greatest positive potential first and shelve others for consideration in a future year. Of course, this is not an absolute because other considerations, such as maintenance necessity or market potential, may also factor into a decision to approve a project.

Internal rate of return (IRR) uses the concepts practiced when calculating a bond's yield to maturity. This calculation equates the present value of a project's expected cash inflows to the present value of a project's expected costs or:

PV inflows = PV investment costs.

In this calculation, the rate of return is an unknown; if calculated manually, it can only be found by a series of trial-and-error calculations that substitute different variables for the rate of return until the equation is equal on both sides. Obviously, this can be a tedious and potentially long calculation. Advanced financial calculators or spreadsheet packages have simplified the use of this method. To calculate IRR using a calculator or spreadsheet program requires only entering the cash flows; the calculator can find the IRR. Most advanced financial calculators will explain how to input the data for finding IRR in their accompanying instruction book. Since the actual input methods vary, we can't describe them all here. A business will likely chose those projects with the highest IRR, unless there is some other logical business reason to choose a project with a lower IRR.

The **profitability index** looks at the relative profitability of any project by comparing a project's present value of benefits to its per-dollar costs. Essentially this is a cost/benefit ratio. The formula for this calculation is as follows:

$$PI = \frac{PV\ benefits}{PV\ costs}$$

Any project with a PI greater than one is an acceptable project.

Estimating Cash Flows

All the methods for evaluating capital projects require cash-flow estimates. The results depend on the quality of the estimates. Many variables go into these estimates, which require input from many different departments. The marketing department generates sales forecasts for capital project inflows based on their research, projecting price, advertising costs, economic state, competition, and consumer acceptance. The engineering and product development departments project capital outflows for new products. Outflow projections for operating costs of all types of projects are developed by cost accountants, production experts, human resource specialists, and purchasing and other departments involved in company operations.

All the methods for evaluating capital projects require cash-flow estimates.

ZapMail Optimism Results in Poor Cash-Flow Analysis for FedEx

A classic example of a poorly analyzed pet project that resulted in a major loss is the Federal Express Corporation's (FedEx) foray into fax services. In the early 1980s, FedEx developed a new service called ZapMail. Customers would arrange for fax delivery through a FedEx facsimile machine for a cost initially set at $35 for a fax up to ten pages. When its customers balked at the cost, FedEx lowered its price to $25, but customers still decided to buy or lease fax machines directly for a few hundred dollars and then fax as many documents as often as they wanted. FedEx invested $300 million upfront in ZapMail and incurred operating losses of $132 million with revenues of only $33 million in its second year of operation (fiscal year 1986). After those dismal results, the project was killed. How did FedEx go so wrong in its cash-flow analysis? Marketing managers did not properly research market potential. They thought their competition would be the other delivery services, when instead the competition was the customers themselves who chose to buy their own fax machines.

Forecasting is not an exact science, and especially for large or complex projects, major errors can be made. Cost overruns are a common aspect of most major projects. Sales forecasts are little more than crystal ball gazing, especially if the project being considered is for a totally new product. While major corporations can absorb the cost of a mistake when introducing a product line that doesn't take off, a small company can go under.

Finance's primary role in the capital budget planning process is to:

1. Coordinate the information gathered by the various departments involved in developing the cost-flow estimates.
2. Make certain that estimates used for economic assumptions are consistent among all departments participating in project planning.
3. Seek to eliminate any biases in the forecasting process. For example, when a proposal is a known pet project for a particular manager, finance must more carefully scrutinize the cost-flow projections from this manager to be certain these projections are not too optimistic.

When developing cash-flow estimates, finance must also be watchful of costs that could skew the numbers incorrectly. These include sunk costs, opportunity costs, the effects on other parts of the company, tax effects, salvage value, and inflation adjustment.

Sunk costs, costs already spent or committed prior to the approval of the project, should not be part of the capital budget decision-making process for a new project. For example, suppose a company is considering whether to go forward with the construction of a new facility. Design plans for the facility have already been completed and the bill has been paid to the design firm. When developing cash-flow estimates to make a decision whether to build the facility, the costs for the design plans should not be included. Those are sunk costs and the decision to build or not to build will not be affected by future cash flows of these design plans. Although the decision not to build will result in a loss of the cost for developing the design plans, if the economic situation has changed and it is questionable that the new facility will be able to generate the cash flows necessary to justify its cash outflows, the company should put the brakes on the project and accept the smaller loss related to the design costs.

Opportunity costs are costs related to alternative uses for the assets that will be tied up in the proposed projects, whether cash or non-cash (such as land). For example, suppose the company owned the land on which it planned to build the new facility. While the cost of purchasing that land is a

Accepting Your Sunk Cost Mistakes

"In the corporate world, sunk costs are in play in a big way when you're agonizing over whether to continue to invest in a money-losing project or shut it down. Or when you're torn between walking away from existing, highly usable production equipment and investing in newer, faster, more efficient machines.

"As a general rule, shutting the project down or walking away from the old machines is exactly what you should do. Investments should be based strictly on the course of action that promises the highest future rate of return."

—*IndustryWeek* columnist Karen Kroll in a column published December 4, 2000 sunk cost and would not be included in the analysis, the decision to use that land for the new facility is an opportunity cost. Instead of building on that land, it might be possible for the company to sell that land at a profit and generate additional cash inflow. This opportunity cost should be factored into the decision-making process.

Effects on other parts of the company involve considerations for the impact of any capital budgeting expense that impacts other existing company operations. For example, if building the new facility means that the company will no longer need an older facility, the costs of closing down that facility should be factored into the capital budget decision-making. There could be cash inflows, such as the sale of the old facility, as well as cash outflows, such as labor costs related to relocating or laying off employees.

Tax effects can have a major impact on a company's cash flows, so they must be factored into any capital budget decision-making. Finance should work closely with accounting and the company's tax attorneys to be certain the tax impact has been factored into the cash-flow analysis.

Salvage value relates to the market value of the asset at the end of the project's useful life. Part of a project's cash inflows could be the sale of the asset once the project is completed; this inflow should be factored into the cash-flow analysis.

Inflation adjustment is required for most capital-planning cash-flow analysis. Inflation is a part of operating in almost every country. When calculating costs or inflows over a number of years, these numbers should be adjusted for inflation.

Just to give you an idea of the variables that would need to be considered when planning to replace old equipment, here is a sample worksheet:

> Finance should work closely with accounting and the company's tax attorneys to be certain the tax impact has been factored into the cash-flow analysis.

Net Cash Flows at the Start of the Project

    Cost of New Equipment   _____

    Market Value of Old Equipment   _____

    Tax Effect on Sale of Old Equipment   _____

    Increase (Decrease) in Net Working Capital   _____

    Total Net Investment   _____

Operating Inflows During the Life of the Project

	YR1	YR2	YR3		Final Year
After-Tax Decrease in Costs	____	____	____	.....	____
Depreciation on New Machine	____	____	____	.....	____
(Depreciation of Old Machine)	(____)	(____)	(____)	.....	(____)
Change in Depreciation	____	____	____	.....	____
Tax Savings from Depreciation	____	____	____	.....	____
Net Operating Cash Inflows	____	____	____	.....	____

(After-Tax Decrease in Costs Plus Tax Savings from Depreciation)

Cash Flows in Final Year of New Machine

    Estimated Salvage Value of New Machine   ____

    Tax on Salvage Value   (____)

    Return of Net Working Capital   ____

    Total Cash Flows at End of Project   ____

| Net Cash Flows | ____ | ____ | ____ | ..... | ____ |

Cash-Flow Analysis

    Payback Period   _____

    IRR   _____

    NPV   _____

Profitability index would not be relevant to this decision-making process, so it would not be calculated. For each capital budgeting process, a worksheet laying out all relevant cash inflows and outflows would be developed. Category 1—Maintenance of Business Assets (repair or replacement of old assets)—is the easiest type of analysis. More extensive analysis is needed for the other categories, and the possible line items for a cash-flow analysis worksheet would be much greater depending on the number of variables to be considered in the capital budget decision-making process.

Analyzing Risks

Risk analysis for capital budget decision-making falls squarely on the shoulders of the finance department. As we discussed in Chapter 9, investors expect a higher return when there is a greater degree of risk in buying a stock or bond. The same is true for capital budgeting. Finance managers must measure the risk of capital projects and incorporate these risks into capital budget decision-making.

In analyzing risks, a company must consider the variability inherent in cost-flow analysis and the risks associated with that analysis. It also must consider how errors in this cost-flow analysis could impact the firm's overall cash flows and finally how the decision could impact the firm's perceptions in the marketplace. As we discussed in the earlier sidebars, FedEx and LILCO both suffered dramatic losses in their cash flows because of bad capital budget decision-making. These types of mistakes happen across the country in companies almost every day.

When analyzing the risk of a project, businesses must consider the risks on a stand-alone basis, as part of a firm's overall cash flows and its market risk or how the project could impact a firm's stock price. To assess a project's risk, firms can use these analytical techniques:

Sensitivity analysis seeks to determine how much the NPV will change in response to various output changes, provided everything else stays constant. For example, when assessing whether to introduce a new project, the project values for unit sales, sales price, fixed costs, and variable costs will be estimated. Then the sensitivity of various questions will be asked, such as if sales fall 20 percent below the expected level, what is the impact on NPV? Or, if

> In analyzing risks, a company must consider the variability inherent in cost-flow analysis and the risks associated with that analysis.

the projected product price per unit falls, what will the impact be on NPV? Looking at the sensitivity of each of the key variables, executives will have a good idea of the potential risks.

Scenario analysis looks not only at the sensitivity of NPV to changes in the key variables but also at a range of likely variable values finding worst-case and best-case scenarios. For example, for deciding the worst that can happen a worst-case scenario will assume that unit sales will be lower than anticipated, costs will be higher, and the sales price will be lower. The best-case scenario will look at the best of all possible worlds, projecting higher sales than anticipated, lower costs, and increasing sales price. When the analysis is completed, executives will be presented with worst-case, expected-case, and best-case scenarios, and each scenario will be assigned a probability of occurrence. The limitations of this type of analysis are that only three possible scenarios are considered, even though in reality there are an infinite number of possibilities.

Monte Carlo simulation, developed by mathematicians who were working on the risks of gambling, uses a powerful computer simulation program. Inputs are entered for a number of variables with a probability distribution for each uncertain variable, such as unit sales, fixed costs, variable costs, and sale price. Data for costs that are considered fixed with no variables are also entered, such as the depreciation for needed equipment. Using these data, the computer then develops possible project NPVs and makes up a probability distribution for these NPVs.

While these analytical techniques can give the executives some help in making a decision, the final decision will be based on subjective judgment criteria built up over years of prior business experience. The weakness of all these types of analysis is that it is not easy to come up with working variables on which executives can absolutely depend because of the uncertainty of the cash-flow variables.

Executives clearly realize they can't find the ultimate risk analysis tool. Instead, they use these tools as a means to estimate risk as one part of the capital budgeting process. In most cases, capital projects will last a number of years and their potential can and should be reassessed yearly during the capital budgeting process. The **decision-tree analysis** is the one method commonly used for assessing a project over several years. With this analysis, goals are set for the project on a yearly basis. If the project meets its yearly goal, the next phase is implemented; if not, the project is stopped. At each assessment point in the tree, NPVs are assigned as well as the probability for either the success or failure at each decision-tree point.

As part of any risk analysis, a company must also consider the impact abandonment might have on NPV and project risk. When a company can easily abandon a project without major contract or equipment commitments, the risk is minimal. But if the project requires signing a long-term agreement that cannot be easily canceled, such as building a new plant or purchasing expensive equipment, the abandonment costs rise dramatically, as do the risk factors. The key to minimizing the abandonment risk is to have various decision points on the decision-tree that allow executives to consider abandonment with the least amount of abandonment risk.

> When a company can easily abandon a project without major contract or equipment commitments, the risk is minimal.

Market risk for an individual project is difficult to measure, but two analytical techniques can be used:

- **Pure play method** tries to find comparable companies that produce only one product similar to the one being considered. This method assumes that the market risk for these single-product companies will aid their company with calculating market risk. Companies will normally find it difficult to locate an applicable single-product company, so this technique is rarely feasible.
- **Accounting beta method** is a fallback method when the pure play method is not feasible. Instead of using market data to calculate a project beta, companies use accounting data that uses historical data that can easily be found for publicly owned companies.

Planning Capital Budgets

While it is advisable to incorporate risk analysis methods into the capital budgeting process, all companies realize that ultimately risk assessment will be a judgment call.

For this reason most companies use a four-step process to develop a risk-adjusted NPV for proposed capital projects:

1. Chief financial officer working with his staff develops an investment opportunity schedule (IOS) and a marginal cost of capital (MCC). The IOS schedule plots the IRR for each project in descending order versus the amount of new capital needed to finance it. This graph will give management a quick overview of each project's potential compared with others under consideration. The MCC seeks to identify the incremental costs of each dollar of additional financing as the capital budget increases.

2. Armed with an IOS and MCC, the MCC scheduled is then adjusted to reflect the risk of the divisions proposing the projects. For example, if a low-risk division is proposing a new project, it will receive less of an adjustment than a high-risk division's new project.

3. Projects within each division are then grouped into three categories based on these adjusted figures: high risk, average risk, and low risk.

4. Using these risk-adjusted figures, each project NPVs are then recalculated so a risk-adjusted project cost of capital can be determined.

While none of these figures can be a guarantee, they do arm executives for comparable measurements that can be used to plan the capital budget. When all is said and done, however, the ultimate development of the capital budget will be based on the judgment calls of the key company decision-makers. Executives will have to ration available funds for capital projects among the various capital project proposals, deciding which projects to include in the current capital budget year, which projects to shelve for a future budget year, and which projects to reject completely.

> **Chapter 11**

Long-Term Financial Funding

Part One

Part Two

Part Three

Part Four

Part Five

Part Six

Using Newly Issued Common Stock

Decisions involving capital expenditures always involve the use of long-term funding. How these projects will be financed, whether by debt or equity, is crucial to all long-term financial planning for a company. In addition to discussing these options in this chapter, we'll also review alternative financing tools including warrants, convertibles, options, and futures.

Issuing new shares of common stock offers a company numerous advantages:

- **No obligation for fixed payment**—A company is not obligated to make any fixed payments on a periodic basis. While a company may eventually decide to pay dividends, they are not required as part of a stock offering. Bonds or other debts do require interest payments.
- **No fixed maturity date**—A company is not required to pay off the stockholders, as it would be required to pay off debt holders.
- **Creditors view common stock positively**—When assessing a company's creditworthiness, creditors see common stock as a shield against losses. The sale of common stock can raise bond ratings, lower debt costs, and increase the possibility of using debt in the future.
- **Stock can be sold on better terms than debt**—Certain types of investors prefer common stock because typically they expect a higher return from that stock with the prospect of capital gains and dividends than could be expected from debt or preferred stock. Common stock, which represents ownership in the firm, is viewed as a better hedge against inflation than bonds or preferred stock. While common stock normally increases in value during inflationary periods, the opposite is true for bonds or preferred stock.

But there are disadvantages for issuing common stock:

- **Control of the company is weakened**—When new common stock is issued, voting rights are extended to new stockholders and possibly even control of the company. If a company's owners or managers are concerned about losing control with additional equity financing, they will avoid issuing new stock.

- **Profits must be shared with new stockholders**—When new common stock is issued, the new stockholders will have the right to share in any profits generated by the cash investment in the company's expansion. Bondholders and preferred stockholders will not get any increase in their potential returns, which are fixed payments no matter how much additional profit is generated from their cash infusion.
- **Issue costs are higher**—The costs to underwrite and distribute common stock usually are higher than underwriting and distributing bonds or preferred stock.
- **Dividends are not deductible**—Companies cannot deduct dividends as an expense of doing business, while they can deduct interest paid on bonds or other debt.

Small companies in which only a few people own stock—usually the company founders and key managers or partners—are considered to be privately owned or closely held corporations. These shares of stock are not actively traded in the open market. You won't find much written about a private company's assets or performance, because they are not required to provide public reports, as are publicly owned corporations.

America's Largest Private Companies

Each year *Forbes* magazine publishes a list of America's largest private companies. All companies on the list must have revenues over $1 billion and cannot have widely owned public stock. Topping the list for at least the past five years is a company founded in 1865—Cargill sells agricultural and industrial products and has about 100,000 employees. The members of the Cargill and MacMillan families jointly own common stock for the company.

The second largest private corporation is Koch Industries, which owns a group of companies engaged in trading, petroleum, asphalt, natural gas, gas liquids, chemicals, plastics and fibers, chemical technology equipment, minerals, fertilizers, ranching, securities, and finance. The Koch family owns and runs the company.

Mars, with top candy sellers including M&M's, Snickers, and Milky Way (to name a few), ranks number three on the *Forbes* list. Members of the Mars family own the company. Mars's products are sold in 100 countries, and the company maintains facilities in 60 countries.

Most larger corporations are owned by a large number of investors who are not active in the actual management of the company. As private companies grow and the need for additional capital increases, many seek to go public so they can raise additional capital. Going public requires meeting the regulations and disclosure requirements of the Securities and Exchange Commission. There are pros and cons to this decision.

The advantages of going public include:

- **Diversification**—Owners of a privately held company may wish to diversify their investments by selling shares of stock so they can then invest in other vehicles. This reduces the risk of their portfolios.
- **Liquidity**—Owners of a privately held company can't sell their stock easily, so it is not a liquid investment. If an owner needs to convert stock in a privately held company to cash, he or she will not find it easy to locate a buyer.
- **Raise cash**—When a private company needs additional capital to expand, it must either find a creditor or get its existing owners to buy more shares. Getting outside investors to put money into a private company without offering them voting rights is a difficult, if not impossible, task. To raise a large chunk of additional capital from outside investors, a company must usually consider either giving up some portion of ownership rights to new private investors or going public.
- **Establish market value**—Selling stock helps a company establish its value in the marketplace. This can be particularly valuable to a family after the death of the business owner as the family tries to sort out inheritance tax issues with state and federal tax appraisers. A publicly owned company has a clearly established market value per share, while a privately owned company may end up battling with tax appraisers as to the true value of the shares.

Going public is not always the best decision for a company. There are some disadvantages:

> Most larger corporations are owned by a large number of investors who are not active in the actual management of the company.

- **Reporting costs**—Publicly owned companies must file quarterly and annual reports with the SEC and/or state agencies. Preparing these reports is costly and may not be worth it for small firms.
- **Disclosure**—Public companies must report operating data giving competitors information that managers would prefer not to share. Also, more information is known about an owner's net worth in a public company than in a private company. Publicly owned companies must disclose the number of shares held by their officers, directors, and major stockholders.
- **Benefits**—Owners of privately held companies have more flexibility when it comes to setting benefits, paying high salaries, hiring relatives, and arranging private financing using company assets. Once a company goes public, these arrangements must be disclosed; stockholders have the right to file suits if they believe company assets are being misused.
- **Control**—Once the owners of a private company sell stock that represents more than 50 percent ownership, there is the risk of losing control of the company.
- **Undervalued in the marketplace**—Small companies whose stocks are not frequently traded in the marketplace will not offer much liquidity and the sales price of the stock may not be truly representative of the company's value.

The actual decision to go public is a major milestone in the life of a company and changes its operations. While owners of a privately held company are more likely to make decisions that look toward long-term growth prospects, once a company goes public many shareholders look for more immediate gratification and capital growth. Rather than looking at the impact of a decision over a five- or ten-year horizon, which may be more common in privately held companies; public companies must be concerned about how their quarterly results will be viewed by their investors. Many public companies are forced to seek short-term solutions that raise immediate profits but may not be the best decision for the long term.

Using Preferred Stock

A hybrid between common stocks and bonds is a financing vehicle called preferred stock. Technically preferred stock is an equity, but it has properties that resemble both stocks and bonds. As with a fixed-income security (such as a bond), a stream of income is provided in dividends; sometimes this amount is fixed and sometimes variable depending on the type of preferred stock.

Preferred stockholders are paid after bondholders but before common stockholders in the case of bankruptcy and liquidation. Dividends for preferred stockholders are not legally binding, as is interest for debt holders, but unpaid dividends accumulate and must be paid before dividends for common stockholders. Non-cumulative preferred stock is sometimes issued, which means missed dividends do not have to be paid.

About a third of the time, preferred stock is sold as convertible into common stock at the option of the stockholder. Usually this is done by some agreed-upon conversion rate set at the time the stock is sold. Today other variations on preferred stock include:

Using the MIPs Alternative

Monthly income preferred stock was first introduced to the corporate world in October 1993 by Goldman Sachs and today accounts for almost 70 percent of new preferred issues. MIPs give companies the advantage of repackaging subordinated debt as preferred stock, which improves their standing with rating agencies. In addition, at least so far, the IRS has permitted the issuer to deduct the preferred dividends on MIPs as interest for tax purposes. Therefore, the firm can increase its equity base using MIPs at an after-tax cost that is close to that of long-term debt. In order to create an MIP, a special-purpose subsidiary of a parent firm sells the preferred stock to the public and then lends the proceeds to the parent. The interest the parent firm pays on the loan to the subsidiary is deductible as interest, while the interest is used to pay the preferred dividends to the buyers of the MIPs. The interest income received by the subsidiary is not taxable, because it was organized as a tax-free entity.

- **Variable-rate preferred**—Dividend rate is tied to current market interest rates.
- **Auction-rate preferred**—Dividend rate floats and is established by auction every four to seven weeks.
- **Retractable preferred**—Usually issued for a set term with a par value that will be paid by the issuer to the shareholder at the end of the term.
- **Participating preferred**—A rare type of preferred that includes some share in the firm's earnings.
- **Brokerage house preferred**—Securities sold by a brokerage house under such acronyms as MIPs (monthly income preferred) and QUIPs (quarterly income preferred) securities.

Preferred shares are sold with a par value, similar to bonds, which must be paid to preferred shareholders in the event of bankruptcy before the common shareholders get any share of the assets remaining. Most preferred shareholders do not have voting rights, but if a company has not paid promised dividends for a specific period (normally four, eight, or ten quarters), preferred stockholders generally get the right to vote for directors of the company. This feature definitely motivates managers and directors to pay dividends even though, like bond interest, they are not required. Also, like bonds, some preferred stock is issued with a call provision, which gives the issuing corporation the right to call the stock for redemption. Usually the call provision is set at a value above par value.

For a company, the advantage of using preferred rather than common stock is that the potential future profits will not have to be shared by the common stockholders, and if for some reason dividends can't be paid, the company is not increasing its bankruptcy risk. Nonpayment of bond interest does put the company at risk of insolvency. A major disadvantage is that the preferred stock has higher after-tax costs because the dividends are not tax deductible, as is interest expense. If a company does not need the interest tax write-off, which is true for many start-ups that have significant expenses to write off, the non-deductibility of dividends is not as important as the flexibility of not having to pay out dividends.

From the investor standpoint, the primary advantage preferred stock offers is the possibility of a steady income stream that is generally higher than a bond, as well as ownership rights higher than those of common stockholders. Disadvantages include returns limited by preset dividend levels, usually with no rights to profit sharing and no way to enforce the payment of dividends legally. Today a common use of preferred stock is in exchange for cash from venture capitalists and other early-stage investors in a new company.

Using Long-Term Debt

Traditionally there are two types of long-term debt available to companies: term loans and bonds. A term loan is a loan in which the borrower agrees to make a set number of payments over a set period, usually including both interest and principal payments. At the end of the term, the loan is paid in full. Bonds, as we discussed in Chapter 9, require periodic interest payments with a par value paid in full at the maturity of the bond.

It is quicker and easier to get a term loan than it is to orchestrate a sale of bonds. Term loans are negotiated between the borrower and the lender. For major companies, lenders can be banks, insurance companies, or pension funds. Since loans don't have to meet the extensive registration and sales process as bonds, they are cheaper to get and can be arranged much more quickly. Interest terms for loans can be at a fixed or variable rate.

Bonds are much more costly to issue. Before being issued, bonds must be registered with the Securities and Exchange Commission, which is both a costly and lengthy process. Once that is completed, bonds are then sold on the public market, which also delays how quickly a company can get cash from the bond issue. There are numerous types of bonds:

> It is quicker and easier to get a term loan than it is to orchestrate a sale of bonds.

- **Mortgage bonds**—Companies pledge assets as security for the bond and are usually used to buy a land or a building. If a company defaults on this type of bond, the bondholders can foreclose on the underlying asset.
- **Debentures**—Unsecured bonds are known as debentures, which include no specific lien on property. Bondholders of debentures have rights to property not already pledged under a mortgage bond. Companies that hold most of their assets in inventory, or types of assets not tied to land or buildings, will use this form of bond.

- **Subordinated debentures**—These types of debentures are subordinate (or inferior) to more senior forms of debt, such as debentures or mortgage bonds. In the event of a bankruptcy, holders of subordinated debentures would not be paid until the higher-level debt holders are paid.
- **Convertible bonds**—These bonds are convertible to common stock at a price fixed at the time the debt is issued. Conversion is at the option of the bondholder. By issuing convertible bonds, companies can offer a lower coupon rate in exchange for giving investors the potential of sharing in profits if the bonds are converted.

Leasing

Sometimes companies prefer to use funding that will not appear on their balance sheet or directly impact their borrowing potential. Leasing equipment or buildings is one alternative because lease payments are shown as part of operating expenses but do not always appear on the firm's balance sheet. There are four types of leases:

- **Sale and leaseback**—A company sells an asset to another company and then leases back the property. This is a mortgage alternative. The payments are set to return the full value paid for the property plus a return on the investment.
- **Operating lease**—With this type of lease, the company offering the equipment provides both financing and maintenance. This lease is commonly used for office equipment, computers, trucks, and cars. Payments are not fully amortized (will not pay off the equipment) and will not recover the full cost of the equipment. They usually include a cancellation clause with the return of equipment expected at the end of the lease.
- **Financial or capital lease**—This type of lease provides financing but does not provide maintenance, as does an operating lease. Payments are based on the value of the asset plus a return on the investment. Cancellation is usually not allowed. At the end of the lease term, a company can renew the lease, usually at a reduced rate, or buy the asset based on terms set up in the lease.

- **Combination leases**—Many lease variations available on the market today combine features of the key types of leases mentioned here. These types of leases are called combination leases.

Leasing offers a number of advantages for a company. Loans usually require an initial cash down payment on equipment, while a lease often requires none. Companies may have to agree to restrictive covenants that require the company to maintain certain financial ratios that restrict future borrowing options. If a customer violates these restrictions, the lender can demand payment in full, even if all payments are made on time. Leases do not contain restrictive covenants; as long as the company makes its lease payments on time, there is no risk of early demand. When equipment is bought using a loan, the company bears all the risk that the equipment may lose value because it is replaced by new technology. The lessor owns leased equipment, so the company can choose not to purchase the equipment or renew the lease at the end of the agreed term. While many of these aspects may make the lease seem more attractive, each factor must be weighed against other capital financing needs of the company, as well as whether lease or loan terms make better economic sense for the company in the long term.

Leases offer companies a greater tax benefit than loans because the entire payment can be written off as an expense, whereas on a loan only the interest is deductible. The IRS can decide that a lease is actually a loan and this benefit will be lost. The IRS will rule that a lease is a loan if:

> Leases offer companies a greater tax benefit than loans because the entire payment can be written off as an expense, whereas on a loan only the interest is deductible.

1. Total lease payments are made over a relatively short period and approximately equal the total cost of the asset.
2. The lease provides that the equipment can continue to be used for its useful life with minimal renewal payments.
3. The lease includes a purchase option with favorable pricing.

If you are considering leasing as an option for your company because of the greater tax benefits, be certain to verify that the lease provisions will pass muster with the IRS. Ask your lawyers or tax accountants to review the lease provisions before signing a deal.

The ownership provisions at the end of the lease are a key factor in whether a leased item is listed as an asset. If one or more of these conditions exist, the lease must be capitalized and shown on the balance sheet:

- Ownership of the property leased is transferred from the lessor to the lessee as part of the terms of the lease.
- At the end of the lease, the asset can be purchased for less than its true market value.
- The lease is written for a term that is equal to, or more than, 75 percent of the asset's life.
- The present value of the lease payments is equal to, or greater than, 90 percent of the initial value of the asset.

If you are considering using a lease to avoid listing the debt on the balance sheet, be certain your lease provisions meet the necessary accounting disclosure rules. Even if a lease does not have to appear on the balance sheet, there are disclosure rules for operating leases so that investors can adjust for leases when considering a firm's debt-to-equity ratio.

Considering Alternatives

Companies also have a number of alternatives for raising cash that do not fit into the more traditional stock, bond, or lease options. These alternatives include options, warrants, convertibles, and futures. We'll briefly describe options here, but if you are interested in learning more about options, go to the Chicago Board Options Exchange Learning Center (*www.cboe.com/LearnCenter/*).

Options—Options are contracts that give a holder the right to buy (or sell) an asset at some predetermined price within a specified period. Both warrants and convertibles are types of options.

Warrants—Warrants are a type of option that gives a warrant's owner the right to buy a stated number of shares of the company's stock at a specified price. These are generally distributed with debt instruments to entice investors to buy a firm's long-term debt. Warrants do have the potential of bringing additional capital to the firm if the warrant owners decide to purchase stock at some future date.

Convertibles—Convertible securities are bonds or preferred stock that can be exchanged for common stock at the option of the holder under terms and conditions specified at the time the convertible is issued. Unlike warrants, convertibles do not have the potential of bringing additional cash into the firm, but they do have the advantage of lowering expenses of interest (if a bond is converted) or dividends (if preferred stock is converted).

Futures—Futures establish a fixed price for an asset the day the future contract is issued, which guarantees that the asset can be sold or purchased at some time in the future at the fixed price. No matter how high or low the price goes, the parties on both sides of the future must carry out the contract at the agreed-on price. This differs from options, where the buyer of the option has the right to buy or sell the option, but is not required to do so. The Commodity Futures Trading Commission (*www.cftc.gov/cftc/cftchome.htm*) is a good place to start if you want to learn more about futures.

Long-Term Financing Decision-Making

When making decisions about what type of long-term financing to use, a company must consider these critical issues: target capital structure, maturity matching, interest rate levels, company forecasting, debt restrictions, and the availability of collateral. Each of these factors will play a critical role in the finance department's recommendations for the best capital fund-raising options.

> Companies should establish a target capital structure that establishes the optimal mix of debt and equity for the firm.

Target capital structure—Companies should establish a target capital structure that establishes the optimal mix of debt and equity for the firm. When new long-term financing is being considered, whether to use debt or equity will depend on how the new financing will impact this target structure. Too much debt could make it more difficult and more expensive to take on new debt, while too little debt may not be a good use of funds and available leverage. In setting this target structure, a company should look at averages for the industry averages, as well as companies with similar markets and goals.

Maturity matching—When deciding to issue bonds, a company has the flexibility of deciding the term for the debt, which can be five, ten, twenty, or thirty years. The most common date of maturity is to match the debt's maturity to the life of the asset being financed. Other considerations may include management's forecast of future interest rates and the maturity of other debt already issued.

Interest rate levels—When interest rates are low and appear as though they may be rising, managers are more likely to issue long-term debt. When interest rates are high and likely to be going lower, managers will decide to use shorter-term debt with the hopes of refinancing that debt at lower rates in the near future.

Company current and forecasted position—When a company's current financial position is poor, it will most likely try to avoid issuing new long-term debt. Not only will new debt cost more with higher interest rates required to attract new bond investors, but bond-rating agencies could also lower a company's rating after new debt is issued. If a company is currently in a strong position but forecasts problems in the future, that company would be more likely to issue long-term debt when it can get the more favorable rates.

Existing debt restrictions—When companies enter into debt contracts, frequently there are restrictions placed on the company by its lenders that require the firm to maintain a certain current ratio, debt ratio, or other restriction that limits its ability to seek new debt financing. Before considering new debt, a company must review any existing debt restrictions to be certain it will not be breaking previously agreed-on contract terms.

Availability of collateral—Usually a company will find it is cheaper to finance using secured, rather than unsecured, debt. To save money, a company may decide to raise long-term funds using existing collateral to lower interest rates and get better debt terms.

Now that we've reviewed all the options available for a company to raise new funds, the next chapter will review how to manage the working capital raised.

> **Chapter 12**

Managing Working Capital

Part One

Part Two

Part Three

Part Four

Part Five

Part Six

Capital for Daily Operations

While we've been talking primarily about planning and raising long-term capital, a major part of the finance department's work actually involves managing working capital, which relates to the use of current assets and current liabilities. Not all capital is raised using long-term debt. Much of the capital needed for daily operations is raised using short-term debt, especially in businesses whose product is seasonal. These businesses may have a short-term need for a cash infusion to develop product for the next season, which can be paid off quickly as the inventory is sold. Long-term debt would never be needed for this type of working capital.

Finance must establish working capital policies, determine sources for raising working capital, understand the impact that accounts receivable and inventory have on the need for additional working capital, and put controls in place not only to ensure that working capital is being used effectively but also to minimize the use of current liabilities by instituting proper working capital controls.

Establishing Working Capital Policies

When developing policies for working capital, finance must address two key issues:

1. What is the appropriate level for current asset accounts?
2. How should the company finance its current asset needs?

Companies can choose to institute a liberal financing policy that carries large amounts of cash, marketable securities, and inventory. Usually this type of policy is matched with credit policy that provides rather liberal standards for customers to buy on credit, which also means a high level of accounts receivable. A more conservative approach would be the opposite of the liberal approach that minimizes holdings of cash, marketable securities, inventories, and receivables. Most companies chose a working capital policy somewhere between these two extremes.

When a company can regularly and accurately predict its sales, costs, lead times, payment periods, and other aspects of operation, the managers will most likely decide to keep current assets at their minimum levels. This policy minimizes the need to raise short-term capital—reducing costs and risks and increasing profits. If the working capital policy is too tight though, it can result in lost sales and increased production costs if materials or inventory are not available when needed. Sales can also be lost to overly restrictive credit policies. Establishing the appropriate working capital policies is critical to a company's success. While finance may take the lead in developing these policies, other department managers should have a critical role in assessing the impact of any new working capital policies on the operations of their individual departments.

Working capital needs vary for each company depending not only on its individual operations, but also on the state of the economy in general. Businesses whose products are seasonal or cyclical must carefully plan for production and sales needs that match their seasonal or cyclical needs. If a company is very dependent on a robust economy for sales success, it must pull back its production if the economy shows signs of weakness. When the economy begins to strengthen, working capital policies can be readjusted to be sure the company doesn't miss sales opportunities. Monitoring economic situations is a critical part of any finance manager's workday.

> Working capital needs vary for each company depending not only on its individual operations, but also on the state of the economy in general.

Raising Working Capital Financing

Working capital financing can be raised using short-term or long-term debt. Speed, flexibility, cost, and risk are all factors in deciding what type of debt is best to use.

- **Speed**—A company can obtain short-term debt much faster than long-term debt. Financial institutions require a more thorough examination of a company's assets and future prospects before making a long-term loan.
- **Flexibility**—Short-term debt provides more flexibility and should be used especially if the need for cash is seasonal or cyclical. Costs for long-term debt are higher. There are usually prepayment penalties if the company wants to pay off the long-term debt earlier. Long-term debt usually comes with restrictive provisions that limit other future debt decisions.

- **Cost**—Interest rates are usually lower for short-term loans than for long-term loans. Also the costs of obtaining short-term debt are lower, especially if a company is considering the more expensive possibility of issuing bonds.
- **Risk**—A company's risks can be higher with short-term debt because interest rates are not guaranteed and can rise rapidly, while a long-term debt issue will have a fixed interest rate expense that is not affected by market fluctuations. Also, a firm that borrows heavily using short-term debt may find itself in a weak financial position if the economy changes expectedly and the firm is unable to repay its debt. This could force the firm into bankruptcy or into using less favorable debt terms.

> Short-term financing can come from four major sources: accruals, accounts payable, bank loans, and commercial paper.

Short-term financing can come from four major sources: accruals, accounts payable, bank loans, and commercial paper. Accruals can include an influx of cash waiting to be used for future payouts, such as taxes and employee paychecks. While this type of cash is "free," it must be available when the company needs to make those accrual payments.

Buying things on credit and increasing a firm's accounts payable account is the most common way companies finance their short-term working capital needs. Many companies rely heavily on using accounts payable for short-term needs; estimates for this time of funding are about 40 percent of all short-term working capital needs. If payments are missed, the interest on these types of accounts can be very high, and there is the risk that a vendor or supplier may cut off future purchases a company needs to make.

Short-term bank loans, which usually appear on the balance sheet as notes payable, are the second most common way companies get additional short-term working capital. In fact, even though banks do make long-term loans to companies, the bulk of their lending is on a short-term basis. Almost two-thirds of bank loans to companies mature in a year or less. The most common loan to businesses is a ninety-day note, which can be repaid in full or renewed at the end of the ninety-day period. Banks usually renew these loans if the company requests the extensions, but they will refuse if the company's financial position has deteriorated.

Other short-term bank financing includes lines of credit from a bank and revolving credit from another corporation. Lines of credit usually involve an informal agreement between the bank and a company that permits the company to draw on that credit line as needed. Usually a maximum line of credit is determined at the beginning of each year, and the company either draws down on that line when working capital is needed or pays down the line when extra working capital is available. Revolving credit for a company is a formal line of credit between a firm and another company, usually one of its vendors or suppliers. A maximum line of credit will be agreed to by contract, and the company either buys on credit within that revolving line or pays it down as working capital becomes available.

Commercial paper is another way companies raise short-term capital. These are unsecured promissory notes issued by large companies and sold to other business firms, insurance companies, pension funds, money market funds, and banks. Commercial paper generally matures in one to nine months. The interest rates fluctuate depending on the marketplace, usually 1½ to 2½ points above the prime rate or a half point above the T-bill rate. Not many companies can use commercial paper. This form of financing is usually restricted to a small number of large corporations that are considered good credit risks.

Secured short-term loans are also a possibility for a small company, especially if their financial conditions are weak. Firms can use marketable securities, land, buildings, equipment, inventory, and accounts receivable as collateral for these types of short-term loans. Most short-term loans are secured using inventory or accounts receivable. Other types of collateral are used for long-term loans.

Understanding the Impact of Accounts Receivable and Inventory

Typically, companies hold about 20 percent of their assets in accounts receivable and another 20 percent in inventory. The effectiveness of managing these two key asset types is critical to effectively using working capital.

Accounts Receivable

Obviously, every company prefers cash sales, but competitive pressures usually create the need to offer credit to customers. Granting credit will increase sales, but the critical task of finance is finding the right balance of developing a competitive credit policy while maximizing the cash flows of the firm. As was discussed earlier, when calculating the accounts receivable turnover ratio, the volume of credit sales and the time it takes to collect on those sales are critical factors in managing accounts receivable. Finance must regularly monitor the turnover ratio and if the number of days to collect on accounts continues to increase, some adjustment may be needed in the established credit policy.

Companies that have excess capacity and low variable production costs can extend credit more liberally, but those operating at full capacity with a slim profit margin would likely maintain stricter credit policies. There are four variables to consider when establishing credit policy:

1. **Credit period**—length of time you allow customers to pay for their purchases.
2. **Credit standards**—minimum financial strength customers must show to open a credit account and how the company will verify financial strength (such as credit check and credit scoring).
3. **Collection period**—how tough or lax the company will be in collection of slow-paying accounts. Follow-up standards should be set for how customers will be contacted if they have not paid. For example, sending a letter when the account is thirty days late, making a phone call when it's sixty days late, and using a collection service for accounts over ninety days late. Also, at what time in the process will the customer be cut off from buying on credit?
4. **Discounts**—whether to offer discounts for accounts paid early. Offering cash discounts, such as "2/10, net 30" (which is common), can entice new customers who prefer to work with companies that offer discounts and can also encourage customers to pay early and increase cash flow. The discount would be 2 percent if paid in ten days or the full invoice if paid in thirty days. After thirty days, many companies begin adding interest charges or fees for late payment.

Whenever a company considers changing its credit policy, finance must analyze the proposed change to determine its impact on the profit margin. The key questions are whether the change in policy will increase sales revenues and at what cost. For example, if a company decides to ease its credit policy to increase sales, what will that change cost? There will be additional staffing costs to manage the accounts receivable. There could be additional bad debts that might need to be written off when easing credit policy. There could be additional discounts that will need to be offered to encourage early payments. All these factors will need to be analyzed to determine whether the credit policy change will actually result in increased profits. If a stricter policy is being considered, then finance must look at the possible impact on lost sales versus the reduction in bad debt and staffing costs with reduced accounts receivables to manage.

There are three common measures used for monitoring accounts receivable: the average collection period, aging schedules, and the payment pattern approach.

The **average collection period (ACP)** is calculated by looking at a payment history and determining what percentage of your customers pay within the discount period (assume ten days), what percentage pay within thirty days, and what percentage pay late. For example, ABC Company found that 40 percent of its customers take advantage of the discount, 50 percent pay within thirty days, 8 percent pay within sixty days, and 2 percent pay in ninety days or more. When a company is sixty days late, the account is closed and no additional credit is offered. The money is written off as bad debt, and the account is transferred to collections. To calculate their average collection period:

$$ACP = 0.4(10 \text{ days}) + 0.5(30 \text{ days}) +$$
$$0.08(60 \text{ days}) + 0.02(90 \text{ days}) = 25.6 \text{ days}$$

If finance notices that the ACP increases in number of days, then further research would be needed to determine the reason for the increase. Quickly noticing any shift in ACP and understanding the reason for the difference is critical to good working capital management.

Aging schedules break down a company's receivables by age of account. These schedules are developed from the accounts receivable ledger. Most companies that use aging schedules have designed a report that can be generated by computer on a periodic basis. The report would look something like this (for comparison, we'll use the same assumptions used for ACP):

Age of Account	Value of Account	Percentage of Total Value
0–10 days	$1,000,000	40%
11–30 days	1,250,000	50%
31–60 days	200,000	8%
Over 60 days	50,000	2%
Total Receivables	$2,500,000	100%

If finance notices that the percentage of late accounts is increasing, further research would be needed to discover the reasons for the increase. Quickly picking up any deterioration is crucial to working capital management.

The **payment pattern approach** looks at accounts receivable data to see if there is a pattern indicating that customers are slowing down their payments. Both ACP and aging schedules can be affected by the company's sales levels, so red flags could be raised when they're not necessary or missed completely during periods of high or low sales volumes. The payment pattern approach first breaks down sales and collection data by month. Then finance uses the data to compare quarterly results. Next an analysis is made of the uncollected balances per month and quarter to see if there is a pattern of change. This analysis allows managers to remove the effects of seasonal or cyclical sales variation and construct a clear measure of customers' payment patterns.

Inventory

Inventory management is traditionally the role of production managers, but since finance is responsible for raising the capital needed to maintain inventory levels, which can greatly impact a company's profitability, there are concerns that must be addressed from the finance prospective. Basically, three critical questions must be answered:

1. How many units should be ordered or produced at any given time?
2. When should items be reordered? For example, determining when the inventory falls to x number of units, new items should be ordered or produced.
3. What types of items need special attention?

Icon of Just-in-Time Inventory Management

Sam Walton is widely known as the icon of just-in-time inventory management. He knew that minimizing the costs of his merchandising system would be critical to his success. When he had only twenty stores in 1966, Walton attended a computer school run by IBM in New York intending to hire the smartest guy in the class to computerize his operations. His computer database developed into today's premiere just-in-time inventory control system and is second only to the Pentagon's in capacity, according to John Huey, coauthor of Walton's biography entitled *Sam Walton, Made in America: My Story*. The original concept of just-in-time inventory is credited to Taiichi Ohno, a mechanical engineer and manager for the Toyota Motor Car Company in the 1950s. Effective just-in-time inventory management can result in cost reductions, increased speed to market, and identification of bottlenecks in the company's systems, but in order for the system to be properly implemented, a company must build strong relationships with its suppliers to be sure they will cooperate and become a partner in the process.

Before even answering these three critical questions, finance managers must understand the costs of inventory, which includes carrying costs, ordering, shipping and receiving costs, and costs of running out of inventory. Carrying costs include the cost of capital tied up in inventory, storage and handling costs, insurance, property taxes (if relevant in the state in which the inventory is held), depreciation, and the risk of obsolescence. The costs of running out of inventory can result in lost sales, disappointed customers, and disruption of production schedules if raw materials are not available when needed.

Setting the appropriate order point to be sure inventory will be there just-in-time is critical to working capital management. While you don't want to order inventory too early and tie up too much capital, it can be just as damaging to company profitability not to have inventory on hand when needed. For example, if it takes thirty days from the date an item is ordered until the date the item will be received, then the company must estimate the number of items that will be sold in a thirty-day period and order new items once inventory falls to within that level. Many companies will also plan for safety stock, so the actual order point will be earlier than needed just in case there is an expected jump in sales.

Another factor to be considered when placing orders is whether quantity discounts are offered. For example, if there is a 2 percent discount when more than 1,000 units are ordered and a 5 percent discount when ordering more than 10,000 units, a company must determine whether its sales volumes warrant the higher ordering level to take advantage of the discounts.

The goals of any good inventory management program should be high inventory turnover, low write-offs of obsolete or damaged inventory, few instances of work stoppages, and infrequent lost sales because of lack of inventory on the shelf. Finance must work closely with sales, production, and purchasing to design a cost-effective inventory control system.

Managing Cash and Marketable Securities

Cash is the lifeblood of any business but holding more than necessary can be a drain on assets since most cash accounts do not earn interest. Financial managers must develop an effective cash budget to determine what levels of cash must be held at different times of the year. Some large corporations actually break down their cash budgets based on daily cash needs using extensive computer simulations, but most small companies will develop a cash budget based on monthly or quarterly cash estimates. The primary goal of a cash manager is to minimize the amount held in non-interest-earning accounts. Cash budgeting was discussed in Chapter 6.

The primary reason for holding cash is to cover transactions necessary to carry out business operations, including routine payments and staff salaries. Also, minimum cash balances may be required at the bank in order to qualify for certain bank services. Adequate cash balances can help a company:

- Take advantage of discounts by paying suppliers promptly.
- Improve a company's credit rating by keeping it current and maintaining quick ratios in line with other similar companies in order to get the best credit terms.

> Financial managers must develop an effective cash budget to determine what levels of cash must be held at different times of the year.

- Take advantage of unexpected business opportunities, such as the acquisition of another company.
- Meet emergency needs that can occur because of a fire or strike, or respond to a competitor's marketing campaign.

Marketable securities, including U.S. Treasury bills and bank certificates of deposits (CDs), are some alternatives to holding cash that do yield interest, but not earnings as high as operating assets. They serve as a bridge between cash needs and operating assets. Holding marketable securities allows the cash manager to minimize the amount of cash on hand, while having sufficient liquid assets to respond to any situation where cash outflows exceed inflows. Firms must make the choice between holding sufficient marketable securities or borrowing on a short-term basis as needs arise. The primary reasons to hold marketable securities are as follows:

1. As a reserve for contingencies.
2. To meet seasonal needs.
3. To meet projected future payments, such as taxes or payments for major projects.
4. To park cash in after the sale of a long-term asset until long-term capital plans are made for the money.

Companies with a conservative working capital policy will tend to hold marketable securities and use short-term debt sparingly. Companies with a more aggressive working capital policy will be more likely to use short-term debt rather than holding on to marketable securities. Obviously using debt can be riskier if the economy slows and a company's sales decline, making it more difficult to carry debt payments. Just as with long-term debt, finding the proper balance between current assets and current liabilities is critical for the financial health of the firm.

> **Chapter 13**

Understanding
Management Theory

Part One

Part Two

Part Three

Part Four

Part Five

Part Six

The Beginnings of Management Theory

Managing effectively was practiced for thousands of years, but the actual study of management theory did not start until the late 1800s with the research of two early pioneers in management theory: Robert Owen and Charles Babbage.

Robert Owen, a British industrialist, spearheaded the importance of managing people. Prior to his studies, people were treated in the same way as machinery and equipment with little regard for respect or dignity. He showed that by giving greater attention to workers, businesses would be paid back with increased productivity. He pushed for better working conditions, higher minimum working age for children, and reduced work hours. He even advocated meals for workers. His early lead in this area developed into today's behavioral management theory.

Charles Babbage, a British mathematician, showed more interest in ways to increase production efficiency. Using his mathematical skills, he advocated applying math to finding the best division of labor and the most efficient use of facilities and materials. His work is considered to be the early stages of both classical management theory and quantitative management theory. He didn't forget the importance of rewarding people though. He also advocated a good relationship between labor and management and favored such reward programs as profit-sharing plans.

In this chapter, we'll review the basic management theories—classical, behavioral, and quantitative—and how these theories blend into today's contemporary management practice. All three theories are used in different ways in almost every major company.

Classical Management

Classical management theory is based on two primary ideas: scientific management, which focuses on employees and how to improve their productivity, and classical organization, which focuses on the total organization and how to make it more efficient and effective.

Scientific theory was popular in the late 1800s through the mid-1930s. Recently these theories have been revisited in efforts to cut costs and increase productivity. Four key pioneers—Frederick Taylor, Frank Gilbreth, Lillian Gilbreth, and Henry Gantt—led research in scientific management.

Taylor developed a four-step process that he summarized as the essence of scientific management:

1. Analyze the work situation to determine the work to be done, the workers needed, and the manager's responsibilities.
2. Analyze the tasks to be completed by determining the elements of the tasks, the skills each of these elements require, and the number of workers needed to complete the tasks.
3. Match the workers to the tasks based on skills required for each task.
4. Managers continue to supervise the workers and serve as planners for the work group.

Taylor's work aided manufacturing organizations in developing job specialization and had a major impact on mass-production techniques. Workers' groups argued against his theories saying they were just a way to get more work from each person and reduce the size of the work force.

Frank and Lillian Gilbreth, a husband and wife team, were industrial engineers who furthered the ideas of time-and-motion studies and job simplification. Working together and individually, the Gilbreths developed techniques to improve efficiency. For example, Frank Gilbreth is known for his work in defining the steps in the craft of bricklaying. He specified standard materials and designed scaffolding that placed the bricklayer, bricks, and mortar at different levels, so the work could be done more efficiently. He also broke up tasks so less expensive laborers could be used for tasks such as carrying bricks to the scaffolding and stacking them. He also developed a standard mortar to ensure consistency. These studies

Investigating Taylor and Shop Management Systems

Frederick Taylor's systems became so controversial that in 1911, the U.S. House of Representatives authorized a Special Committee to Investigate Taylor and other systems of Shop Management, after a strike at a government arsenal in Watertown, Massachusetts, in response to new management procedures based on Taylor's work. Taylor is seen today as the first efficiency expert and management guru. At the time, organized labor said Taylor was "a soulless slave driver, out to destroy the workingman's health and rob him of his manhood," according to Robert Kanigel who wrote *The One Best Way: Frederick Winslow Taylor and the Enigma of Efficiency*. Taylor's time-and-motion studies improved productivity but also were thought to increase the monotony of work assignments. The congressional investigation looked at whether his scientific management techniques dehumanized workers.

decreased the number of physical movements and increased the output of bricklayers by 200 percent.

Henry Gantt, an associate of Taylor's, is best known for his Gantt chart, a means of scheduling work that can be used for individual workers or for a complex project as a whole. You can learn more about Gantt charts, which are still used today, online at *http://www.smartdraw.com/resources/centers/gantt/tutorial1.htm*. Gantt's second major contribution to management theory was his pay system, which established a minimum wage plus bonuses for workers who exceeded minimum expectations. Gantt's system also rewarded supervisors whose employees exceeded minimum levels.

At the same time advocates of scientific management were studying ways to improve the efficiency of individual jobs, classical organization theorists focused on improving the management of the entire organization. The leading pioneer in this area was Henri Fayol, a French industrialist who developed the first set of principles for effective management by dividing them into fourteen key guidelines. These guidelines were laid out in his book *Industrial and General Management*:

1. **Division of labor**—Specialization results in efficiency and can be used at both the managerial and technical work levels.
2. **Authority**—Managers must have authority to carry out their responsibilities. This includes authority to command, as well as personal authority developed from experience and intelligence.
3. **Discipline**—People must respect the rules that govern the organization.
4. **Unity of command**—Each employee must report to one and only one superior.
5. **Unity of direction**—Companies should group similar activities under one manager.
6. **Subordination of individuals to the common good**—The interests of individual employees should not be placed before the organization's goals.
7. **Remuneration**—Compensation should be fair to both the employees and the organization.
8. **Centralization**—Power and authority should be concentrated with upper management as much as possible.

9. **Scalar chain**—A chain of authority should extend from the top of the organization to the bottom and should be followed at all times.
10. **Order**—Both people and material resources should be coordinated so they are found in the organization in the proper place at the required time.
11. **Equity**—Managers should be kind and fair when dealing with employees.
12. **Stability**—High employee turnover should be avoided.
13. **Initiative**—Employees should have the freedom to take initiative.
14. **Esprit de corps**—Teamwork, team spirit, and a sense of unity should be fostered and maintained.

Fayol may not have been the first to employ these guidelines, but he was the first to formalize them. He also identified the principal functions of managers as planning, organizing, leading, and controlling, which are still the core management functions today.

These theories are most useful in stable and simple organizations, but they are not as useful in dynamic or complex organizations. By imposing classical management theories across the board in complex organizations, you will certainly find areas of the company in which these practices are not appropriate. Many of the classical management theorists view employees as tools rather than as resources.

Behavioral Management

While classical management theory concentrated on controlling and standardizing employee production, behavioral management theorists concentrated more on individual attitudes and group processes. Behavioral management came in vogue in the 1930s and 1940s and was driven by the birth of industrial psychology and the human relations movement.

The Development of Industrial Psychology

The father of industrial psychology was Hugo Munsterberg, a German psychologist who ran a psychological laboratory at Harvard in 1892 and wrote *Psychology and Industrial Efficiency*, which was translated into English

> Many of the classical management theorists view employees as tools rather than as resources.

in 1913. He believed psychologists could make valuable contributions in the areas of selection and motivation to aid managers. Mary Parker Follett was another early proponent of the role behavior plays in companies. She believed companies needed to be more inclusive when working with employees and managers. These contributions didn't actually form into the field of behavioral management theory until the late 1920s and early 1930s, when Elton Mayo conducted his Hawthorne studies while a faculty member and consultant at Harvard.

Between 1927 and 1932, Mayo conducted behavioral studies at the Hawthorne plant of Western Electric near Chicago. These studies involved manipulating illumination. The illumination for the first group of workers was increased, while a second group being studied continued to work with an unchanged level of illumination. When illumination was increased for one group, Mayo found that productivity went up in both groups. Productivity continued to increase even when the lighting was decreased for the first group until it was decreased to a moonlight level. At a moonlight level, productivity began to decline.

Mayo also tested the classical management theory regarding incentive pay plans. Mayo selected nine industrial workers and devised a plan based on classical management theory that would reward workers based on the number of units produced. While classical management theory assumes each worker would maximize his production to get the largest paycheck, Mayo found workers instead set an informal production level. Anyone who produced above that level was labeled a "rate buster" and those who produced below that level were considered "chiselers." As workers approached the informal production level, their productivity slowed so they would not antagonize others.

Mayo continued his behavioral studies and finally concluded that human behavior was a much more important aspect of management than previously theorized in classical management circles. He proved pay incentive plans did not work because social acceptance was more important than the additional money. Social pressures, as well as individual pressures, played a large role in worker attitudes and behavior.

The Growth of the Human Relations Movement

A product of Mayo's studies still crucial to today's management theories is the human relations movement. Abraham Maslow's theory of "hierarchical needs" still holds a major role in human relations management today. Classical management theorists believed that if you designed a job properly and developed good incentives, you would get the best productivity out of your workers. Leaders of the human relations movement believed that if managers showed concern for their workers it would lead to greater worker satisfaction and ultimately improved productivity.

Maslow's theory of "hierarchical needs" is based on the belief that people are motivated by satisfaction of various needs—physiological, safety, belongingness, esteem, self-actualization. The most basic of these needs is physiological, which includes the need for food, water, air, and sex, or the basic needs of survival and biological function. Next in line is safety, which addresses the needs for a safe physical and emotional environment. When designing a workplace, these needs are addressed in terms of job and economic security. Then comes "belongingness," which in the workplace is satisfied when workers feel accepted by their peers. Next is esteem, which includes a positive self-image as well as recognition and respect from others. At the top of the hierarchical needs is self-actualization, which includes the need for growth and individual development. Maslow believed employees are initially motivated by the satisfaction of their physiological needs, but once these needs are met, safety needs are the motivating factors. As each need is met, the next in line becomes a motivating factor, with self-actualization the highest level.

Proponents of today's contemporary management theories, which we'll discuss later, believe the human relations management theories are too simplistic and don't fully describe work behavior. Some theorists today believe good performance leads to worker satisfaction rather than the other way around. Most theorists believe that, even with its limitations, the behavior

Meeting Maslow's Hierarchical Needs in the Workplace

As a manager, you can take steps to meet employees' needs in the workplace. To meet physiological needs, offer workers a decent working environment that includes restrooms, adequate lighting, good ventilation, and comfortable air temperature. Safety needs are best satisfied when workers believe their employment will continue, have a way to express grievances, and are offered adequate benefits packages for insurance and retirement. To satisfy belongingness needs, managers can promote events that encourage social interaction. Esteem needs are served using job titles, job assignments, and office sizes, as well as reward programs and other recognition opportunities. Self-actualization is probably the most difficult need for managers to satisfy, but including a worker in decision-making that impacts his or her career can aid in the realization of meeting individual goals.

management theory helped managers to realize the importance of addressing behavioral issues in the workplace.

Quantitative Management

Quantitative management theories are an outgrowth of techniques learned during World War II related to the movement of troops and equipment during the war, as well as the deployment of submarines. Basically, quantitative management theory depends on quantitative techniques to solve workplace problems and make management decisions. There are three distinct areas of quantitative management: management science, operations management, and management information systems.

Management science focuses on the development of mathematical models to solve problems and make decisions, most commonly in production settings. For example, a mathematical model will be developed on different variables whose values can fluctuate. As each value changes, a manager can use the model developed to determine the impact on the production process.

Operations management, which is less mathematical than management science, is used more broadly in the management of the organization and is not tied as directly to production management. Tools that fall under this category include network modeling, queuing theory, breakeven analysis, and simulation. While these techniques are commonly used in production, they can also be used in finance, marketing, and personnel management. McGraw-Hill manages a good site online for current stories and information in the area of operations management: *http://www.mhhe.com/business/opsci/pom*.

Management information systems (MIS) focuses on the information provided to managers, usually using an integrated database on a computer system that aids managers with decision-making. MIS enable the flow of information in a company allowing managers to request reports about company operations depending on their clearance level, such as line supervisor, middle management, and executive management. The amount of information available to a manager depends on their level of access. For example, marketing managers can get basic information about production and inventory levels without needing to make a call to the department heads, saving time for both the marketing managers and the production and inventory managers.

Quantitative management techniques definitely add to the decision-making ability of managers, but they do not explain or cannot predict the behavior of people. No doubt its tools are an important part of the planning and control process for any company.

Integrating Management Theories

While each of these management theories—classical, behavioral, and quantitative—added to the quality of management techniques employed today, they are not considered competing or mutually exclusive theories. Today these theories are integrated into management structures within companies, using the most appropriate aspects of each theory for the particular management issue being solved.

Classical management theories are used in organizations to solve questions related to efficiency and productivity, provided managers do not depend too heavily on these theories and follow the strict or narrow interpretations that resulted in boring and unsatisfactory jobs. Behavioral management theories help solve questions related to organizational behavior and people management. These theories are used today for motivation, leadership, company communications, and developing group processes. Quantitative management theories focus on concerns related to modeling, operations management, and management information systems. These useful techniques help managers do their work more effectively and efficiently.

Contemporary Management

New management theories are constantly being developed. The three most frequently studied are known as the X, Y, and Z management theories. In the 1960s, Douglas McGregor developed

From War Theory to Management Tool

Robert McNamara, while working as a statistician for what was then the Army Air Force, was one of the first to employ quantitative management techniques. He was assigned the problem of determining how to get aircraft produced, delivered, crewed, fueled, and repaired around the world during World War II. A big problem was how to get the planes located in Europe to the Pacific, where they were most needed in 1945. McNamara was responsible for gathering the information and doing the calculations. He decided it was cheaper to build new planes for the Pacific than fly the old ones half way around the world. He used quantitative management techniques to make this decision. McNamara applied the quantitative techniques he developed during the war at the Ford Motor Company after the war. He later went on to be secretary of defense under Presidents Kennedy and Johnson.

theories X and Y. Theory X, also known as the autocratic style, or "hard" management, is based on the assumption that the work force is lazy and will avoid work whenever possible. Theory Y, also known as the participative style, or "soft" management, takes the opposite view, that people are creative and enjoy work. Theory Z, developed by William Ouchi in the 1980s, also known as the "Japanese" management style, combines the participative style of management seen in the Japanese business culture with successful aspects of the American style of management. Ouchi also emphasizes job rotation, broadening of skills, generalization rather than specialization, and continuous training.

> Managers who buy into theory X manage people with pressure and control that usually requires the use of threats of disciplinary action to motivate staff.

Managers who buy into theory X manage people with pressure and control that usually requires the use of threats of disciplinary action to motivate staff. These managers also believe that employees will only respond to monetary incentives to perform at higher levels. Their decision-making is authoritative; only after decisions are made do they inform employees of any changes. This type of manager shows little concern for worker's attitudes toward any decision and focuses solely on getting the job done.

Managers who buy in to theory Y encourage worker participation in decision-making, better use of employees' creativity, and involving workers in more of a teamwork approach. Workers under this type of leadership are comfortable working in an environment that allows creativity and opportunities to be involved in organization planning. People are willing to accept responsibility and seek increased authority. Two types of leaders have developed under this style of management: democratic and consensual. The democratic leaders allow groups to vote on decisions. The consensual leader encourages discussion in the group and seeks group consensus.

Most organizations will have some departments run under theory X and some under theory Y, depending on the tasks and types of employees hired to complete the work. Positions filled by workers who are more highly skilled and better educated tend to be run using theory Y, while departments fill with less skilled workers tend to be run using theory X.

Theory Z draws on aspects of both American and Japanese management styles. Ouchi found that American and Japanese firms had seven important differences:

1. Length of employment
2. Mode of decision-making

3. Location of responsibility
4. Speed of evaluation and promotion
5. Control mechanisms
6. Career path specialization
7. Concern for employees

Where Japanese companies usually offer lifetime employment and collective decision-making, American companies usually offer shorter-term employment and individual decision-making by the lead supervisor or manager. Ouchi wrote about these differences in a book entitled *Theory Z—How American Business Can Meet the Japanese Challenge.*

Companies that buy into the theory Z approach generally believe that people are self-motivated not only to do their work but also to help make the company succeed. This differs from the companies that believe in the X and Y theories, which tend to group people into type X or type Y categories. Theory Z managers have a greater degree of trust and are more willing to let their workers make decisions, while theory X or Y managers tend to retain a great deal of control even though theory Y leaders allow more participation. Under theory Z, conflict in an area is settled by discussion, collaboration, and negotiation. Theory X managers would settle conflict using their power. Theory Y managers would probably encourage more participation in conflict resolution, but they would use negotiation strategies to solve the problem.

Also in the 1980s, Kenneth Blanchard introduced the "One Minute Manager" approach. He suggests there are three secrets of management:

- One minute objective setting
- One minute praising
- One minute reprimand

He also espouses the ABCs of management. *A* is for *activators*, which are actions that must be taken by the manager before employees can accomplish a goal. *B* is for *behavior*, which relates to what a person says or does. *C* is for *consequences*, which are shown by the manager through actions such as praising, reprimanding, or setting a new objective. Spencer Johnson popularized Blanchard's theory in a book by the same name, *The One Minute Manager* with an introduction by Blanchard, which was published in 1983.

In the 1990s, the idea of management by empowerment came into vogue. Kenneth Blanchard is also involved in this movement and wrote the book *Empowerment Takes More than a Minute* with John Carlos and Alan Randolph. This style of management is explained in greater detail in their second book, *The 3 Keys to Empowerment*. This type of management encourages employees to do their work without needing to seek approval from their supervisors. Proponents of this theory believe empowerment gives employees a greater sense of responsibility and achievement that results in reduced delays in workflow and reduction in the workload of the manager. Managers use exception reporting to spot red flags and deal with problems.

The success of these contemporary theories, as well as new theories being developed today, will not be known for many years. Managers must always keep a watchful eye for articles on management theory and incorporate ideas that best fit their staffs and work environment.

> **Chapter 14**

Setting Goals and Strategies

Part One

Part Two

Part Three

Part Four

Part Five

Part Six

PART FOUR   MANAGEMENT

▧ CHAPTER 13 Understanding Management Theory ▪ CHAPTER 14 Setting Goals and Strategies ▧ CHAPTER 15 Building Your Organization ▧ CHAPTER 16 Leading Your People ▧ CHAPTER 17 Putting in Controls

Instituting a Planning Process

Figuring out where you want your company or department to go and developing strategies about how you plan to get there are critical elements for any company to succeed. Formulating organizational goals are paramount and must be done carefully as the first step in an overall planning process for the company. Once goals are determined, strategic plans can be developed, which are then turned into action plans. In this chapter, we'll review the planning process, how to set goals and objectives, and how these goals and objectives are used to develop strategic plans and finally action plans.

Before a company can even begin its planning process, though, it must first determine purpose, mission, and objectives. The purpose is its overall basic goal. For example, the purpose of most for-profit businesses is to earn a profit for the business's owners.

Next the business must determine its mission, which is a statement about how the company will fulfill its purpose. A mission statement sets the tone for the business, giving all employees a cohesive idea of what you want to accomplish with the business. Briefly, the mission statement should say why the company does what it does and how you want the company to be perceived by the general public.

Just to give you an idea of what a corporate mission statement might look like, here is one from IBM:

At IBM, we strive to lead in the creation, development and manufacture of the industry's most advanced information technologies, including computer systems, software, networking systems, storage devices and microelectronics.

We translate these advanced technologies into value for our customers through our professional solutions and services businesses worldwide.

Here is Sam Walton's vision for Wal-Mart:

Sam Walton built Wal-Mart on the revolutionary philosophies of excellence in the workplace, customer service and always having the lowest prices. We have always stayed true to the Three Basic Beliefs Mr. Sam established in 1962:

Respect for the Individual
Service to Our Customers
Strive for Excellence

As you can see, mission statements are brief—usually just one or two sentences. If you are wondering how to go about developing a mission statement for your company, American Express has developed a tool to help small businesses create their own mission statement: *www.americanexpress.com*.

Setting Goals and Objectives

Once a company has developed its mission statement, the next step is to set its goals and objectives. Goals should be specific and concise, and they should include a time factor. Usually goals fall into four major areas: financial, environmental, participant, and survival. In a formal presentation, the goal will be a general statement about what you plan to achieve, and the objectives will include specific numbers about how you plan to get there.

Financial goals relate to profits and costs. These goals would include sales targets, profit targets, and productivity levels. For example, a financial goal could be to increase sales, cut costs, and increase production. The stated objectives would be to increase sales by 10 percent, cut costs by 15 percent, and increase production by 5 percent. Financial goals and objectives should be specific with actual target numbers.

Environmental goals relate to how the company will interact with the outside world. These types of goals will not likely be stated in quantitative terms but rather in qualitative ones, such as how the company will meet its social responsibility. Goals in this area can also relate to attaining increased market share or overall growth plans in relation to the company's outside competitors.

Developing the Wal-Mart Cheer

Sam Walton developed the Wal-Mart cheer after visiting a factory in Korea. Each morning he saw workers do a company cheer while doing calisthenics together, and he decided to try to practice something similar at Wal-Mart. He developed this cheer:

Give me a W!
Give me an A!
Give me an L!
Give me a Squiggly!
Give me an M!
Give me an A!
Give me an R!
Give me a T!
What's that spell?
Wal-Mart!
Whose Wal-Mart is it?
My Wal-Mart!
Who's number one?
The Customer! Always!

Walton said about his cheer, "My feeling is that just because we work so hard, we don't have to go around with long faces all the time—while we're doing all of this work, we like to have a good time."

Participant goals focus on the people inside the company. Goals can relate to decreasing absenteeism or turnover. Objectives could include cut employee turnover by 5 percent over the next year.

Survival goals relate to the actual survival of the company. These are overall goals that you put in place to assure the company will be alive and financially well at the end of the year.

Goals can be set in three different time frames: short run, inter- mediate, and long run.

Goals can be set in three different time frames: short run, intermediate, and long run. Short-run goals are those the company plans to attain in a one-year period. Intermediate goals are those the company plans to attain in more than one year but less than five years. Long-run goals are those that have a horizon that is longer than five years. These time periods are not set in stone. A small business could decide short-run goals are to be met within a six-month period. Intermediate goals are to be met within a year. Long-run goals are to be met within two years. Whatever time frame works within your business is acceptable.

Some companies are shifting to establishing goals that mesh more easily with the strategic planning process. Using this breakdown, there are five primary areas: business posture, business mix, market share and growth rate, resource allocation and risk analysis, and social issues.

- **Business posture goals** would include overall goals related to growth, stability, and survival.
- **Business mix goals** focus on the combination of products and services an organization plans to market.
- **Market share and growth rate goals**—Market share relates to what percentage of the overall market for any one product or group of products the company plans to capture. Growth rate relates to the rate of growth the company can realistically plan to attain over a given time period.
- **Resource allocation and risk analysis goals**—Resource allocation goals relate to how the company plans to divide its limited resources. For example, a company can determine one of its goals is to retain all profits to grow the business rather than pay dividends. Risk analysis looks at the risk of planned courses of action.
- **Social issues goals** focus on a company's social responsibility, which has become an issue of greater importance to maintain a good corporate image and attract customers as well as talented employees.

Issues involving protection of the environment or consumers' rights are the key areas that many companies attempt to address today.

Nothing is set in stone as to how business goals must be structured. Use the information noted here as a guide, but develop your goals using a structure that makes the most sense for your company. The key is not to put up any barriers to effective goal setting. This can happen in a number of ways, including establishing inappropriate or unattainable goals, overemphasizing quantitative or qualitative goals, and instituting improper award systems.

Inappropriate goals—Some goals can create a situation in which trying to attain one goal could actually harm another aspect of the company's operations. For example, setting a goal to increase the pay of all executives by 25 percent may result in either cutting pay for others or reducing profits to shareholders. Sometimes these goals can even lead to illegal actions, such as a goal to drive a competitor out of business or to evade environmental regulations to save money.

Unattainable goals—These are goals that set the bar too high and ensure failure. By setting unattainable goals, companies can actually create a morale problem and decrease sales or productivity. Goals should challenge the company and its employees, but they should be attainable with hard work and focus.

Overemphasis on quantitative or qualitative goals—Quantitative goals are more easily measured. Some managers may reward their employees by their achievements in meeting quantitative goals without considering successes in qualitative goals. For example, suppose a company sets a quantitative goal of increasing sales by 10 percent and improving customer relations. One salesperson met the 10 percent goal, but he did so by sales tactics that actually hurt customer relations. Another salesperson increased sales by 8 percent, but she used tactics that improved customer relations. Rewarding solely on the quantitative measure because it is easier to calculate may overlook the potentially harmful long-term tactics of the salesperson who met the goal. The key to avoiding this barrier is to be sure that any employee evaluation considers both quantitative and qualitative goals set by the company.

Improper reward systems—These are situations in which poor goal setting may actually result in better rewards for an employee than the reward given to an employee who sets appropriate goals but fails to meet them. For example, one salesperson sets a goal of increasing sales, while another salesperson specifies a goal of increasing sales by 10 percent. In an improper reward system, the first person set a goal of increasing sales and actually increased his sales by 2 percent. He met his goal and is rewarded. The salesperson who set a more specific (and actually more proper) goal only increased sales by 8 percent. She did not meet her goal and does not get a reward. Companies must be certain that setting and meeting goals and rewards for doing so are looked at consistently across business lines.

Many companies are using their goal-setting process as a successful management tool under a system credited to Peter Drucker that is called *management by objectives* (MBO). Managers establish individual goals for their staff in collaboration with each employee. Attainment of these goals is then used during the evaluation process of each employee's performance. This technique gives employees a role in setting their goals and understanding what is expected of them.

To use the technique of MBO, companies must first set overall goals for their business. Then working with each department, managers set goals for individual departments. Once those are in place, managers work collaboratively with their employees to set specific goals. This collaborative goal setting is accomplished using a five-step process:

1. **Communicating business and department goals**—Once the overall goals are set, managers or supervisors meet with their employees to communicate these goals and ask each to develop their own goals for how they believe they can contribute to helping the department meet its goals and objectives.

2. **One-on-one meetings**—Next, managers and supervisors will meet one-on-one to develop a set of goals and objectives specific to each employee, melding ideas the employee has developed with department goals and objectives.

3. **Writing proper goals**—Managers or supervisors should help each employee write proper goals that are specific, concise, and time-related. Also the goals should be measurable.

4. **Review goals**—Managers or supervisors must be certain employees develop goals that are attainable and that will actually help the department and company meet its goals. Counseling employees may be necessary to reach this objective.

5. **Determine resources**—Once goals are set, the manager and employee must determine the resources that will be needed to meet the goals and objectives. If, for some reason, the resources will not be available, the goal may need to be revised. By the end of the process, both the employee and the manager or supervisor must agree that not only is the goal attainable but that the resources will be available to attain that goal.

Once the goals are in place, the manager or supervisor will meet periodically with each employee to be certain all is on track. For example, quarterly meetings may help pick up any problems the employee may be facing, so solutions can be developed early and the problems fixed. This avoids the potential of total failure to meet goals and gives each employee a better possibility of attaining their stated goals.

Finally, the entire process begins anew at the end of the year when the manager or supervisor evaluates how well the employee did to meet his or her goals. They then discuss both successes and failures and how to improve performance during the next year. Most times, this evaluative session will lead to the planning of the next year's collaborative goals.

Proponents of management by objectives believe this process improves employee motivation by clarifying expectations, allowing employee involvement in setting these expectations, and rewarding employees based on these objectives. Critics of the process believe that top executives may implement MBO but not actually support it, and they reduce its effectiveness by delegating it to lower management levels. Others create an extensive quantitative system that requires lots of paperwork and record-keeping, which results in a lack of commitment by all involved.

The Role of Strategic Planning

Once the organization's goals are set, the next step in the planning process is to develop the strategies for meeting those goals. Policies for meeting the major long-term organizational goals are developed at the highest level in a

> Once the goals are in place, the manager or supervisor will meet periodically with each employee to be certain all is on track.

process called strategic planning. During this process, top-level mangers match the resources and skills available to the business with the opportunities present in the external marketplace.

As part of strategy formulation, companies must analyze their environment and organization in order to understand how a company's strengths and weaknesses impact its ability to compete in its environment. This is commonly known as a SWOT analysis, which stands for *strengths, weaknesses, opportunities,* and *threats.* Internally, the analysis looks at a company's strengths and weaknesses; externally, it surveys its opportunities and threats.

Strengths: When looking at a company's strengths, executives look for the company's advantages, what it does well, and determine the relevant resources including financial and human assets. Basically the company is looking for strengths that give it a competitive advantage, such as patents, brand names, customer reputation, cost advantages, staffing (for example, top research and development people), and distribution networks. A strength must be unique to the company. Although producing quality goods may seem like a strength, if the production of quality goods is common among the company's competitors, then it is not a strength but a requirement in order to be successful within the company's external environment.

Weaknesses: In analyzing weaknesses, executives look for areas of the company that need improvement. They must be realistic about what the company does badly and what areas of competition the company must avoid. Examples of weaknesses could include the lack of patent protection, weak brand name, poor customer reputation, a high cost structure in some areas of production or operations, or poor distribution channels. In this organization analysis, companies review the quality and quantity of its human and physical resources, and its financial strength. As part of the strategic planning, the company must decide how to overcome these weaknesses, either through partnering with a vendor, developing better internal resources, or possibly even deciding not to continue operations in a particularly weak area.

Opportunities: When looking at opportunities, executives look at interesting trends and possible opportunities these trends create for the company. These trends could include changes in technology or markets, changes in government policy that could impact the company or the field in which it operates,

In analyzing weaknesses, executives look for areas of the company that need improvement.

or changes in social patterns or lifestyle that may suggest new opportunities. If the company is considering international expansion, it may find that removal of certain trade barriers could create a new opportunity.

Threats: When considering external threats, executives look at the possibility of new entrants into its areas of operations, the competitive relationship among dominant firms in the industry, changing technology that could impact the company's position and standing in the marketplace, and the possibility of substitutes that are either on the market or about to be released. Executives will also look internally to see if any of the company's weaknesses could pose a threat to their strategic planning. For example, could bad debt or cash-flow problems make it difficult to carry out their strategic plan? Or could the lack of a strong research and development function make it impossible for them to respond to the threat of new technology? New government regulations or trade barriers may also be a threat to future operations.

When the analysis is completed, companies can develop what is known as the SWOT matrix:

	Internal Strengths	Internal Weaknesses
External Opportunities	S-O Strategies	S-O Weaknesses
External Threats	S-T Strategies	S-T Weaknesses

S-O strategies listed in the matrix would include opportunities that fit well into the company's strengths and would be good opportunities to pursue. For example, a strong cash position may offer the opportunity to begin research and development in a new product area.

S-O weaknesses would include strategies to overcome weaknesses so the company could pursue new opportunities. For example, recognition that the company lacks patent protection for its primary product line may result in the decision to use its research and development team to pursue new product designs and patents.

S-T strategies would include ways the company can use its strengths to overcome potential threats in the marketplace. For example, news stories about a new product line to be introduced by a competitor may result in using the company's strong research and development team to find ways to overcome that threat.

S-T weaknesses would identify defenses the company could put in place to prevent the firm's weaknesses from making it susceptible to outside threats. For example, recognition of weak brand identity may result in the development of a strong brand marketing campaign.

Some critics of the SWOT analysis believe that it can oversimplify the planning process. Not all strength and weakness or opportunities and threat clearly fit into this organized matrix. Whether a company actually formalizes the use of the SWOT matrix, the analysis done to identify strengths, weaknesses, opportunities, and threats is crucial to the strategic planning process. Once this analysis is done, strategic planning takes place on three levels: corporate, business, and functional.

Corporate Strategy

Corporate strategy is also known as *grand strategy*. This strategy charts the course of the organization as a whole. The top executives will develop strategies for what types of businesses the company will compete in, deciding the scope of the company and how its resources will be deployed. The most popular approach to determining corporate strategy is the business portfolio matrix developed by the Boston Consulting Group (BCG) in the early 1970s. This process involves three steps: identifying strategic business units, classifying these units in a matrix, and developing strategies for each of these units.

Strategic business units are parts of a company that have their own mission. They can include a single unit or a set of related units. An SBU will have its own set of competitors and its own unique strategy.

Unit classification involves categorizing each SBU based on its rate of growth and market share. The development of this process can be credited to the Boston Consulting Group, which classifies SBUs into four categories: stars, cash cows, question marks, and dogs. Stars have a large share of a high-growth market. These SBUs require a large cash influx to support their growth spurt. Cash cows are SBUs that have a large share of a mature market with low growth potential. Money is not needed for growth or expansion;

instead these SBUs generate cash that can be used in other parts of the business. Question marks are SBUs with low market share in a high-growth market. When looking at question marks during the strategic planning process, executives must decide whether to commit the resources to make the question mark into a star or reduce the investment in the question mark and de-emphasize its role in the company, possibly even closing down the unit. Dogs are at the bottom of the heap. They have a small share of a low-growth market. These are the top candidates for shutdown. For example, slide rules were a star at one time, but they became a dog as the market for the product collapsed.

Once each unit is classified, the company develops a business portfolio matrix using these classifications by plotting the SBUs within the matrix designed by BCG:

High Market Growth Rate Low	Stars	Question Marks
	Cash Cows	Dogs
	High Relative Market Share Low	

The Founder of SBUs

General Electric founded the concept of strategic business units (SBUs) in the 1970s. Its managers realized that they needed a framework for managing GE's large and diverse organization. The idea of viewing the company as a portfolio of businesses developed into what is today known as the SBU. GE managers identified forty-three SBUs within the company. Other large corporations, including Union Carbide and General Foods, quickly adopted the concept. For example, one SBU identified was GE's food preparation appliance producers (this includes toaster ovens, ranges, etc.).

Weaknesses of Strategic Planning

Henry Mintzberg pointed out the weaknesses of strategic planning in his 1994 book, *The Rise and Fall of Strategic Planning: Reconceiving Roles for Planning, Plans, Planners.* Mintzberg believes that strategic planning actually caused the failures of some SBUs and companies. He argues that there are three fallacies of the planning model: predetermination, detachment, and formalization. The concern he expressed regarding predetermination is the weakness he sees in trying to forecast the future and then trying to adapt or control that predicted future. He disagrees with the detachment of planners from operations, which he says creates a reliance on hard data to the exclusion of soft data. He also objects to the formalization of strategy making; he does not believe that systems can be designed that will detect all the gaps or problems, consider all the stakeholders, and encourage a creative corporate environment.

Unit strategies—Once each SBU has been identified and classified, strategies for each of the SBUs can be developed. For a star, executives must decide the level of resources that will be needed to take advantage of its growth opportunities. For a cash cow, executives must develop strategies that maintain its market share, while milking the division's cash flow for other growth opportunities. For a question mark, executives must decide whether to develop strategies to improve the question mark's chance of success or to decrease resources and reduce its future potential. For a dog, the executives must decide whether the SBU can be turned around or if it's time to pull the plug.

As the matrix gained acceptance and was more widely used, weaknesses were found in its design. These weaknesses relate primarily to the fact that the matrix is based on market growth rate, but there are other factors in determining competitive advantages. For example, sometimes a dog is divested before a company realizes that it was actually helping another SBU maintain or gain market share.

Newer models that relate to business intuition, growth, and diversification are constantly being tested. The followers of the intuitive model believe that consensus based on experience, values, and organization norms may be a better path to follow during the strategic planning process.

Business and Functional Strategy

Once corporate strategy is determined, the next level of strategic planning is business strategy. This involves developing strategies for each business unit and how it might best compete within its particular market or industry.

Once the overall decision is made about how each SBU fits into the long-range business plan, business units can then develop their strategies for fulfilling the vision of the executive team. Strategies at this level will be shorter term and will focus on the growth and operation of the individual unit.

After business strategy is determined for a unit, planning gets down to the third level—functional strategy. At this level, functions within each unit determine strategies for meeting the goals set at the corporate and business levels. At this level, strategies are developed for functions such as marketing, finance, production, research and development, and human resources.

Developing and Implementing Plans

Once all the strategies have been decided, the last step in the planning process is to develop action plans to implement these strategies. There are three types of action plans: tactical, single use, and standing.

- **Tactical plans** systematically implement the overall strategic plans set by the organization. These can be compared to the battle plans of wartime with the overall strategy being winning the war.
- **Single-use plans** are developed for one-time use and are not likely to be repeated. These plans include programs for a large set of activities and projects, which are smaller in scope.
- **Standing plans** determine how to carry out a course of action that is likely to be repeated regularly and for a long period. For these plans, companies will develop polices that serve as a guide for the action, operating procedures that will set standards for how to carry out the action, and rules and regulations that will govern the long-term operations.

In addition to developing action plans, companies must determine time frames for each of the strategies, whether they are long-range, intermediate, or short-range planning. Short-range planning involves plans with a time frame of one year or less. Intermediate planning relates to time frames of one to five years, and long-range planning is for strategies whose time frame is longer than five years.

Along with strategic plans, companies must also develop contingency plans, which are alternative courses of action in case the original set of actions does not work, is unexpectedly disrupted, or is no longer appropriate. Planning for how the company will deal with emergency situations or in times of disaster also falls under the aspect of contingency planning.

> **Chapter 15**

Building Your Organization

Part One

Part Two

Part Three

Part Four

Part Five

Part Six

PART FOUR   MANAGEMENT

■ CHAPTER 13 Understanding Management Theory ■ CHAPTER 14 Setting Goals and Strategies ■ CHAPTER 15 **Building Your Organization** ■ CHAPTER 16 Leading Your People ■ CHAPTER 17 Putting in Controls

Basic Building Blocks

As companies implement their strategic plans, critical decisions about how to build the organization must be made. These decisions will not only impact a company's chance of success, they will also have a major impact on employee morale and how employees perceive the work environment, which ultimately will lead to increased or reduced productivity. In this chapter, we'll review the basic building blocks of organizational structure and design, and then talk about strategies for handling change.

Among the key building blocks that are part of every organizational structure are the following: work specialization, departmentalization, setting up lines of authority, and finally designing line and staff positions. How companies develop their building blocks impacts the entire tone of the organization and the way people will work within that organization.

Work Specialization

First, an organization must decide to what degree they want to break down and divide the tasks required to implement goals and strategies. Adam Smith first introduced this concept of work specialization to the work force in his 1776 book, *Wealth of Nations*, in which he described how work specialization in a pin factory improved productivity. In that factory, one man was responsible for drawing the wire, a second for straightening it, and a third for cutting it and performing additional specialized tasks until the pin was ready for market. Smith claimed that using work specialization increased productivity and that ten men produced 48,000 pins per day.

Moving closer to modern-day management techniques, Henry Ford's use of work specialization on the automobile assembly line is the classic example of a highly specialized work environment. This concept drove the workplace until automation gradually took over many individual tasks; machines were able to replace assembly-line workers in many companies doing work more quickly and consistently.

Assembly lines are not the only jobs in the workplace that are impacted by the degree of work specialization a company wants to build into its organizational structure. Specialization also plays a part in dividing up organization tasks in finance, marketing, accounting, and administration. Companies can either develop their personnel as generalists who learn a number of different tasks and can cover for each other throughout the organization or as specialists in one particular task with no opportunity to move around. Some people work best when given one task to do with no interruptions, while others prefer more variety in their work.

Companies must determine how specialized each staff position will be and then match the people they hire based on their personalities and skill sets. Smaller companies tend to encourage employees to train in a number of tasks so they can fill in as needed. As companies grow, greater work specialization becomes part of the organization because there are more people who can jump in and do the work if someone is out.

Some key reasons to introduce work specialization in today's work force can still be traced back to Adam Smith's original studies. These reasons include individual dexterity, decreased transfer time, specialized equipment, and decreased training costs.

- **Individual dexterity** relates to the concept that employees who learn and do one simple task repetitively will become proficient at that task and do it well and fast.
- **Decreased transfer time** relates to the concept that an employee will lose time as he transfers from one task to another, but specialization

The Father of Economics and Work Specialization

You may not think of Adam Smith, an economist and philospher in the 1700s, in the context of management and work specialization, but it was actually his writings that form the basis for much of the theory in the area of work specialization. Smith was the son of a comptroller of customs in Scotland. He studied philosophy at the University of Glasgow and taught logic and moral philosphy at the university in the 1750s. He gradually moved to the field of economics in the 1760s, which culminated in his classic book, *The Wealth of Nations*. This work did much to reinforce his image as the father of modern-day economics.

in only one or two tasks will decrease the time the employee loses to transferring from one task to the next.

- **Specialized equipment** relates to the need to train on and operate a specific type of machinery or equipment. Many times when using specialized equipment as part of a work assignment, the employee will focus solely on tasks that require the operation of that specialized equipment.
- **Decreased training costs** relates to the fact that specialization reduces the costs of training new employees. Obviously, it takes less time to train a person to do one or two tasks then to do many tasks.

While work specialization has been shown initially to boost efficiency and performance, it can also create situations of low morale and ultimately reduced productivity. This happens because employees become bored and dissatisfied if their work becomes too specialized. As you are designing positions in your organization, take into consideration the level of specialization in the design and be certain enough variety is designed into each job to avoid the workers' becoming too specialized and bored with their jobs.

> While work specialization has been shown initially to boost efficiency and performance, it can also create situations of low morale and ultimately reduced productivity.

Setting Up Departments

Once you have an idea of the tasks you will need to fill in an organization, the next step in building the company is to group these jobs into logical departments. Departmentalization can be designed around functions, products, locations, or customers. Although we're using the name *department* here, companies may use various designations such as divisions, units, sections, or bureaus.

Functional departmentalization is used when an organization builds itself around various functions, such as finance, production, marketing, operations, and research and development. This is the most common structure in smaller companies. The key advantages of this form of departmentalization is that each department can be staffed with specialists in that particular function and supervision is easier because the manager of that function only needs to be aware of one set of skills. Functional departmentalization also makes it easier to coordinate the work within the function. Disadvantages to this structure include slower and more bureaucratic decision-making, concentration on a particular function rather than on the needs of the organization as a whole, and greater difficulty in determining accountability and performance in meeting the overall corporate goals.

Product departmentalization is used when an organization builds itself by grouping its staff around its products and the activities needed to ensure the success of those products. These types of groupings are seen in organizations as the company becomes larger. For example, General Motors groups its departments by product lines, such as the GMC truck division, Chevrolet division, Cadillac division, and so on. Each of these divisions includes the key functional areas, such as production, finance, marketing, human resources, and research and development. The key advantages of this type of departmentalization include grouping activities around a product makes it easier to integrate and coordinate the needs of the group, decision-making can be faster and more effective, and monitoring the performance of individual products groups is easier, which increases accountability and makes it easier to determine a group's impact on the profitability of a particular product.

Location departmentalization, which is based on physical location, is not used as frequently as product or function departmentalization when building a company. This type of departmentalization may be found more commonly in distribution organizations, in which each department is focused on a particular location, such as the northeast, southeast, northwest, southwest, and central regions. A small local company may set up its departments based on city or country coverage. The major advantage of this organizational structure is that the company can respond more easily to customer needs in a particular region, but a larger administrative staff may be required to manage this more diverse structure.

Customer departmentalization is used in companies that want to structure their employees based on activities to satisfy various customer groups. For example, this is common in financial organizations that group their departments by loan areas, such as consumer loans, commercial loans, and agricultural loans. Larger banks also have departments that focus on serving other customers such as credit card operations, large businesses, and small businesses. The advantage of this type of structure is that employees are trained in the skill sets needed to satisfy a particular type of customer. For example, the skills needed to evaluate the personal assets of an individual before approving a consumer loan are much different than the skills needed to evaluate a business's balance sheet before approving a commercial loan. The big disadvantage of this structure is that a large administrative staff is needed to integrate the activities of the various departments.

These are the four most common departmentalization groupings. Two others are infrequently used: *departmentalization by time* and *departmentalization by sequence*. If a company divides itself by time, departments are based on shifts and a plant manager is assigned to each shift that has his or her own functional departments. This is most commonly used in a manufacturing company. Departmentalization by sequence occurs when departments are grouped based on a sequence of customers, such as credit card companies that are departmentalized by customer name. For example, one department is responsible for credit checks on customers whose names begin with *A–D,* the second for customers whose names begin with *E–H,* and so on. Large companies will use multiple types of departmentalization. At the highest level, for example, the departments may be grouped by production lines; within those lines, the next level of departments may be grouped by function, time, sequence, or location. When building your company structure, the key to determining that structure is what works best to meet your company's goals and objectives and implement your strategic plans.

Authority and Delegation

Once you've decided on your departmentalization plan, the next key decision is how to pattern the authority given to each. This relates to the amount of authority you maintain at the upper rungs of the organization versus the amount you delegate to others in the organization. In a small company, the owners tend to maintain strong control and most of the authority. As organizations grow, this is no longer realistic and owners must give up the reins through delegation.

The primary reason to delegate authority down the line of command is to enable managers and other employees to get the work done more quickly. Managers who learn to delegate reduce their workload and put the decision-making ability in the hands of employees who most likely are closer to the situation and have a better understanding of how to solve the problem. For example, a manager's subordinate may have special training on a product line or geographic area. By recognizing this expertise and delegating authority to the specialist, the manager will make better use of his resources and provide a work environment that results in better overall decision-making for the organization.

Delegation allows managers to assign responsibility for various tasks to subordinates. By doing so, the manager grants authority to the subordinate to make key decisions related to that responsibility. Finally, this delegation creates a situation in which a subordinate is accountable for his or her actions.

There are some risks in delegating authority. From the manager's perspective, this can be a problem if the manager is so disorganized that he or she finds it difficult to plan work and cannot delegate tasks. Some managers fear delegation because they believe that if an employee does too well, he or she may threaten their own chances of advancement. Other managers will avoid delegation because they just don't trust their employees.

Some employees are reluctant to accept delegation and the responsibilities that go with it. Some employees fear that they will fail and that this failure could result in reprimand or disciplinary action. Others believe the rewards being offered for taking on that responsibility are not worth accepting the

Managing by Exception

Managers who are successful at delegating tasks often use a technique called "management by exception." This requires continuous evaluation of business performance, timely communications, and proactive exception alerts. For example, if the growth target for a particular product line is 15 percent, a proactive alert will be generated if the target is missed by 10 percent in any one quarter. The manager of this product line would then take a closer look at the problem and meet with others responsible within the product line to identify the weaknesses and fix the problem.

added burden. Still other employees like to avoid risk, and they prefer that their manager takes all the responsibility.

There are no easy solutions to these problems that can develop as managers try to delegate responsibility. Most problems can be solved through good communication between the manager and his or her subordinates. As an organization delegates more and more of its authority down the line, the key to success is to provide good employee training so everyone understands their responsibilities, authority, and accountability, and how that will impact their standing in the organization. Quick and effective individual counseling when problems are recognized along the delegation chain can help minimize the problems. Ultimately, responsibility for delegating flows back up the chain to the higher-level managers, so it is in their best interest to be sure the entire concept of the delegation of tasks is working within their area of authority.

Centralization Versus Decentralization

In additional to delegating along staff lines, a company can also be decentralized or organized centrally. Decentralization relates to the amount of power systematically delegated to various departments or managers versus maintaining power centrally at the upper levels of an organization.

If an organization decides to decentralize, then authority will be delegated as far down the chain of command as possible. A centralized organization will keep all power at the top. In reality, no organization is completely decentralized or centralized, and most organizations drift between the two types of structure depending on various challenges or changes. Factors that can impact whether a company decentralizes include the external environment, the organization's history, the risk of decision-making, and the abilities of lower-level managers.

- **External environment**—Companies that face a greater complexity and uncertainty within the environment of operations tend to decentralize their power into the hands of managers most familiar with different aspects of their environment. For example, as financial institutions merge with various businesses such as banking, insurance, and brokerage operations, they are more likely to decentralize responsibilities for each of the vastly different types of markets.

- **Organization history**—Companies tend to continue to follow historical patterns. An organization that has always run with a strong centralized structure will likely continue operating that way, while a company that has always operated in a decentralized manner will usually continue to do so. In order to change this historical method of operations, a company usually needs to bring in a strong leader.
- **Nature of the decision**—As the potential risks of a decision increase or become more costly, the decision-making power is more likely to be held at the top levels of management.
- **Abilities of lower-level managers**—If higher-level mangers do not trust the lower-level manager's ability to make solid decisions, they are more likely to hold decision-making power at the top of an organization.

There is no hard or fast rule about whether it is better to centralize or decentralize an organization. Both types of structures are successful. Most companies use a combination of centralized decision-making to take advantage of economies of scale or reduce the risk of certain types of decision-making, while decentralizing other aspects of business operations so lower-level managers and their staff can respond more effectively to customer needs.

Tall or Flat

Another key decision you must make when organizing your business is whether you want that organization to be tall, with many levels of management, or flat with key managers reporting to the top and only one other level with supervisors. For example, in a tall organization, two top managers would report to the president. The next level might have three managers reporting to each of the two top managers and followed

Changing the Corporate Structure of Home Depot

The shift in leadership from the cofounders of Home Depot, Arthur Blank and Bernard Marcus, to former General Electric executive Robert Nardelli is a classic case of using a change in leadership to spark a shift from decentralization to centralization. Home Depot's organizational structure under the leadership of Blank and Marcus was entrepreneurship and decentralization to the lowest levels of management. Each store manager was given a great deal of autonomy to build the store as he or she saw fit, considering the location and customers. Robert Nardelli, used to a centralized management structure at GE, shifted Home Depot's structure to a more centralized base primarily to take advantage of centralized purchasing and other economies of scale that could raise profit margins. Initially, there was fear and resistance to the change, but Nardelli is now widely recognized for taking Home Depot to the next level of profitability.

by another level with four supervisors reporting to each of the three managers above them.

When trying to determine how tall or flat your organizational design should be, there are several things to consider: the competence of your managers, the dispersion of your employees, and the degree of supervision needed for each employee. If your managers are competent and well trained, you will be more comfortable allowing them to manage more of your employees. Also well-trained employees tend to need much less management time, so managers will have the ability to manage more employees. When this type of organizational environment exists, companies tend to have a flatter management structure.

If your employees are widely physically dispersed, a taller structure will be needed in order to effectively manage the employees. This becomes a big issue when parts of the organization are located in numerous parts of the country. This structure is most common in organizations with a large sales force, a greater number of retail stores, or a widely dispersed distribution network. The more locations a company has, the greater the need for a taller structure; otherwise managers will be spread too thinly, trying to travel to different parts of their region.

Managers who supervise employees with lower levels of skill usually need to spend more time supervising, so they cannot effectively manage as many people. These situations usually require a taller organizational structure as well.

Other factors that affect the span of the management structure include how much interaction a manager must have with his or her subordinates. Any work situation that needs a considerable level of interaction for subordinates to do their jobs means a manager will be able to supervise fewer people effectively. If the company has developed a fairly comprehensive set of standard procedures, a manager can supervise more people and the organization can be flatter. If few standardized procedures exist, however, a taller organization with more managers will be needed. The same is true when tasks are similar. Also if new problems frequently arise within an organization, more management involvement will be needed to decide how to handle these problems. If new problems are rare, a flatter management structure can be put in place.

Essentially how tall or flat your organization will be depends on how much individual attention each subordinate under each manager will need.

> If your employees are widely physically dispersed, a taller structure will be needed in order to effectively manage the employees.

As a manager needs more time either to manage employees or to do other tasks, such as paperwork or planning, he or she will have less time to effectively manage subordinates.

Staffing

Finally when determining employee positions, a company must decide whether an employee will have a line or staff management role. Line roles include positions in the direct chain of command, such as vice presidents of each of the function areas. Staff roles include employees who provide a particular expertise, advice, or support to the line managers. Line managers usually have a great deal of authority over a major business unit, while staff managers serve as advisers to line managers but have a lower degree of authority that does not directly impact the overall mission of the organization.

Once the managerial organization is in place, managers can then develop their staff plans for the areas of the organization that fall within their responsibility. This includes human resource planning, recruitment, selection, and placement of employees, orientation, compensation, training and development, and performance appraisals. Managers must also decide how they want to design employee positions depending on the degree of work specialization desired. In addition, they will need to determine work schedules and how flexible they want these schedules to be.

Some managers will prefer to design their operations in a team or group environment, while others will choose to work in a more traditional way. No matter how the manager designs his or her function, dealing with conflicts that arise will be a primary role that falls on the manager's shoulders. Finding effective ways to reduce or resolve conflict is a key goal of any manager.

Organizational Design Options

In addition to determining organization structure, a company must also decide on its organization design. This looks at how the various structures within an organization will interact. There are a number of theories that impact organization, including classical organization, behavioral perspective, contingency approach, and contemporary trends.

Designing Contemporary Organizations

One of the leaders in contemporary organizational design is Dr. Jay Galbraith, a professor at the International Institute for Management in Lausanne and senior research scientist at the Center for Effective Organization and professor of Management and Organization at the University of Southern California. His specialties include organization design and change and development with an emphasis on international partnering, including joint ventures and network organizations. His work has included the formation and development of joint ventures between Asian and Western companies. Dr. Galbraith directed his own management-consulting firm before joining the USC faculty. He has also been a faculty member of the Sloan School of Management at the Massachusetts Institute of Technology and the Wharton School at Pennsylvania University. He has been a consultant to numerous companies and entities in the United States, Europe, Asia, and South America.

- **Classical organization** is based on a great deal of authority held at the top of the organization with a strict division of labor, a consistent set of rules, a vertical chain of command, and advancement based on expertise. These types of organizational designs tend to be bureaucratic.
- **Behavioral perspective** grew out of the human relations movement. These organizations are driven more with leadership, motivation, and communications. Employees are given a greater deal of involvement in decision-making, goal-setting, and control processes.
- **Contingency approach** is based on the assumption that organization design should be based on situational factors. With this approach, two factors play a dominant role: technology and size.
- **Contemporary design trends**—These include matrix design, which involves superimposing a product-based structure on a function structure. In this type of design, employees will often report to a functional manager and to one or more product managers. To learn more about contemporary views in this area, one good book to read is Jay Galbraith's *Designing Organizations: An Executive Guide to Strategy, Structure, and Process Revised*. Another contemporary view focuses on the link between strategy and design. Henry Mintzberg, who questioned the role of strategic planning, believes there are actually five forms of organization design that can result from different types of strategy. These five forms include simple structure, machine bureaucracy, professional bureaucracy, the divisionalized form, and the adhocracy. You can learn more about his theories in his book *Structure in Fives: Designing Effective Organizations*.

Organization design will have the greatest impact on a company's culture, which drives the internal environment of any organization. A company's culture includes how employees perceive the organization and will have a great impact on employee motivation and productivity. For example, if employees see their company is viewed as cold and uncaring, they will be less likely to display loyalty to the organization and more likely to look for ways to minimize their output. Companies that are viewed as warm and caring usually have more highly motivated employees with a higher level of productivity.

Dealing with Change

All organizations will face periods of change. There are many reasons for change. Externally, change can occur because of new competitors, new products, political influences, new laws or regulations, or court decisions. Mergers and acquisitions can cause change both from external and internal forces. Internally, organizations face major changes when new goals are set or company leadership changes.

Generally, organizations that plan well for handling change use a seven-step process:

1. **Recognition of the need for change**—The first step in the process usually begins after complaints from employees, customers, or vendors. Or need for change may be realized when a company sees a sales slump, high turnover, labor strikes, productivity decline, or external forces, such as a court injunction or patent approval of a new product developed by a competitor.

2. **Establishment of goals for the change**—Once the need for change is recognized, management must then establish goals to be accomplished when dealing with making the changes. Goals will include ways to maintain market share, restore employee morale, reduce turnover, and settle a strike (if it is part of the force for change). Other possible goals could include the identification of new business opportunities or plans to enter new markets, depending on the forces related to the need for change.

3. **Diagnosis of the reason for the change**—The next step is to be sure management understands all the reasons behind the need for change. For example, if management notices that the turnover rate for employees is rising, in addition to developing goals for the change, they must look internally for

the reasons, such as noncompetitive pay packages, poor supervisors, or inferior working conditions.

4. **Select the technique that will be used for the change**—The techniques used to deal with the change will, of course, be related to the reasons for the change. For example, if during the diagnostic process, management determines their pay package is a primary reason for the higher turnover, their technique to solve the problem may require the need to develop a new reward system.

5. **Plan to implement the change**—Once the technique is chosen, management will have to plan the way it wants to implement the change. Issues to consider here will be costs of the change, how the change will impact various parts of the organization, and how much employee participation management wants to include in the planning process. Whatever is decided about the level of employee participation, planning good communications strategies as part of the implementation is critical.

6. **Implementation of the change**—Once all the plans are in place, the company then can implement the change, making sure all employees are aware of the need for change and how it will directly impact them.

7. **Evaluate the success of the change and follow up to fix any problems**—After implementation of the change, the last crucial step is to evaluate how effective the process was and how well the change was received within the organization. During the evaluation phase, any problems that are found should be fixed quickly to ensure the change receives wide acceptance throughout the organization.

No matter how well a change is planned, management can expect to see resistance to the change. Factors driving this resistance will include uncertainty about how the change will affect people's jobs and their future with the company. If a change impacts the future of a unit or manager, self-interest will take hold and resistance could result in efforts to derail the change and cause it to fail. Feelings of loss can also be an underlying factor of change, as employees see a loss of work arrangements to which they have become accustomed. Others may fear a loss of power, status, or security when a change is implemented.

The best ways to overcome resistance to change is through employee participation as early as possible in the change process, through communication of the change, and by implementing training to educate employees about the change and how it will impact them. Introducing a change gradually can also help ease some of the resistance and tensions that may become evident during the change process.

There are numerous levels of change. Structural changes will impact the basic components of an organization, including a decision to centralize or decentralization parts of a company. Change can also impact many other aspects of the organization's structure, including the span of management, job designs, and work schedules. Technological changes relate to changes in equipment, work processes, work sequence, information processing systems, and automation. People-focused changes relate to changes planned to enhance employee skills and performance. The most stressful form of organization change is one that relates to decline and possible termination. This could be the result of poor management, obsolescence, competition, adverse economic conditions, or new government laws or regulation.

Organizational structures and designs can have a positive impact and enable growth and improve employee morale. On the opposite side, organizational structures and designs can create a cumbersome work environment, boring jobs, low morale, and poor productivity levels. While you may think that spending a lot of time designing an organization and developing its structures may slow your ability to build your company, in the long run taking this time and doing it carefully to best match the needs of your market environment and your employees will give you the best chance of success for your company.

Finding Change Leaders

One of the gurus of change management is Jon Katzenbach, who wrote the book *Real Change Leaders: How You Can Create Growth and High Performance at Your Company*. *Publishers Weekly* wrote: "Numerous corporations are downsizing, restructuring or revamping. Yet the steps taken to do so may limit the resulting organizations' ability to further adapt, because workers with superior skills are terminated and middle managers with leadership skills are eliminated. Katzenbach argues that the key to changing performance capability in dynamic companies is a new breed of middle manager—The Real Change Leader (RCL). Common characteristics of RCLs are outlined and illustrated with examples. The RCLs connect three forces of organizational change: top aspirations, work force productivity and marketplace reality. This book is highly recommended to all corporate executives who want to learn about effective leadership in large organizations."

Leading
Your People

Part One

Part Two

Part Three

Part Four

Part Five

Part Six

PART FOUR   MANAGEMENT

■ CHAPTER 13 Understanding Management Theory ■ CHAPTER 14 Setting Goals and Strategies ■ CHAPTER 15
Building Your Organization ■ CHAPTER 16 Leading Your People ■ CHAPTER 17 Putting in Controls

Essential Leadership Skills

Leading your people to build an effective organization is more than just giving orders and expecting them to be followed. Motivating your employees to want to do their job and to do that job the best way they can is critical. Being able to provide that level of motivation shows specific types of leadership traits. You must also learn the dynamics of group management and how to communicate effectively. This chapter will help you learn critical techniques to motivate your employees, be a strong leader, manage groups, and communicate effectively.

Motivating Employees

In Chapter 13, we reviewed behavior management theories and what motivates employees. As was discussed in that chapter, Maslow's theory of "hierarchical needs" is based on the belief that people are motivated by the satisfaction of various needs (i.e., physiological, safety, belongingness, esteem, self-actualization). While you might not think that as a manager you are responsible for meeting an employee's personal needs, employee satisfaction has been shown to improve performance, reduce absenteeism, and minimize turnover.

> Organizational reward systems can help a manager ensure that his or her employees' needs are being met.

Organizational reward systems can help a manager ensure that his or her employees' needs are being met. Formally, most companies have a mechanism in place for evaluating employee performance and rewarding good performance through pay, promotions, benefits, and status.

Edward Lawler, director of the Center for Effective Organizations at the University of Southern California's Marshall School of Business, believes there are four major factors that influence employee satisfaction and job attitude:

1. How much employees think they should receive compared to how much they actually receive.
2. Comparing the rewards they receive to the rewards others receive.
3. Misperceiving the rewards they believe others receive. For example, if an employee believes a coworker is making more money than he or she actually is, this can create dissatisfaction.

4. Recognizing that each employee has a unique set of needs and that satisfying each employee's needs will likely require a different set of rewards.

This style of management by reward is directly tied to the expectancy theory of motivation, which basically rests on two factors—how much we want something and how likely we believe we are to get it. Lawler, working with David Nadler, developed this framework as a key diagnostic approach for managing within the expectancy theory framework:

1. Behavior is determined by a combination of forces in the individual and forces in the environment.
2. People make decisions about their own behavior in organizations.
3. Different people have different types of needs, desires, and goals.
4. People make decisions among alternative plans of behavior based on their perceptions of the degree to which a given behavior will lead to desired outcomes.

The expectancy theory model suggests that motivation leads to effort, which when combined with employee ability and the working environment ultimately impacts performance. When all is going smoothly, the employee expects that his or her efforts will lead to high performance and just rewards or outcomes that will have value to that employee.

Lawler and Nadler developed a seven-step process based on expectancy theory that a manager can use to motivate his or her employees:

1. Figure out the outcomes each employee is likely to want.
2. Decide what kinds and levels of performance are needed to meet organizational goals.
3. Make certain that desired levels of performance are attainable.
4. Link desired outcomes and desired performance.
5. Analyze the situation for conflicting expectancies.
6. Make sure rewards are large enough.
7. Make sure the total reward system is fair to all.

Expectancy theory is just one of the key motivational theories. Another is equity theory, which contends that people view their outputs and inputs as a ratio and then compare their ratio to others. While none of this is quantitative and is built primarily on an employee's perception, the net result of this comparison is that the employee can either believe that he or she is being equitably rewarded, under-rewarded, or over-rewarded. When an employee perceives an equitable reward, he is not likely to seek a change in his work situation; he will likely seek changes if he believes he is being under-rewarded and he may seek changes if he believes he is being over-rewarded.

When an employee perceives she is being under-rewarded, her actions may include decreasing effort, asking for a raise, or leaving the job. An employee who believes he is being over-rewarded may exert more effort or reduce output to equal others. This theory holds that, in order to provide the proper motivation, managers must be certain their employees perceive the rewards systems as being equitable and fair.

The third theory impacting motivation is reinforcement theory. This theory is fairly straightforward. It is based on the assumption that when an employee's results are rewarded, those results are likely to be repeated, and if an employee's results are punished, those results are not likely to be repeated. For example, if an employee wants a raise and starts working harder, which results in getting that raise, she is likely to repeat that behavior the next time she wants a raise. If, for some reason, the employee worked harder because he expected a raise and then didn't get the raise, he will be unlikely to try working harder again. Instead he may try other tactics to get a raise. There are four elements of reinforcement theory:

> An employee who believes he is being over-rewarded may exert more effort or reduce output to equal others.

1. **Positive reinforcement** encourages a behavior by providing desirable results. When a manager sees an employee behaving in a way that she wants to encourage, praise can be a strong reinforcement. Pay raises, promotions, and other awards are all strong methods of positive reinforcement.
2. **Avoidance** encourages a behavior by allowing an escape from undesirable results. For example, an employee may show up for work on time to avoid the possible consequences for being late.
3. **Punishment** weakens a behavior by providing undesirable results. For example, an employee who regularly shows up late for work

could be docked pay. By using punishment, a manager hopes the unpleasant consequence will change the employee's behavior. Punishment can result in resentment and hostility, so most managers will use this as a last resort and try other types of reinforcement.

4. **Extinction** weakens a behavior by not providing desirable results. For example, an employee is known for being a clown in the office. Initially, the manager laughs at the behavior, which reinforces it. But if the behavior becomes disruptive, the manager instead ignores the behavior, which may encourage the clowning to stop.

Developing an effective reward system is critical for any organization. Lawler has identified four major characteristics of an effective reward system:

1. The system must meet a person's physiological and security needs (Maslow's theory).
2. The system must compare favorably with rewards offered by other similar organizations. Managers should keep abreast of rewards, compensation, and benefits offered by similar companies.
3. The distribution of rewards must be fair and equitable within the organization. Perceived inequity is likely to result in low morale and poor performance.
4. The system must recognize that different employees have different needs and develop a reward system that is flexible enough to recognize this and reward employees appropriately.

Thomas Wilson's 1994 book, *Innovative Reward Systems for Changing the Workplace,* concludes that positive reinforcement is the most effective tool for encouraging desired employee behavior. He believes this tool stimulates people to take action in exchange for something they consider valuable.

Wilson developed the SMART criteria that managers should use when developing reward programs. SMART is an acronym for *s*pecific, *m*eaningful, *a*chievable, *r*eliable, and *t*imely. *Specific* means that there should be a clear connection between rewards and actions. *Meaningful* means that achievements will be rewarded and will provide an important return on investment to both the performer and the organization. *Achievable* means that an employee's or group's goals must be within reach of those expected to perform the task. *Reliable* means that the program should operate according to expected principles and stated purpose. *Timely* means that recognition and rewards should be provided frequently enough to make performers feel that they are valued for their efforts.

Other types of motivational techniques are also being used in the workplace. As discussed in Chapter 14, management by objectives and goal setting is a good way to involve employees in determining what efforts are required, how those efforts will be measured, and how these efforts will lead to rewards. Managers also commonly use behavior modification based on the reinforcement theory.

Some companies are using a flexible workweek to give employees more freedom to set their time, control their work schedule, and meet other personal needs. This flexibility can enhance an employee's self-respect and improve performance. Job design can also play a major role in employee satisfaction, motivation, and performance. Two goals can be satisfied with careful job design: work gets done in a timely and competent manner, and employees are motivated and challenged.

Leadership Traits

Although there are no key management studies that have shown what constitute effective leadership traits, psychologist Raymond Cattell, who was a pioneer in the era of personality assessment, developed the Leadership Potential Equation in 1954. His equation was developed during a study of military leaders and is still widely used today to determine the traits of an effective leader. Cattell's traits include the following:

- **Emotional stability**—Leaders must tolerate both frustration and stress and be able to deal with anything they are required to face. They must be well adjusted and have reached a level of psychological maturity.
- **Dominance**—Leaders are assertive in both their thinking and their ability to deal with others. Most are competitive and decisive. They also enjoy overcoming obstacles.

- **Enthusiasm**—Leaders are used to thinking quickly on their feet and tend to be uninhibited. Most are active, expressive, and energetic with an optimistic outlook that is open to change.
- **Conscientiousness**—Leaders have a high standard of excellence and an internal desire to do their best. They also need order and tend to be very self-disciplined. Most are dominated by a sense of duty.
- **Social boldness**—Leaders tend to be risk-takers. They are generally thick-skinned and socially aggressive. They are responsive to others and have a good deal of emotional stamina.
- **Tough-mindedness**—Leaders are usually insensitive to hardship and are poised. They are practical and logical. Many do not seek sentimental attachments and are comfortable with criticism.
- **Self-assurance**—Leaders are self-confident and resilient. They are secure and free from guilt. They usually are not affected by prior mistakes or failures. They have little or no need for approval from others.
- **Compulsiveness**—Leaders are controlled and precise in their social interactions. They are protective of their integrity and reputation. They have considerable foresight and are careful when making decisions or determining specific actions.

In their 2003 survey, Right Management Consultants found the top five leadership traits cited by employees were honesty (24 percent), integrity/morals/ethics (16 percent), caring/compassion (7 percent), fairness (6.5 percent), and good relationships with employees, including approachability and listening skills (6 percent).

The U.S. Small Business Administration developed basic personality traits that a leader must have in order to motivate others and lead in new directions. In addition to envisioning

Honesty and Integrity Are Key

In a 2003 study, Right Management Consultants, a worldwide career transition and organizational consulting firm, found that honesty and integrity are the two most important leadership traits. Chris Pierce-Cooke, worldwide director of Right's organizational consulting practice, said, "Employees today are looking for strength of character in their leaders. They want to shake off the hangover of last year's corporate scandals and financial sleight of hand and be reassured that their leaders are honest, ethical and caring individuals. Employees are confronted with continued layoffs, a spotty recovery and three years of stock market declines. But they are not looking for leaders with a magic wand or a quick fix. Instead, they seem to be yearning for fundamental leadership principles, lessons on honesty and goodness that they were more likely to have learned in elementary school than in business or law school."

the future and being able to convince others to follow that vision, leaders must demonstrate:

Leaders must be able to deal with the rapid changes that are part of the world today.

- **High energy**—Leaders must be willing to put in long hours. Some travel is usually a prerequisite for leadership positions. They must also remain alert and stay focused.
- **Intuitiveness**—Leaders must be able to deal with the rapid changes that are part of the world today. These changes are often combined with information overload. Leaders must realize that they can't "know" everything and that reasoning and logic won't get them through all situations. Leaders must learn the value of using their intuition and trusting their "gut"" when making decisions.
- **Maturity**—Good leaders must recognize that personal power and recognition is secondary to the development of their employees. Mature leaders recognize that more can be accomplished by empowering others than by ruling others.
- **Team orientation**—Business leaders put a strong emphasis on teamwork. Top leaders create an adult/adult relationship with their employees that fosters team cohesiveness rather than promoting an adult/child relationship with their employees.
- **Empathy**—Leaders are able to put themselves in others' shoes. By developing an ability to be empathetic, a leader is able to build trust. Without trust, leaders will never be able to get the best effort from their employees.
- **Charisma**—Leaders use charisma, an almost larger-than-life persona, to arouse strong emotions in their employees. They are able to define a vision that unites and captivates their employees. Leaders use this vision to motivate employees to work toward a future goal and tie this goal to substantial personal rewards and values.

While few leaders are born, to become a leader requires a lot of self-discipline and work. People who choose to become leaders frequently seek a mentor who can help them develop the traits they need to lead. Others take on leadership roles as early as high school or grammar school and build their personality traits.

There actually have been no successful management studies that scientifically define leadership traits. Most of the theories were developed in the field of psychology or through anecdotal studies of successful leaders.

Managing Groups

Many companies are using group structures for decision-making rather than depending on decisions made by just one person. These include executive committees, design teams, marketing planning groups, as well as a myriad of other types of groups. Most decisions made by these groups are done by finding a consensus rather than by vote. Today's managers must learn how to lead this type of business structure, as well as how to be an effective part of someone else's group.

There are a number of advantages to group decision-making, including:

1. The group forms a large knowledge base with a greater number of years of total experience.
2. By depending on group input, more alternatives are suggested as the group looks for a solution.
3. By involving more people in the decision-making process, there is greater buy-in for the final decision and a greater chance for success.
4. With more people involved in the decision-making process, the communication of the decision to others in the organization is improved.
5. In most cases, the decision made by the group involves a more thorough analysis of the problem with a greater chance of success.

But, there are some disadvantages of the group process as well. These include:

1. Making decisions by committee usually takes longer and the process can be more costly than if one person makes the decision.
2. The group decision may result in an undesirable compromise.
3. One individual in the group may dominate the decision-making process, which essentially renders the group process useless and a waste of time and money.

4. Groups can be consumed by a process of groupthink, which is a situation in which the group desires consensus and cohesiveness rather than taking the time and enduring the possible initial conflict to find the best solution. A group leader can avoid this by encouraging the members to consider all alternatives and by holding back her position so divergent views can be presented and considered. Some group leaders will even encourage a member of the group to be a devil's advocate to ensure full consideration of all topics.

Not all groups make decisions using the same methods. There are a number of common styles, some more successful than others. What will work in your organization depends on the personalities of the people involved in the group, especially that of the group leader. Here are the most common styles to look for when you are involved in a group decision-making process. As a manager, the key is to understand the group dynamics in play and to determine how to best influence the outcome given the dynamics:

Autocratic or directive style—A leader using this style will define and diagnose the problem without seeking input on these aspects of a problem. Then he will present solutions, evaluate what is presented, and see alternative solutions. The leader will then choose among the alternatives proposed. While this style is easiest to manage from the viewpoint of the leader, it will likely generate less significant input from the participants.

Autocratic with group input—As is the case with the autocratic style, the leader will define the problem and diagnose its cause. The key difference is that after making that presentation, she will seek information from the group to gather more information about the cause. The leader will present a list of potential solutions and seek data from the group to evaluate each possible solution. Ultimately, the leader will decide on which alternative solution will be chosen. This style of group management does encourage more participation than the autocratic style, but it still leaves most of the power in the hands of the leader and may result in fewer alternatives with less critique of those alternatives, especially once the leader signals which alternative seems best.

Autocratic with group review and feedback—When using this leadership style, a manager defines the problem, diagnoses the causes, and determines

> What will work in your organization depends on the personalities of the people involved in the group, especially that of the group leader.

the solution. Once he makes all these decisions, a presentation is made to the group to communicate the information, review the solutions, and seek feedback. While this style may be an effective way to communicate a decision, it will not encourage significant input if the group disagrees with any of the points.

Individual consultative style—The leader meets with each member of the group individually to define a problem share information with the group. She seeks ideas regarding the problem, its causes, and potential solutions by meeting individually with the members. Usually, she will seek input for alternative solutions from individuals based on their area of expertise. Once she gathers all the information, the leader will make the final choice about which alternative to use and communicate that decision either individually or in a group setting. This style of group management does not take full advantage of group dynamics in defining problems and finding solutions, but it does give the leader strong control of the decision-making process.

Group consultative style—This style of group management is almost identical to individual consultative style. The key difference is that the leader shares his definition of the problem with the group as a whole rather than individually.

Group decision style—The group leader presents her definition of the problem to the work group and then encourages the group to diagnose the causes of the problem. Once the group agrees on the causes, it works as a whole to develop solutions, evaluate alternatives, and choose the appropriate solution. This process will encourage greater participation, but for it to succeed, the leader must have accurately defined the problem or be open to input that the definition might be wrong.

Participative style—The leader serves primarily as a facilitator allowing the group to define the problem, determine its causes, develop solutions, evaluate alternatives, and choose the appropriate solution. While this style gives the leader the least amount of control, it will benefit from the greatest degree of group participation and buy-in for the solution.

Leaderless team—This type of group has no designated leader but instead has been formed as a leaderless team. This style of group management is most often found in research and development settings with top professionals each offering their own expertise to solve problems. Many times, a different leader will emerge for each problem, depending on the problem and expertise needed. The group will define the problem, diagnose its causes, develop solutions, evaluate them, and select the best alternative. While this style takes full advantage of group dynamics, it can take longer for the group to find its working style and develop its problem-solving processes.

Modeling Group Dynamics

Forming an effective group can be a difficult process.

Forming an effective group can be a difficult process. The Tuckerman Model of Development, which was defined in 1965, is probably the one most commonly recognized. There are four stages to the model: forming, storming, norming, and performing.

In the forming stage, the group is just getting to know each other and members are becoming oriented to the group's goals and procedures. At this stage, the group leader must be certain that each member has plenty of information. The leader also helps break the ice and helps members get acquainted with each other and with the responsibilities of the group.

In the storming stage, group members will start questioning the task demands and even exhibit some hostility to both the tasks and the leader. If a leader tries to suppress the tension, he could end up with bitterness and resentment. If a leader allows the storming to go too far, the group could be filled with anxiety and tension. The critical step for the leader is to find a balance and use conflict management techniques to get past this stage.

In the norming stage, the group begins to work together and build a strong relationship. The leader works to encourage this relationship and build a team based on unity of purpose and shared responsibility.

In the performing stage, the leader's main role is to encourage cooperation. The group performs using problem-solving themes and develops a relationship based on interdependence and trust. Once the group reaches this stage, the group is functioning efficiently and can work to achieve its goals. The group can stay at this productive stage by constantly defining new problems and finding their solutions.

Brainstorming

Many groups that use a participative style or leaderless team use a process called brainstorming to make decisions. There are six basic steps to this process:

1. **Define the problem**—The brainstorming session starts with a request for suggestions about the most important problem. No criticism of anyone's suggestions is allowed at this time in order to encourage everyone's participation and not take the risk of discouraging a potentially useful point. All suggestions are written on a board or other mechanism that allows the group to see the full list as it is developed. Problems that are similar are grouped together. Once that is done, the group prioritizes the list and puts the most important problems at the top.

2. **Determine the solution**—Once a problem is defined, the next step in the process is to determine the best solution. Using the same process of defining the problem, the group brainstorms possible solutions. Again similar solutions are grouped together. Then the group can look at the alternatives and pick the best solution.

3. **Develop a plan**—Once the solution is defined, the group uses the same brainstorming process to develop a plan. First suggestions are encouraged and written down for all to see. No suggestions are criticized during this process to encourage the greatest degree of participation and creativity. Suggestions are grouped by their similarities and the list is rearranged with the best suggestions on top. A final plan can then be developed.

4. **Identify resources and limitations**—Once the group agrees on the plan, they need to discuss the resources on hand to carry out the plan, as well as any limitations they might see to successfully implementing that plan. The group may need to alter the plan to fill any gaps in resources or deal with any limitations found.

5. **Design plan implementation**—Once the group determines they have a workable plan, they need to develop strategies for implementing the plan. Assignments of responsibility need to be made to ensure that someone takes responsibility for each aspect of the implementation. While the group as a whole will implement the plan, it is important to have a point person for each task identified as part of the plan to ensure success.

6. **Summarize the decisions**—At the end of the meeting, the group leader (either one who was designated prior to the start of the session or one who took a leadership role as part of the process) should summarize each of the steps: the problem or problems identified, the solutions found, the plans developed, the methods to be used to implement the plan, the resources that will be available, the limitations that have been identified, and the strategies for implementing the plan. Finally, a list of the key tasks and who will be responsible for each should be listed. This summary should be typed and distributed to each member after the meeting either by the leader or by someone he or she designates.

Instituting Effective Communications

Managers must learn to communicate effectively with their staff and their superiors. There are four basic elements to effective communication: feedback, awareness, credibility, and empathy. Feedback is probably the most important element. By encouraging feedback, a manager allows her staff to ask questions, to seek clarification, and to express opinions. In that way, she can quickly tell whether the message was understood and if there are any problems with the message.

The second most important aspect of communications is to be aware of how the message might be received. For example, an investor may be very pleased to learn of a big jump in profits, while the employees may be disappointed to learn there was a major jump in profits if it did not come at the same time as bonuses or raises. The manager must always think not only about what he wants to say, but also about how it will be received by parties with different underlying interests in what is being said.

Listening Is as Important as Talking

To communicate effectively, managers must develop strong listening skills. Employees need to believe that they are being heard and their concerns are being addressed. You should always prepare some open-ended questions so that employees feel comfortable expressing their opinions about the message.

Be attentive as employees give their feedback, and make sure that your body language gives the employee a clear sign you are listening. Make eye contact and take notes about what is being said. Even if what the employee says angers you, avoid making a comment that could lead to more tension. Acknowledge what the employee says by asking follow-up questions, nodding your head, or summarizing the key points you believe the employee was making.

If the employee disagrees with you, ask open questions to understand how the employee wants to proceed. Develop a plan of action that clearly shows you've heard what the employee has said and that you will take his or her concerns into consideration. Often communication problems can be avoided as long as employees believe their concerns have received a fair hearing.

For any message to be effective, the person sending the message must have credibility. If a manager constantly tells his staff this project must be done this way and by this date and then changes his mind a few days later by asking for a different deadline or a different method for completing the task, his credibility will suffer unless he communicates why there is a change. He must be reasonable with the new deadline if a major change is requested to maintain both credibility and respect.

This leads to the final element—empathy. Any time a manager is conveying bad news, she must realize her employees will be disappointed or unhappy. Before passing on the bad news, the manager should carefully consider what the likely response or responses could be and convey the message while being sensitive to the employee's feelings and possible reactions.

Many managers don't like to convey bad news and delay doing so as long as possible. This helps to feed the grapevine, an informal communications channel in almost every organization. Generally when there is a lack of information about a subject that is creating concern in the organization, people tend to fill that gap with speculation of their own using the grapevine. Managers should get to know what is passing on the grapevine and respond to information that is definitely not accurate by effectively communicating the correct information.

Managers can actually make use of the grapevine if they get to know the key people who fuel the grapevine and use that knowledge to help get accurate information back into the loop. Keeping your ears open for what is on the grapevine is a good way to find out about employee concerns, get reactions to change, and actually improve decision-making and effective communication.

Leading people is probably the most challenging aspect of any manager's responsibilities. While a person could have been a very effective and productive employee, moving up to the role of managing people is not for everyone. Get to know yourself and how you interact with people. Try out your leadership skills outside the workplace in volunteer work or through professional organizations. If you would like to be a manager, hone your leadership skills before you are promoted to that role in the workplace.

> **Chapter 17**

Putting in Controls

Part One

Part Two

Part Three

Part Four

Part Five

Part Six

PART FOUR   MANAGEMENT

■ CHAPTER 13 Understanding Management Theory ■ CHAPTER 14 Setting Goals and Strategies ■ CHAPTER 15 Building Your Organization ■ CHAPTER 16 Leading Your People ■ CHAPTER 17 **Putting in Controls**

Organizational Controls

After careful strategic planning, you want to be sure that your plans are carried out effectively. The only way to be certain is to put organization controls in place. Most controls focus on four basic areas: physical resources, human resources, information resources, and financial resources.

Physical resources include inventory management, quality control, and equipment control. In the area of inventory management, you must put in controls that will maintain the right amount of stock. Quality controls ensure that your products or services are provided at the level of quality expected by your customers. Equipment control ensures that your employees have the right kinds of equipment and facilities to do their jobs.

Human resource controls ensure that hiring practices and placement services adequately meet the needs of your departments. These controls also ensure that training and development functions meet the needs of your staff and keep your staff up-to-date on industry changes. Finally, human resource controls focus on how employee performance is appraised and review the compensation structure of the company.

Information controls make sure that information is in the hands of the various departments when needed. Also, there should be controls in place to make certain that sales and marketing forecasts and results are accurate; that production scheduling is meeting the demand for your product; and that economic conditions are monitored with methods to adjust strategic plans if conditions differ dramatically from initial expectations.

Financial controls not only impact the accounting and finance departments directly; they also play a role in the entire operation of the organization. While making sure that the company has cash on hand when needed and that company assets are properly expended, financial controls also play a role in all other controls. For example, financial controls are one of the key ways to be certain that inventory is not growing too rapidly, resulting in increased storage costs. Finance may also be the first to notice there is a human resources problem if costs for hiring and firing start increasing. Sales discrepancies also will most likely be caught first at the finance level, if red flags are raised when sales goals are not met or if sales far exceed projections. Although a company may be happy to see sales goals exceeded, it must also be sure that these positive results are based on true numbers and not falsified sales results.

In this rapidly changing world and complex business environment, adequate controls are paramount. A company can't decide on a series of strategic goals and magically expect the company to meet them. Changes in the economic environment require constant monitoring of goals and adjustments throughout the year to be sure departments are on target. Controls also help avoid the compounding of errors by finding a problem quickly before a large loss of assets has a major impact on a company's bottom line. In this chapter, we'll review the types of controls you can put in place, how you can use those controls to manage strategically, and then discuss the control techniques and methods most appropriate for four key areas: budget, operations, human resources, and marketing.

Types of Controls

Companies use controls that are self-monitoring as well as controls that require manual monitoring. One example of self-monitored controls is a just-in-time inventory system that is managed using a computer program. The program will continue ordering products or raw materials until inventory hits a certain level. Ordering will then be automatically stopped until inventory falls to a certain level. Companies that have a just-in-time inventory system that requires manual monitoring usually produce big-ticket items such as planes or major manufacturing equipment. For example, with this type of system, products and raw materials are ordered by purchasing only when an actual sale has been confirmed.

Controls can be put in place at three different levels: preliminary, screening, and post action.

Preliminary controls focus on either the quality or quantity of resources before they become part of the system. For example, to control the quality of its managers, some companies will only promote staff members who were hired right out of college and developed through its own management training system. Some companies require rigid standards that must be

Playing with the Sales Numbers

Time Warner's takeover by AOL will probably go down as one of the most famous cases of a major corporation being fooled by creative sales bookings. AOL had booked millions of dollars of deals as revenue that turned out to be nothing more than unfounded paper trails. Even as information about these deals surfaced, AOL continued to count millions of dollars in ad revenues from dot-coms that even its advertising salespeople were beginning to realize would never be paid. Negotiations to shift revenue from one division to another also helped improve the bottom line for its online business. Ad sales that were sold on behalf of eBay, the online auction site, were booked as AOL's own revenue. AOL also bartered ads for computer equipment with Sun Microsystems to make its revenue appear to be higher. Many more instances of creative sales bookings are coming to light as Time Warner digs deeper into AOL's finances. This case clearly shows a lack of good financial, and human resources, controls at AOL.

met by any products that are produced by an outside company and that carry the company's brand name.

Screening controls require quality control reviews at various stages of production. For example, a manufacturing plant will set up various points during the production process at which product components are checked to be sure that they meet quality standards and work properly. The Japanese proved the value of this method of control with their car manufacturing. Japanese companies encourage their workers to inspect parts through the production process and reject any part that is defective. At the same time, U.S. car manufacturers were only inspecting cars at the end of the product line. These controls are the most popular types of controls in today's manufacturing environment.

Postaction controls look at the quality of outputs after production, which was more common in Detroit when the only inspection was after completion of a car. Less complex products, such as light bulbs or batteries, can be monitored successfully upon completion. Postaction controls are not as effective as preliminary or screening controls; their primary purpose is to help management improve future production results. For example, if at the end of a product line too many light bulbs are defective, the manager knows there is a problem in the line and she must find the problem and correct it before more resources are wasted.

> Postaction controls are not as effective as preliminary or screening controls.

Most organizations use a combination of these types of controls, implementing the type of control most appropriate for the desired outcome. The key is to determine the standards desired and implement controls that will help monitor those standards. For example, a fast-food restaurant may determine that all tables must be cleaned within five minutes after a customer has left the table. If a manager sees tables not being cleaned within that standard, he knows that a corrective action must be taken.

Controls and standards can be put in place at all levels of an organization. Sales goals are most commonly quantified and monitored in organizations, but many more types of standards can be established and monitored. This can include how quickly customers will be greeted or what level of recovery a hospital wants to achieve for its patients.

Once standards are established and clearly communicated to staff, then it's important to set up a method for measuring performance that is both transparent and carried out consistently. For example, a sales manager will have goals for daily, weekly, and monthly performance. Mechanisms must be in place to be able to quickly monitor success rates, so any divergence from goals can be quickly assessed. Production managers could have standards established based on volume, cost, and quality. Measurements should be able to pick up any problems quickly so they can be fixed before a large number of production items are defective.

Employee measures can be based on quality and quantity output, which is simple when measuring sales results or production quotas, but much more difficult for departments such as research and development. Many companies struggle with measurements for creative and research teams, and often settle on some form of peer review as the most appropriate measure.

The most effective control systems are integrated with the planning process. Goals and strategies for meeting those goals are set. Then action plans are developed for each department or functional area that has clearly measurable components. These measurements become part of the control system. The key is not to be rigid with the controls put in place. There must be flexibilities in the system that allow for changes that alter initial expectations.

Getting information in a timely way is another component of a good control system. The frequency needed depends on the type of performance being measured. For example, a well-established product may only need inventory monitoring at top management levels quarterly or annually, while a new product would need to be monitored more frequently as management determines the product's viability.

Controlling Strategically

When developing control mechanisms, it's important for managers to think strategically. There are three key elements of strategic control: effectiveness, productivity, and managerial performance.

Effectiveness

Deciding how to measure effectiveness is not easy. Researchers have developed four models for measuring effectiveness:

1. **Systems resource approach** focuses on how a company acquires its assets in order to compete effectively in the marketplace. For example, if there is a shortage of raw materials, the company would prove its effectiveness if it were able to get the raw material it needed to continue operations.
2. **Goal approach** focuses on meeting set goals. For example, if the company sets a goal of increasing sales by 15 percent and meets that goal, then the company was effective.
3. **Internal functioning approach** focuses on how smoothly the company operates without straining the organization. An organization with this approach will seek to maintain employee satisfaction and morale with a low level of internal conflict.
4. **Strategic constituencies approach** focuses on satisfying outside groups that have a stake in the organization such as investors, suppliers, and financial institutions, in addition to employees and managers. This approach depends on feedback from all its constituent groups to determine how effective the company operations are.

Productivity

Measuring productivity is considerably easier than effectiveness, because productivity is a quantitative measure that looks at the actual level of output of goods and services. When comparing the productivity of different areas of the company, some standards need to be established. For example, a clothing chain should calculate average sales for each square foot of retail space. Stores that are meeting or exceeding the sales level would have a good level of productivity. Stores that are not meeting those numbers would be red-flagged as having a problem using the control system. Managers would then look more closely to find out what the problem is in the red-flag stores.

Managerial Performance

Few people can truthfully and effectively monitor their own performance. Many companies that want to assess their managerial performance hire an outside consultant to evaluate how well the company is doing. Consultants meet first with management to determine the scope of the study.

Then they hold stakeholder meetings with groups that have a stake in the business, such as suppliers, vendors, employees, managers, customers, and financial institutions. Next, the consultant reviews the written policies and practices to be sure that what is being communicated in writing matches the stakeholders' perceptions. Then, the consulting firm looks at a number of benchmarks to compare various company measures with other companies in similar businesses in terms of inputs (workload, cost, and human resources), outputs (work performed, revenue generated, and service levels provided), and efficiency measures (cost per employee and cost per unit of service). The consulting firm then prepares a preliminary report and presents it to the management team as well as to some of the key stakeholders. After getting feedback on the conclusions and recommendations of the preliminary report, a final report is submitted that lists the key findings with recommendations for improving performance.

Productivity is the easiest area to measure and a control system for measuring this area is found in almost every company. Effectiveness measures are more qualitative. Small companies can benefit by learning more about each of these approaches and implementing them as appropriate within their organizational structure. A full management audit is less likely to be done in small businesses, but it may be a good idea if the company's performance is lagging behind its competitors and if management wants to have an outside auditor come in and assess what the problems may be. The money spent may be just what is needed to get the company back on track.

> Productivity is the easiest area to measure and a control system for measuring this area is found in almost every company.

Control Techniques and Methods

Techniques for control are based in four key areas: budgeting, operations, human resources, and marketing.

Budgetary Control Methods

Budgetary controls were discussed in great detail from both the accounting and finance perspectives in each of those sections, so we won't cover them again here other than to say that budgets are the foundation of most financial control systems. How an organization budgets, how much participation an organization allows, and how much ownership each employee feels for the budgeting process definitely impacts how effective budgetary controls will be.

The more involvement people have in preparing budgets for their departments, the greater responsibility they will feel for staying within budget controls. Budgets that are imposed on managers without any significant involvement from them and their staffs will likely be less effective controls than those developed in a participative style.

Operations Control Methods

Operations control methods concentrate on four key areas: operations design, operations coordination, quality control, and inventory control.

- **Operations design** focuses on how work facilities (such as equipment and job assignments) are constructed, arranged, and coordinated.
- **Operations coordination** focuses on what materials and services are needed to do the work of the company efficiently. In setting up controls, companies must determine the materials and parts needed for production operations, and then determine the level of inventory the company should keep on hand and at what point more materials or parts should be ordered. Next, a schedule is set up for parts deliveries and the lead times needed.
- **Quality control** focuses on maintaining the level of quality for the company to keep customers happy. A number of techniques are used to control quality. The two techniques most commonly used are acceptance sampling of finished goods and in-process sampling during production.
- **Inventory control** focuses on finding the optimum level of inventory to avoid shortages, lost sales, and customer complaints without having too much on hand.

Four techniques are most commonly used to measure operational controls: PERT, linear programming, break-even analysis, and queuing theory. PERT (program evaluation and review techniques) helps schedule and manage complex projects by inter-relating the activities and determining the best order of activities, the amount of time needed for each, and ways to minimize costs of the project using a technique called Critical Path Analysis (CPA). Linear programming is another control approach that determines various solutions based on a set of linear equations that represent objectives and constraints. Break-even analysis determines the number of units that must be sold in order to cover fixed and variable expenses. Queuing theory focuses on customer waiting times. This theory seeks to find the optimum number of waiting lines to minimize customer dissatisfaction while minimizing costs. Queuing theory seeks to find the optimum balance. These are all complex theories; if you would like to learn about them, a classic textbook on the subject is *Operations Management* by Jay Heizer and Barry Render.

Human Resources Control Methods

The two primary methods of instituting human resources controls are performance appraisals and the analysis of key human resources ratios. Performance appraisals start with a job analysis to determine the duties and their relative importance. Next, performance criteria based on these duties are developed, which leads to the development of performance standards for the job. Using these standards, each employee is measured on their actual performance and then compared to the standards. Then, the manager meets with the employee, discusses the appraisal, and either rewards the employee for his or her performance, or develops a series of corrective actions if performance is not up to par.

Human resources ratios measure a number of aspects of employee behavior. Ratios are developed for employee turnover, absenteeism, and work force composition. These controls also monitor employee turnover. An acceptable ratio for the type of position within the type of organization is established. For example, a company determines that a 25 percent ratio is normal for clerical positions. If a department is experiencing a steadily

Using the Critical Path

Critical Path Analysis (CPA) is a popular operations control technique that helps you plan all the tasks that must be completed as a part of a project. CPA can form the basis of your schedule preparation and resource planning. As the project progresses, the CPA can be used to monitor the achievement of project goals and to see quickly where fixes may be needed if the project gets off course. Many operations managers prefer CPA to Gantt charts (mentioned in Chapter 13), because CPA formally identifies tasks that must be completed on time in order for the entire project to be completed on time. Others prefer Gantt charts because the relationship of tasks to time is more immediately obvious. Some project planners prefer CPA because it helps them identify the minimum length of time to complete a project and which steps can be accelerated to complete the project in the available time. CPA helps minimize costs of completing a project as well. You can learn more about CPA and PERT techniques at *www.mind tools.com/critpath.html*.

increasing turnover, then human resources will investigate to determine the cause for the higher ratio. Similar techniques are used to measure absenteeism and work force composition. One of the key reasons to monitor work force composition is to be sure there is no sign of discrimination in hiring and promotions.

Workplace Monitoring

Corporate security concerns are increasing the use of workplace monitoring to review employee use of electronic communications. Many employers flash some kind of warning on an employee's screen daily to alert them to the types of monitoring programs in place, such as screening Internet use or e-mail. Employers are expected to inform their employees of corporation policies on inspection and monitoring of communications, but if an investigation involves suspected criminal activity or an alleged breach of company polices, then warnings to the employees being investigated are not required or recommended by information technology standards.

A number of activities can and should be monitored when employees use the company's electronic system for purposes of detecting theft, fraud, or illegal use of software or intellectual property. Surveillance can also be used to prevent unauthorized or unlawful disclosure of confidential business information or trade secrets, to reduce a company's liability from unlawful acts by employees, to maintain productivity, to ensure the quality of goods and services, to protect the reputation and goodwill of a company, to comply with laws and regulations, and to ensure that employees are complying with company security and data protection policies.

Marketing Control Methods

Marketing is another critical function that should have its own set of controls. Not only does it control a significant portion of assets to be spent, its results are also crucial to the success of the company. Two key types of controls used by companies are test marketing and marketing ratios.

Test marketing is used when introducing a new product or service or a major change to an existing product line. Since there is such a huge commitment of resources to introduce a new product, testing public acceptance of the

Failing with New Coke

Test marketing does not always prevent a public relations disaster for a company. One of the more famous examples of test marketing failures was the Coca-Cola's 1985 introduction of New Coke. At the time Pepsi was running a marketing campaign with taste testing that showed its product was preferred in blind taste tests. The new version of Coke was sweeter, with a taste close to that of Pepsi.

product before spending large amounts of money to produce, make, and market the product is always recommended, but even these precautions may not prevent a disastrous mistake. Test marketing will be discussed in Chapter 21.

Market research done prior to Coca-Cola's introduction of a new product had showed that the new formula, the first change in Coca-Cola's secret formula since 1903, was preferred by a large margin in taste tests. When "New Coke" was released, there was a major public backlash complaining that Coca-Cola had killed an American icon, and the company had to rush Coca-Cola Classic back onto the market. Some have speculated that the entire campaign, thought to be a public relations disaster, was actually a planned marketing campaign to reignite public interest in Coca-Cola and get a lot of free publicity. If so, it might have been a brilliant marketing move.

Common marketing ratios that are calculated include market share and profit margin on sales. Market share measures the percentage a product represents of the total market for that type of product. Whenever a company sees substantial changes in its market share, it should quickly investigate why and take corrective actions. Profit margin on sales measures the profitability of products and is calculated by dividing net income by total sales. For example, a company that has total sales of $1 million with net income of $200,000 has a profit margin of 20 percent. Marketing will be covered in greater detail in the next chapter.

The key thing to remember when implementing any form of corporate controls is that they should not be so restrictive that they cause major employee backlash and dissatisfaction. Rather than help a company's bottom line, poorly designed controls can actually hurt it. Also, controls should not stem employee creativity and participation, which can also hurt a company's long-term growth potential.

> **Chapter 18**

Understanding
Marketing

What Is Marketing?

For some, marketing is a mysterious process that magically gets a product into the public spotlight and onto the shelves. In reality, it involves a great deal of planning and extensive implementation strategies. In this chapter, we'll review what marketing actually entails, review marketing management philosophies, discuss the goals of marketing, and introduce the idea of marketing sectors.

When asked to describe marketing, most people will mistakenly identify it with selling and promotion. That is actually the function of the sales department. In some companies, sales is a function of marketing; in other companies, the two functions are separate and distinct even though, of course, they must coordinate their activities.

The key responsibilities of a marketing department are to determine the needs and wants of the consumer and find ways to satisfy those needs and wants within the product areas that match where the company wants to focus its attention. Marketing tasks include an assessment of consumers' needs and wants, market research, and product development. We'll be covering these tasks in this section of the book.

Needs and Wants

First, you should understand the difference between needs and wants. Needs represent something a person must have in order to satisfy the basics of life; food, clothing, housing, and safety are the core basic needs. These are just a part of the basic human makeup and not something creative advertising has instilled in the consumer.

Wants, on the other hand, are not required for the basics of life but instead are shaped by a person's culture, personality, and social environment. For example, a person needs to eat some source of protein to satisfy hunger and maintain a healthy body, but he wants to get a cheeseburger at his favorite fast-food joint because of effective marketing campaigns.

As countries develop, the wants of their population increase as more wealth is accumulated and more money is available for discretionary spending. Marketers take advantage of this by creating wants by piquing curiosity, interest, and desires. In order to maintain success and stave off competition, marketers must stay focused on the need that their wants are satisfying. For example, a person needs to bang in a nail. A manufacturer may create an aura around a particular type of hammer, creating a want to buy that hammer. The manufacturer must stay focused on the need to bang in the nail, follow customers' changes on the type of tool they want to satisfy that need, and be sure the product continues to meet the need. If a better or more effective tool to meet the need is introduced, the manufacturer will find customer loyalty can be stolen quickly.

In Chapter 4, we discussed the economic concept of supply and demand. Marketing focuses on meeting customer demand and assisting a company in determining what levels of manufacturing will be needed to meet that demand. One key component of consumer demand is purchasing power. While consumers may have many wants, they can only buy what is within their power to purchase based on available funds. It is true that in today's culture, consumers are laden with credit card debt because they have spent more than they make, but eventually they must stop spending when credit availability is exhausted.

In addition to having the purchasing power to buy a product, a consumer must also want the particular product a company is offering. Consumers look for quality but frequently buy on price. Consumers also look for variety. While last year's product model may meet their needs, their wants may look for some change just to add variety to their life. Understanding these product variables and designing products accordingly is a major focus of marketing.

Products are defined by marketers as anything that can be offered for consumption that meets a want or need. Marketers must know what the consumers' needs are and then develop a series of products that will meet those needs by creating wants. For example, women may need to look attractive, but they will want a series of products to make that happen including lipstick, eyeliner, and other makeup items. A product

Can Consumer Debt Levels Predict a Slowdown?

Economists have watched with alarm as consumers rack up the highest debt levels in history. U.S. consumer debt has doubled over the past ten years, according to the Federal Reserve Board. Consumer debt hit $1.98 trillion in October 2003, up from $1.5 trillion three years earlier. This figure represents credit card and car loan debt but excludes mortgages, and it means that U.S. households carry an average of $18,700 on credit cards and car loans. When mortgage debt is added to this number, the total exceeds $9 trillion. Without a significant increase in job opportunities, this problem is likely to worsen. Even though interest rates are at historic lows, consumer buying is slowing as consumers are leveraged to their maximum. Some economists are calling these debt levels a dangerous bubble about to burst, one that could have even more negative impact on the economy than when the stock market bubble burst in 2000.

line would be defined as a series of products that meet that need to look attractive.

Consumers that look to fulfill their needs and wants form what is called a market, which is essentially all the potential buyers of a particular type of product or service. A market can be made up of a service, a product, or anything else that consumers consider of value. Consumers are not only individuals. Businesses and government agencies are also consumers of other businesses' products.

> A market can be made up of a service, a product, or anything else that consumers consider of value.

Once a company has identified its product and markets, it is up to marketing to determine the best ways to market that product to the consumer by creating wants for the particular product by knowing the customers' needs. So taking this description full circle, marketing is the process by which activities including product development, market research, distribution, communication, pricing, and service are combined to satisfy consumer needs and wants through developing strategies for selling a company's products.

Marketing Management Philosophies

There are a number of philosophies that drive the management of marketing—the production concept, the product concept, the selling concept, the marketing concept, and the societal marketing concept.

The **production concept** is based on the fact that consumers favor products that are available and affordable. Based on this theory, marketing managers concentrate on production efficiency and effective distribution networks, spending very little time on determining customers' actual needs and wants. Marketing using this philosophy can be successful in situations where demand exceeds supply or where the product's price is high and the best opportunity to capture increased market share is by finding production methods that can bring the price down to attract more customers. Henry Ford is probably the best-known practitioner of the production concept. In developing his Model T, he concentrated on production techniques that would help bring the cost of his car down and create a vehicle that most people could afford. He was known for frequently joking that a customer could order a Model T in any color as long as it was black.

The **product concept** is based on the product itself and ways to improve its quality, performance, and features to attract buyers. This concept tends to create too narrow a focus with marketing managers concentrating on a product's features without considering what benefits a consumer is seeking from the product. Marketing managers working from this philosophy may spend too much time adding features to their products and not enough time worrying about what consumers actually need and want. The disappearance of slide rules and the companies that manufactured them is a classic example of how this type of myopia can kill a company's future. The slide-rule manufacturers believed engineers wanted a slide rule, but what they really wanted was a way to do their needed calculations. Slide-rule manufacturers totally missed the challenge to their market share from pocket calculators and paid the price with the demise of their companies.

The **selling concept** places making the sale first and takes the view that consumers are unwilling customers whose opposition to a product must be overcome during the sales process. For example, insurance salesmen frequently try to push a particular product that the customer does not necessarily want and use a hard sales approach to close the deal, often building on a customer's fears rather than his or her wants and needs. These types of sellers misrepresent their product or services and companies that practice this method often end up with high customer dissatisfaction.

The **marketing concept** is the most consumer driven. Rather than focusing on the needs of the seller, the marketing concept focuses on the needs of the buyer. Marketing managers who subscribe to this concept believe satisfying the consumer is what will drive a company's marketing success. When using this approach, a marketing manager starts by defining the market and analyzing the needs and wants of the market. Products are then developed around meeting those needs and wants in a way that is better than what the company's competition is doing—or at least is marketed creatively to make the customer believe the product is better than others in the marketplace that are designed to satisfy the customers' needs and wants.

Ray Kroc was a fifty-two-year-old milkshake machine salesman before he decided to buy seven restaurants owned by Richard and Maurice McDonald. He was impressed with their concept of how to run a fast-food restaurant. He decided to use their strategies for fast-food

McDonald's Mastery of the Marketing Concept

When you look at the success McDonald's has had at selling a basic human need and want—the hamburger—so that it is known worldwide, you can see how much of a master Ray Kroc was at using the marketing concept. He was a master at knowing how to serve people and adapting quickly to consumers' needs and wants.

design and combine it with a plan to sell franchises to others who could duplicate the design in other markets. Kroc developed the method for teaching the McDonald's concept for running a fast-food restaurant by creating Hamburger University, which offers a degree in hamburgerology with a minor in French fries. Franchisees and their staffs learn the basics of the McDonald's methods and must practice them in their own restaurants, which created a level of expectations for customers whenever they entered a McDonald's.

The **societal marketing concept** adds an additional component to the marketing concept—the belief that the company's product should contribute to the betterment of society as a whole. Marketing managers who practice this philosophy believe a company needs to go beyond meeting a customer's needs and wants and also consider the societal impact of a product. With greater emphasis on environmental impacts, population growth, resource shortages, social services, and other societal concerns, a company must market its product by showing that it is concerned with any of these problems that might be related to the product and its impact on society. Exxon learned that difficult lesson after the *Valdez* oil spill, which not only cost them billions to clean up but lost them significant market share that took a long time to recover. Oil companies today focus a great deal of their advertising dollar on building their image as a protector of the environment and keep a close watch on their safety records. Companies that practice this philosophy believe they must carefully balance the needs of society with the needs of the consumer in order to build a strong profit margin. Today even small companies get involved in local activities that show they are serving their communities through sponsoring walks to benefit research on particular diseases or other charitable causes to improve their image in the community and attract more customers.

You will need to understand these concepts and how you will develop your marketing plans based on them before setting the company's goals.

Goals of Marketing

Marketing and its impact are viewed very differently depending on your perspective. Buyers want to find quality products at a reasonable price that can be bought near their home. Sellers need to attract customers and satisfy their needs through an effective marketing program. Governments and other public interest groups seek to control marketing programs to be sure they are accurately promoting products that are safe and reliable and do not harm the environment. Public interest groups in particular serve as watchdogs to protect consumer interests.

A poorly designed marketing program can hurt more than it helps if it generates charges that the company is hurting the environment with its product, attempting to sell unnecessary wants, or teaching greed to children. For example, tobacco companies must be particularly careful about how they market their products and be certain the public does not perceive they are targeting children. Government regulators can force companies to recall products if they are found to be defective. Since marketing can impact even those who will never buy the product, companies must be careful to target the markets appropriately and avoid stirring up controversy unnecessarily.

When setting up goals for a company's marketing program, four alternatives for maximizing results are usually considered: consumption, consumer satisfaction, choice, or lifestyle.

Consumption—Marketing programs with this goal focus on stimulating consumption with the hope of creating maximum production and profits for the company's owners or shareholders. With this goal in mind, companies seek to get people to consume more and more. Coca-Cola's advertising strategy that focused on getting people to consume its products for breakfast rather than consuming a cup of coffee is an example of stimulating a new level of consumption through creating a new desire.

Dell Builds Its Market Share on Choice

Dell Computer's direct marketing model is one of the best examples of how a marketing program based on customer choice can be a successful marketing strategy. Dell believes there are five tenets to this marketing model: (1) the **most efficient path to the customer is through a direct relationship** with no intermediaries; (2) a **single point of accountability** is needed to meet customer needs and deal with any problems swiftly; (3) **build-to-order** allows customers to configure their computer systems exactly the way they want them, which provides customers with the best pricing and latest technology that includes features they really want; (4) **low-cost leader** is made possible because Dell has built a highly efficient supply chain and manufacturing organization that lets them reduce costs; and (5) **standards-based technology** focuses on high-value products and services, which gives customers more flexibility and choice.

Consumer satisfaction—Marketing programs with this goal in mind seek to maximize consumer satisfaction but not necessarily consumption. They believe that pushing consumers to buy more and more without worrying about whether customer satisfaction is being met by this additional consumption can possibly backfire. Companies find it very difficult to design a program around this goal because it is so hard to measure consumer satisfaction. In addition, satisfaction is a very personal issue that differs with each person, making it impossible to determine an optimum level of consumption. Even though it's rare that a marketing program is designed solely around customer satisfaction, most companies do work the concept of satisfaction into most of their ads.

Choice—Marketing programs with this goal in mind seek to maximize product variety and consumer choice. This can be a costly route for a company because the production costs of manufacturing a greater variety of products are usually much higher, and there are increased costs for carrying additional levels of inventory. Other disadvantages are that consumers might be turned off by the higher prices required to sell the products at a profit or they may not want to spend the time it takes to evaluate the various products and find the one that meets their needs. Also, this can result in cluttering the market with too many products that are essentially the same. This style of marketing can actually add to consumer frustration and anxiety. Yet for some products, choice is just what the consumer seeks. For example, personal computer manufacturers have found that allowing customers to build their own systems with exactly the accessories they want is a great way to gain market share.

Lifestyle—Marketing programs with this goal focus on quality of life, seeking to sell the product with the theme that it will improve a person's quality of life. You will frequently see this style used to market housing developments. Another product type that uses this marketing goal is mattresses that promise to improve the customer's life. In many cases, lifestyle-marketing programs involve luxury products.

Marketing techniques are not only used by for-profit business. Non-profits and governmental organizations also see the value of marketing and use it to promote their programs and services. For years, one of the most visible nonprofit marketing campaigns has been the Christian Children's Fund, which runs dramatic ads on television to get donors to adopt a child. The federal government's anti-drug campaign is a good example of how government agencies use marketing strategies to promote their projects. Recruiting for the volunteer U.S. military also shows how slick marketing campaigns can help governments achieve their goals.

> **Chapter 19**

Developing Your Marketing Plan

Part One

Part Two

Part Three

Part Four

Part Five

Part Six

Successful Marketing Strategies

Once you know the goals of your marketing effort, the next step is to design your marketing plan, develop your marketing strategies, and determine how best to implement your marketing plan. The first step in this process is to analyze the market opportunities for your company and its products or services and to select your target markets. You then need to determine what type of market mix best fits your goals, and consider how your marketing plans will meld with your strategic plans so you can develop competitive marketing strategies. Finally, you need to build the market research and information systems that will enable you to successfully implement your plans. In this chapter, we'll review the key components of developing and implementing a marketing plan.

Analyzing Your Market Opportunities

Every businessperson looks for new opportunities to grow his company or the product that he is marketing. Many find new opportunities reading the local newspaper or from success stories of businesspeople marketing similar products in other parts of the country. Others develop ideas by observing problem situations and finding a solution that works. All these approaches are valid, as well as any other way you find new marketing opportunities. But, once found, you must analyze the opportunity, figure out if it fits your overall company goals, and develop a plan to maximize its profit potential.

One common planning tool for analyzing market opportunities is called the *product/market expansion grid*. This tool helps companies identify new marketing opportunities by approaching the question from four possible directions: market penetration, market development, product development, and diversification.

Market Penetration

Market penetration is used to find new market opportunities by finding ways to increase sales of the current product without changing that product. This tactic is most commonly accomplished by convincing users of similar products made by another company to switch to its product. For example,

Pepsi wins a contract for its products to be sold exclusively in a fast-food chain, thereby ousting Coca-Cola products. Not only does this increase Pepsi's sales to those customers at the restaurant, but it also introduces customers not familiar with Pepsi to its products in the hope that these customers will buy Pepsi products for home use as well. Ultimately, if the tactic works, Pepsi will increase its market penetration and its share of the overall soft drink market. Other ways to increase market penetration include cutting prices and improving advertising to attract more customers to the existing product.

Market Development

Market development is used to find new market segments for the company's products. This can be done by looking for new demographic markets, such as developing a marketing campaign to attract teens or seniors to a product they do not currently use. Another way to develop new markets is by institutional marketing, that is, working with a complementary business that might agree to sell your product. For example, if you market a product for cleaning the interiors of cars, you can contact car dealerships and see if they will sell your product in their parts stores. In addition, you can develop your market reach geographically by opening stores in new locales.

Another way to develop new markets is by institutional marketing, that is, working with a complementary business that might agree to sell your product.

Product Development

This method involves deciding to grow your business by improving your existing products or introducing new products to the market segments in which you are already successful. For example, if you market tools for the home repair market, you can look to improve the function or quality of the tools you make or you can introduce new types of tools to customers who already trust your brand.

Diversification

Diversification involves a decision to grow your company by starting up an entirely new product line outside your current market focus (such as introducing a line of floor coverings for the home improvement market if your product has been totally focused on tools) or reaching totally new market segments (such as introducing tools for professional builders if your current tools are primarily made for the home repair market). Michael Porter, in his book *Competitive Strategy*, indicates five key factors to consider when looking at diversifying your company:

High barriers to entry—Markets that have a high barrier to entry—such as patented product lines, high initial start-up costs, strong governmental barriers, purchase of property in highly visible locations, or strong existing brands—can be a difficult stretch for a new competitor. If you are considering entry into one of these markets, you must carefully weigh whether you have the resources to build the brand and compete. A recent example of how superior locations can rapidly build a market was seen when UPS acquired Mail Boxes Etc. and instantly had excellent store locations throughout the U.S. market, cutting deeply into FedEx's market penetration by being able to offer more local service at a lower price than Mail Box Etc. stores offered previously. FedEx appears to be answering the challenge by buying Kinko so it can compete more directly with UPS's new local stores.

Weak competitors—If you identify a segment where you believe the competitors are weak, this could an excellent opportunity for diversifying your product line.

Weak substitutes—If you develop a product for which there are few substitutes or the existing substitutes are less satisfactory for customers, you have found a potential gold mine for growing a new product line until someone else decides to compete directly with your product.

Weak buyers—If you are looking to enter a market segment where the buyers are weaker or less organized, you have a greater profit potential. Most consumer products represent a weak buyer segment. The buyers rarely can demand a lower price.

Most consumer products represent a weak buyer segment.

Weak suppliers—If you are looking to enter a market where the suppliers are less organized or weaker, you have a greater potential to build a profitable new product line by developing your supply chain. If purchases of the product are few, then the buyers can be stronger than the suppliers. One example of this type of market is the garment industry's dependence on only a few top retail chains. The buyers have a greater control over the pricing because they can easily switch to another supplier, thereby being able to negotiate lower prices.

Evaluating Opportunities

Once you have identified a new market opportunity, your next step is to evaluate that opportunity and determine how well it fits into your company's strategic goals, which includes your profit goals, sale volume goals, sales growth goals, and brand identification goals. If you believe the new opportunity melds well with your existing goals, then you need to ensure the opportunity is feasible with current resources. If it is not, can the opportunity be undertaken within a reasonable cost structure? There are three key issues to test:

1. **Financial capital**—The first question to ask before taking on a new marketing opportunity is whether you have the financial capital to fund the costs. If the answer is no, can you get those resources at a reasonable cost without putting your existing business at risk? As long as you can answer yes to this question, move to the next test.

2. **In-house resources**—Next, you must ask yourself whether the company has the necessary production facilities and in-house knowledge to successfully produce and market the product or service. If these resources do not exist in-house, can you obtain them at a reasonable cost without hurting your core business? As long as you can answer yes to this question, move on to the next test.

3. **Distribution capacity**—Finally, you must ask yourself whether you have the distribution capacity to successfully get the new product or service into the marketplace. If you answer no to this, you must ask yourself if it can be obtained for a reasonable cost without hurting your existing business and its products. If you answer no to this final question, then you should pass on the opportunity. If you answer yes, it's time to develop a marketing plan for the new opportunity.

After deciding you do want to take on the new marketing challenge, you then have to determine which markets you want to target. There are four key steps to determining your target markets: testing demand, determining segment, deciding on targets, and finding a market position. We'll be covering target marketing in greater depth in Chapter 21.

Testing demand—This involves researching the current marketplace and determining its current size and its future potential. First, you must identify the similar products or services that are currently available in the marketplace and estimate their current sales levels. Next, you must gaze into the future and determine what the growth potential is for the market. For example, if you are considering introducing a new retirement planning service, you would like the demographics of the age groups that might be looking for help with retirement planning. Given the percentage of the population that is nearing retirement age, this is definitely a growth market. We'll talk more about market research later. Once you've researched the current and potential market, you need to calculate your estimates of current demand and forecast what you think future demand might be.

Determining segment—This involves grouping potential consumers into logical market segments either on the basis of geography (cities or regions), demographics (such as sex, age, income, or educational level), personality traits (such as social class or lifestyle), or consumer behavior (such as buying behavior, wants or desires, or product use). By determining these segments, you can decide how best to market to each segment. Basically, you are

How the IRS Uses Market Segmentation

Even the IRS depends on market segmentation to do its work. One good example is a project being carried out by its Tax Exempt and Government Entities Division to identify the needs of various market segments and develop tools it can use to assist these segments in complying with the tax code. In November 2002, the division initiated a market segment study on five tax-exempt organization market segments: business leagues, labor organizations, religious organizations, social clubs, and social service organizations. The study sought to capture information about the activities and compliance levels of these segments. The IRS will use the information to develop specific materials to aid these various segments with compliance, as well as to set up criteria specific to auditing the various segments.

looking for common threads that you can use to design advertising, product presentation, and other key marketing techniques.

Deciding on targets—Once you've identified the potential market segments, you then have to pick the segments you want to target. You can choose to enter the market in just one segment. For example, the company wanting to offer retirement services may have grouped potential targets by age. The company then decides it wants to target services only to one segment in the beginning, perhaps people in their forties. Another way to group the segments is based on a customer want, such as the desire to retire early, late, or on time. The company could then decide it will target the market by specializing in wants, such as "wants to retire early." The company can also decide to market to all segments that have been identified or to a certain group of segments. The most common way a company starts the development of a new product line is by choosing one segment and then expanding its market by adding segments once the product is viable in the first segment. Choosing which segment makes sense as the next target should be done carefully by considering the successes and failures experienced in developing the first segment.

Finding a market position—After picking a market segment, the company must then decide how it wants to position itself within that segment. To find a position, you must analyze how the companies currently serving the market differ in their positioning by looking at their performance, advertising strategies, pricing, and other aspects of marketing you believe your potential competitors are using. Once you understand the existing market positions of your potential competitors, you need to determine how to position your product within that segment to differentiate it successfully from those already in place.

Developing Your Marketing Mix

After analyzing and deciding on your market target, the next step is to design your marketing mix, which essentially looks at everything you and your company can do to influence its success in marketing a product. Jerome McCarthy, author of the book *Basic Marketing: A Managerial Approach,* introduced a method that is commonly used today to make this assessment, known as the four *p*s: product, place, price, and promotion.

- **Product**—This includes an assessment of how you will position the product by considering its level of quality, features that will be included, options that will be made available, how the product will be styled, the brand name you will use, how the product will be packaged, the variety of sizes that will be offered, the types of services that will be offered, what level of warranty will be included, whether extended warranties will be offered, and finally, what types of return policies will be put in place.
- **Place**—This includes an assessment of the distribution channels that you will use to get your product into the marketplace, whether you will open your own retail outlets or distribute through existing locations, how much inventory you will need and where you will store that inventory, and how you will transport that product when ordered.
- **Price**—This includes determining the optimum selling price; not only considering its costs, but once you know those costs, determining the official list price for the product, whether you will offer discounts and what types of discounts you will offer, whether you will offer credit terms and what those terms will be, what types of allowances you will offer, and how long you will give people to pay for the product.
- **Promotion**—This includes determining your advertising plans, sales force, sales promotions, and publicity for the product.

After collecting information for the four *p*s, you can then determine how to coordinate this information to decide on your marketing mix. Chapters 22 and 23 will delve more deeply into how to develop your products and establish your distribution system.

Developing Competitive Marketing Strategies

Before you even start production, you must decide how to competitively market your product. There are four strategies marketers use: market leader, market challenger, market follower, and market nicher.

Market leaders look to dominate the industry. They must have a substantial market share and extensive distribution arrangements. They become known by their customers as always being on the cutting edge of new technologies or new product designs. The risk leaders take is that they will constantly be the target of new competitors and may even have to battle the government as they build their market dominance. Microsoft comes quickly to mind as the leader in operating system software that is considered by many to have crossed the line from market leader to monopoly, which has left it in the position of constantly fighting off legal challenges as well as competitive challenges. Most times dominance in the marketplace is more commonly challenged when a company seeks the government's okay for a pending merger or acquisition. Market leaders look to expand their market by finding new users for their product, new uses of their product, and greater use by those already using the product. They protect their market share by developing new product ideas, improving customer service, improving their distribution channel, and reducing their costs so they can reduce their prices. Market leaders expand their market share by targeting one or more of their competitors without overstepping legal bounds and getting questioned by government regulators.

Market challengers are those who do not dominate the market but aggressively challenge either the market leader or other competitors to gain market share. After assessing the strength of the competitor or competitors, the market challengers look for weakness in their position and decide on how they will attack. These attacks can include price discounts or price cutting, introduction of a new product that competes more directly with a competitor's existing product, an increase or decrease in a product's quality, improved services for the product, a stronger distribution channel, reduced costs, and intensified advertising and promotion. The battle between Pepsi and Coca-Cola for the leadership position in the soft drink market is a classic example of market-challenger strategies.

Market followers have a strong position, but they do not dominate nor do they seek to do so. Basically, they are content to stay at their current position. They try to ride the coattails of the leader by developing market strategies that parallel what the leader is doing to gain market share. In effect, they let the market leader take the risks and expend the money on research and development, and they just watch the leader's moves carefully to take advantage of the gains the market leader makes with innovative ideas. Burger King is a good example of a company that uses a market-follower position. Frequently when McDonald's successfully introduces a new product line or marketing strategy, Burger King will follow with something similar.

> Market leaders look to expand their market by finding new users for their product, new uses of their product, and greater use by those already using the product.

Burger King Follows McDonald's Diet Lead

Burger King is famous for following the market leads of McDonald's as soon as they appear to be helping McDonald's to build market share. One recent example was McDonald's decision to add diet meals to its lineup. In the spring of 2003, premium salads featuring Newman's Own salad dressing showed up on McDonald's menus. To further improve its image, the company also created the "McDonald's Advisory Council on Healthy Lifestyles," including a number of international experts on nutrition. True to its market-follower style, Burger King followed suit in September 2003 when it introduced the baguette sandwich line, where some choices have fewer than 5 grams of fat; it also introduced a light combo meal line with a side salad and bottle of water instead of the more traditional French fries and soda. Burger King also introduced a new interactive nutrition guide on its Web site giving consumers access to nutritional information on each of its menu items.

Market nichers focus their marketing strategies on just a few target markets and don't try to capture a large share of the overall market. By specializing its products and skills, the market nicher seeks to gain a large enough share of its specialty markets to maintain its profit margin. For these companies, profit margins are more important than market share or total revenue. Market nichers seek to better meet the needs of their specialty markets than the market leaders. Companies using this competitive marketing strategy are usually in high value-added industries that can achieve high profit margins, tend to market high-end products or services at a premium price by building their brand specialty, and tend to keep their costs down because they don't need to spend as much on research and development, advertising, or a large work force in order to compete in the broader marketplace.

Many companies that are just starting up will choose a market-nicher or market-follower position. As they grow, they may decide to increase market share by using market-challenger strategies, and if they hit the jackpot, they may actually make it to the market-leader position. Other companies are content to stay at the market-nicher or market-follower position and enjoy the profits without the additional risk of being a market challenger or market leader. The key for the market nicher or market follower is to be sure they are not going to be the next victim of the market challenger or market leader. Even a market nicher can't just focus on a small part of the market, she must carefully watch what her competitors are doing that could challenge the niche position.

Coordinating Strategic and Marketing Planning

In order for a company to do all this marketing planning, it must be clearly focused on its goals by coordinating its marketing effort with its strategic planning efforts. For this coordination to work effectively, the company's mission statement must be market-oriented and feasible; it must clearly define the direction the company wants to go to achieve its goals and objectives.

The strategic planning process should assess the company's business portfolio annually and decide which businesses should be emphasized in the next year and which businesses should get less emphasis. This does not necessarily mean that strategically the company is shutting down a business, but the company may realize that economic conditions are not ripe to grow that particular business during the next year. Chapter 14 discussed setting goals and strategies.

Once these goals and strategies are set, the marketing team then looks for market opportunities in the businesses that have been deemed worthy of emphasis during the next year. In a well-designed strategic planning process, marketing would most likely have been a major player in helping the executive team identify the businesses with the greatest growth potential.

The marketing department can then use the product/market expansion grid to identify new market opportunities. Next, the marketing team assesses their choices and determines if the company has the financial resources, in-house resources, and distribution channel to successfully develop a market for the new product. If the answer is yes or if the marketing team determines that these resources can be developed at a reasonable cost, then they'll move on to select their target markets by researching demand, forecasting the growth potential for the market, determining market segments, and deciding on market positioning. Then the team will evaluate the development of the market using the four *p*s, and finally the team will determine how it wants to develop its competitive marketing strategies—as a market challenger, a market follower, or a market nicher. The company may also be the market leader or be thinking of using that new marketing opportunity to challenge the market leader.

Getting Market Research in Place

The foundation for the marketing team and its secrets to success will depend on its ability to research the marketplace and properly forecast its growth opportunities. This foundation must be built using a strong market research team. Market researchers collect, analyze, and report on their findings to the marketing managers and key executives. They not only research new opportunities, but they also track the results of existing company products and their competitors to keep a watch on what is happening in the marketplace and alert the company to any challenges that could impact the company's market share. There are many types of market research including advertising research, business economics and corporate research, corporate responsibility research, product research, and sales and market research.

- **Advertising research** includes collecting information about the effectiveness of advertising campaigns, studying the advertising of competitors, and following the way the company is portrayed in the media.
- **Business economics and corporate research** includes long- and short-range economic forecasting, studying business trends, tracking pricing, reviewing locations for plants and warehouses, researching data needed for possible acquisitions, studying opportunities for exporting and other international studies, conducting research on operations, reviewing changes in management information systems, and researching internal corporate questions.
- **Corporate responsibility research** includes reviewing consumer rights studies, ecological impact studies related to the company's product lines, studies of legal constraints on the company's advertising or promotion designs, and studies of political and social issues that could impact the company's products and growth potential.
- **Product research** includes analyzing new product potential and acceptance in the marketplace, analyzing competitive products, testing the market potential and marketing program effectiveness of existing products, and studying packaging design and other physical characteristics of the company's products.
- **Sales and market research** includes measuring the market potential, analyzing market share, determining market characteristics, analyzing sales results, establishing sales quotas and territories, reviewing test market and store audits, organizing consumer panels, studying sales compensation, and studying the effectiveness of promotions (including premiums, coupons, sampling, and special product deals).

A company would need a massive market research staff to do all this in-house. Most companies use outside research groups for at least some of this information. Syndicated-service research firms offer periodic consumer and trade information. The AC Nielsen Company is probably one of the best known in this area. You can find out more about their services at *www.acnielsen.com.* Another key player in the syndicated information service area is Reuters *(www.reuters.com).*

Sometimes a company decides to hire an outside research firm to conduct a customized research project. Many times the company will choose this route if they are considering entering a new market segment or introducing a new product for which they have no in-house researcher. In these types of studies, the company will be involved in the study design, and the final report becomes the property of the company that ordered it. Hundreds of firms offer these services. Word-of-mouth is the best way to find one of these companies. Talk with suppliers and vendors in your product area and see if they have used any of these services and can recommend a company.

The market research process involves a four-step approach: defining the problem, developing the research plan, implementing the market research plan, and interpreting and reporting the findings.

Defining the problem—During this step, the manager and the researcher sit down to define the problem and determine the research objectives. The manager knows the problem, while the researcher understands the tools available to research the problem and how to obtain the information that will be needed to help the manager find solutions.

Developing the research plan—The next step will be to determine exactly what information will be needed and to decide whether the researcher will collect primary data that relates directly to the problem or will depend on outside secondary sources for the information. Secondary sources include internal financial statements, government publications, books, periodicals, and data developed by commercial market research firms. Usually the plan will include a combination of

Mining Your Own Data

New software technologies are making it possible for companies to make better use of the data they collect through a process called *data mining.* These tools can go further than traditional report and query tools of older statistical analysis systems by analyzing the information in new ways to extract hidden predictive information from large databases. Data-mining tools can identify key relationships in a database by looking at trends or patterns in the data and provide warnings or solutions to problems that humans may not even pick up. For example, if a company is trying to determine the attributes of buyers or nonbuyers who visited their Web site, it can use a data-mining tool to review every record in the database, split them into buyers and nonbuyers, and identify the key differences. Once the tool has identified the key attributes, it can rank them by order of importance. Companies can use the mined data to develop strategies for targeting new potential customers.

the two. Obviously, primary data collection is more time-consuming, so the planners would use this method for the data most critical for making a decision and use secondary data when possible. Several approaches are commonly used for collecting primary data. The research approaches include observation of people, actions, and situations (for example, the market research team checks out pricing of competitive products by stopping at various retail outlets); surveys (telephone interviews); and experimental research (testing group responses to various product situations, commonly used to test a new product). Once the researcher develops the plan, she writes it up and presents it to the manager for review. This written proposal will also be used if an outside research firm is going to conduct any part of the plan, so they will fully understand the problem and the information collection that is needed.

Implementing the plan—The next step is actually to implement the plan either by collecting the information in-house or by hiring an outside marketing firm to collect various parts of the information needed. A company maintains greater control of the research project by doing it in-house, but frequently an outside firm that specializes in the type of information needed can do it faster and at a lower cost. This is the part of the research project that will take the most time, will absorb the greatest amount of the costs, and will be the most likely to contain errors. The researcher's primary role is to ensure that the information being collected is accurate and meets the specifications set in the original plan. The researcher must monitor each step to make sure interviewers are not having problems getting cooperation with the respondents or are not inflicting their own biases during the interviewing process or taking shortcuts to speed up the process. If an experimental approach is used, the researcher must be certain the persons conducting the study are not influencing the results and are administering the experiment consistently among control groups. Once all the data are received, they have to be entered and probably coded in order to be able to interpret the results.

Interpreting and reporting the findings—This is the last and most important step in the market research process. The researcher must be careful to interpret the findings accurately, to draw the appropriate conclusions based on the information collected, and to write the report for management. Although the researcher may enjoy working with the numbers and using all the statistical techniques at his disposal, the report developed for management should focus only on the findings and recommendations relevant for management to find a solution or make a decision. Researchers must be careful not to overwhelm management with too much information. Management must look at the information and try not to read the report through biased eyes. Sometimes it can be hard for a manager to accept the information if the results are contrary to what she expected. Once the manager involved in the initial project design has seen the report, the final step is to distribute it to all the managers who might be involved in making any related decisions or who need to know the results for other business reasons.

Now that we've reviewed the basics of how to develop and implement your marketing planning, the rest of the marketing section will focus on critical aspects of the marketing managers' responsibilities including analyzing market approaches (Chapter 20), selecting marketing topics (Chapter 21), developing products (Chapter 22), and establishing a distribution system (Chapter 23).

Researchers must be careful not to overwhelm management with too much information.

> ## ▶ Chapter 20

Analyzing Your Market Approach

Part One

Part Two

Part Three

Part Four

Part Five

Part Six

Understanding Your Marketing Environment

Developing your marketing approach is not only a matter of selecting your targets and developing a plan. Before you even start that process of development, you need to understand the marketing environment—how consumers behave, how consumers decide to buy, and how to approach other organizations rather than just individual consumers. In this chapter, we'll review the key issues you need to understand regarding the market environment you plan to approach.

Just as economics is split into micro and macro components, the marketing environment has similar components: microenvironment and macroenvironment. The microenvironment includes factors that influence the company directly, such as the company's internal environment, the potential marketing channel, types of potential markets, types of competitors, and potential stakeholders or other interested groups and individuals. The macroenvironment includes forces that can have an impact on the company's success, but which the company does not control directly, including demographic, economic, natural, technological, political, and cultural forces.

Microenvironment

As a marketing manager, it is critical not only to know the components of your company's internal environment, but you must also learn how to influence that environment in order to "market" your ideas to other company functions. Yes, you will be marketing ideas internally as well as externally. When marketing attempts to encourage adoption of new strategies or new market approaches, it is actually seeking to change internal thinking. Marketers must know how to use their external marketing internally in order to make this change happen.

This process of internal marketing is geared toward overcoming resistance to change. Marketing managers need to think of internal marketing in the same way as they think of external marketing. The only difference is the customers are the staff, colleagues, and executives within their own company.

Generally, the internal environment is grouped into the five *M*s: *manpower, money, machinery, materials,* and *markets.* Marketing managers must know who influences decision-making within these five groups and learn

> When marketing attempts to encourage adoption of new strategies or new market approaches, it is actually seeking to change internal thinking.

how to communicate their proposals by discovering the wants and needs of each of these components. For example, the finance function controls the money. The first concern in this function will be how much the project will cost and how it will be funded. Before they can be brought on board, the marketing manager will need either to bring them answers or to work with them directly to find the best financial alternatives. This similar strategy will also need to be used to influence other key functions including research and development, purchasing, and manufacturing.

In addition to the internal environment, the marketing team will need to get the suppliers and vendors on board who will serve as intermediaries to reaching the external market. These include the suppliers needed to provide the necessary components to manufacture the product, the intermediaries needed to sell the product to consumers, the distribution channel members needed to warehouse and transport the product to market, the marketing service agencies (market research firms, advertising agencies, media firms, and marketing consultants) needed to build market share for the new product or service, and the financial institutions needed to fund the endeavor.

Next, you will need to understand the types of potential markets or customers you want to attract. These include consumers, industrial markets, governmental markets, and reseller markets (companies that will sell your product because it makes it easier to sell their own goods). An example of a reseller market would be a clothing store that sells another's accessories in order to make it easier for them to sell their own inventory.

In addition, you will need to understand the types of competitors you will face and understand the impact potential stakeholders or other interest groups could have on your marketing success. These include financial, media, government, citizen action, and local community groups.

Macroenvironment

The macroenvironment encompasses all the outside factors that can influence your marketing success but are out of your direct control, such as demographics, economic, environmental, technological, and political factors.

Demographics plays a major role in the potential for any product. Keeping your eye on demographic trends can help you find opportunities as well as recognize red flags where changes could hurt your marketing plans.

For example, the average age of the U.S. population is rising as the baby boomers near retirement. Although this offers new opportunities if you are planning to serve that population, it could also be a red flag if your plans are to focus on a younger age group that makes up a smaller segment of the population. Changes in population, household structures, educational levels, divorce, and marriage all offer marketing opportunities as well as warnings, depending on the product or services you are marketing. Another major demographic shift is from the cold North to the Sunbelt. Population shifts can have a major impact on distribution channels as well as the location of warehousing and retail outlets.

Economics plays a major role in what people can afford to buy. This includes tracking wage changes, debt levels, and saving levels. Also, information about general economic conditions, such as inflation and recession (discussed in Chapter 4), must be a major part of any marketing planning process.

Environmental factors include information about raw material availability; cost of these materials and cost of energy should be key concerns before starting the process of developing and introducing a new product. Your marketing efforts could also be impacted by any environmental problems, such as pollution or discharge of dangerous chemicals, created by new production facilities. Governmental regulations that could impact your production and distribution should be considered as well.

Technological changes must also be tracked. You certainly don't want to spend the time and money developing a new product that is quickly deemed obsolete by a new technological development.

Political pressures can also stall or even stop certain marketing moves. Pending legislation or regulatory changes that could impact your market must be carefully monitored not only for impacts on new product proposals but also for their potential impact on existing products. Also the growth of public interest groups can create a major problem if you are seeking to introduce a product that already has a powerful interest group tracking that particular industry. Understanding the positions of the public interest groups and formulating your advertising and promotions to respond to their concerns can prevent problems from these groups. Green marketing, when companies indicate their products are biodegradable or recyclable, is a good example of how companies are responding to the environmental interest groups.

Consumer Behavior

Everyone wants buyers to buy their product or service, but it's not pure luck that makes that happen. Learning what stimulates buyers to buy and understanding consumer behavior is a critical task for marketers. Four key factors influence consumer behavior: cultural, social, personal, and psychological.

Cultural—These are the values a person learns from his or her family and other key institutions, such as the church or synagogue, that influence character. Within the cultural breakdown, subcultures form such as nationality (such as Irish, Italian, or Russian), religious (such as Jewish or Catholic), racial (such as African-American or Asian), and geographical (such as southerner or New Englander). Social class (such as upper, middle, or lower) can also impact the cultural aspects of buyer decision-making. Marketing campaigns are frequently developed to attract one or more aspects that stimulate buyer behavior because of their cultural biases. For example, today's major cultural shift is a move toward promoting health and losing weight. Marketers in almost every company that can benefit from that shift are jumping on the bandwagon, including restaurants with attempts to add menu items that match diet fads and food packagers with additions to their packaging that promotes items that fit a particular diet fad. Just think about the advertising campaigns you have seen recently from businesses that are trying to take advantage of the new diet craze.

Social—While cultural stimuli relate to learned values, social stimuli relate the pressures a buyer might experience because of the groups to which they belong. These groups include family, religious, professional, social clubs, and union groups. Groups can have a major impact on a buyer's behavior. Most people want to belong to a social group and rarely take action that is not approved by that group. A buyer's family group can have a major influence over her behavior, just ask any real estate agent who has tried to sell a house to a first-time buyer.

Politics Can Kill a Business Plan

The oil industry is still recovering from the *Exxon Valdez* oil spill in Alaska, which mobilized consumer groups, fishermen, labor, and environmental organizations in a battle to halt further oil exploration especially in the Arctic National Wildlife Refuge (ANWR). Prior to the spill, the powerful oil industry was making headway politically, but after the public watched the devastation caused by the oil spill, the anger bubbled over, and to this day the oil industry has had little luck influencing the debate. In addition, the oil industry had promoted Alaska's rugged image and how it had had the technical capabilities to extract oil in this remote and harsh environment while minimizing the environmental impacts. The public no longer believes this advertising, and the oil industry is paying for it with their inability to get legislation passed in the U.S. Congress that will allow them to explore the ANWR.

The Benefits of Showing Two Sides

Many companies assume that they should only show the positive side in their marketing and advertising, but psychologists have actually found just the opposite. Companies that either admit something negative about their own product or admit something positive about a competing product actually significantly improve their credibility. Michael Kamins and Larry Marks studied this concept when they ran an experiment exposing subjects to two different kinds of supermarket comparison ads. One was a campaign you've probably seen many times where the sponsoring supermarket claims to have the cheapest "basket" among all supermarkets compared. Another supermarket admitted that one of its competitors had lower prices, but the service offered by the sponsoring market far outweighed the lower prices. The study showed that consumers rated the supermarket that admitted its competitor had lower prices more favorably.

The family can quickly squash any deal on the table with one quick stop at the house the buyers have chosen.

Personal factors—There are many personal factors that influence buyer behavior including age, lifecycle stage, profession, lifestyle, wealth or lack of it, and personality. Obviously, age or lifecycle will have the greatest impact on what a person buys. A teenager and a fifty-year-old man are certainly going to be looking to buy different goods. But, it's not only an age factor. Families at the stage in the lifecycle where their children are newborns or toddlers are going to look for very different items than families who have teenagers. Marketers are also targeting their promotion and advertising around personal factors and how these personal factors will stimulate buyer behavior.

Psychological factors—A buyer's behavior is also influenced by certain psychological factors, including motivation, perception, learning, and attitudes. Maslow's hierarchy of needs, which was discussed in earlier chapters as a management tool, is also an excellent tool for understanding buyer motivation. How a person perceives a situation will also have a major impact on whether they will make a purchase. If a person perceives that the brochure or sales presentation is truthful, there is a much better chance he will buy. If the person perceives that the brochure or sales presentation is a slick promotional piece that does not provide adequate information to make a decision, she will probably walk away. Two people will perceive the same brochure in opposite ways, depending on personal perceptions. Learning relates to how a buyer's behavior changes as he experiences different things throughout his lifetime. Through this learning process, people develop attitudes and beliefs that will impact their future buying choices.

As you develop your marketing campaigns, think about how each of these factors may influence the target market and develop your plans to take advantage of the consumer behavior factors you have identified. These behavior factors can be a benefit or a detriment, depending on how well you have identified the responses and stimulated the decision to buy. For example, snack advertisers learned long ago that consumers are more receptive to food advertising when they are hungry, so you'll see more snack advertisements in late afternoon or late evening than you will in the morning hours.

The Buyer Decision-Making Process

How a consumer decides to buy a product differs greatly depending on the complexity of product and how it will be used. For example, while a man may be the sole decision-maker for a car that he plans to use for his business, that will not necessarily be the case for the car that will be used by the family. Marketers must understand who will likely influence the decision-making process for their target market and design their promotions to influence not only the buyer, but also the others who may be involved.

Researchers have identified several levels of influence that can impact a buying decision—initiator, influencer, decider, buyer, and user.

- **Initiators** are the people who first suggest that the product should be bought. For example, a teenager who is just entering college may decide that the family needs a new computer.
- **Influencers** are the people whose views and advice may be sought to help make the decision. For example, the parents may seek the advice of a computer-specialist at work to decide on the best brand of computer.
- **Deciders** are the ones who ultimately make the decision about whether to buy, which product to buy, how to make the purchase, and where to make the purchase. For example, the parents will make the choice about the type of computer, the amount they want to pay, and the place they want to buy it.
- **Buyers** are the ones who actually go out and make the purchase. For example, one of the parents will physically go to the store to buy the computer or order by phone or online.
- **Users** are the ones who will ultimately use the product or service. For example, the teenager who first initiated the idea to buy the new computer will be its primary user.

Buying Decision Behaviors

In their book *The Theory of Buyer Behavior*, John Howard and Jagdish Sheth identified three types of buying decision behavior: routinized response behavior, limited problem solving, and extensive problem solving.

Routinized response behavior occurs when consumers are buying low-cost, frequently purchased items. Very little decision-making is involved because the consumer either knows the products, the brands, and, in most cases, her preferences or she decides to buy based purely on price. Consumers rarely give much thought or time to the purchase. Some researchers have also categorized this as low-involvement goods. Marketers for these types of goods must maintain customer satisfaction by consistent quality, value, or service to keep consumers loyal to their brand. To attract new buyers, promotions are usually displays at the point-of-purchase, coupons, and other special pricing or premium offers, such as a free toothbrush with a tube of toothpaste.

Limited problem solving is needed when a buyer is familiar with a class of products but is not familiar with the brand, or when the buyer knows the brands but is buying the type of product for the first time. For example, a photographer wants to buy a digital camera. While he is familiar with the brands and knows his favorites, he is not familiar with the specific features he wants. He will most likely read reviews, ask friends, and question salespeople as he gathers the information he needs to make a decision. Marketers selling products that fit this category will need to promote their products with informational promotions that help fill the buyer's need for information, improve his understanding of the product, and build confidence in the product.

Extensive problem solving is needed when buyers are not familiar with the product and have no idea how to make a purchase decision. The buyer may know the brand names from experience with other products or advertising, but she has no personal experience. Marketers selling products that fit this category must offer opportunities for buyers to learn more about the product and its characteristics, as well as build confidence in the product and the brand. Many marketers of high-end products that fall in this group will even offer customers thirty- or sixty-day free trials in their home as part of their marketing plan.

The Stages of the Buying Process

No matter what buyers are planning to purchase, they all go through the same stages of the buying process: problem recognition, information search, alternatives evaluation, purchase decision, and postpurchase behavior. When buying the simplest products, this could be a very fast process that occurs in a matter of minutes. Buying in the extensive problem-solving mode, however, could take months or longer to make a decision.

1.   **Problem recognition** begins when the buyer determines he has a problem that needs to be solved. This could be a simple need, such as quenching thirst, or a more complex need, such as finding a new home. Marketers need to understand what types of needs, wants, or problems consumers are trying to solve when they choose their product. Learning more about problem recognition will enable the marketer to understand the various internal forces that influenced the consumer to decide to go out and buy a particular type of product. Sometimes marketers are even surprised to find that their product is being used for some use that was never intended, and they find an entirely new potential target market. For example, baking soda was initially marketed for use in baking; it is now marketed as a product that absorbs odors in the refrigerator as well as for other household needs. These new uses were based on what the manufacturer learned from the consumers who were actually using the product to solve problems.

2.   **Information search** will not always be a necessary part of the consumer buying process. In some cases, consumers may know enough and not seek additional information. If they do need information, they will gather it from four possible groups: personal sources (family, friends, or neighbors), commercial sources (advertising, store displays, or salespeople), public sources (reviews, media stories, or consumer-rating organizations), and experimental sources (touching, examining, or using the product). The consumer will seek these sources to learn more about the product. Marketers need to know the sources consumers sought to make a buying decision and the importance they placed on each source so the marketers can more easily influence this stage of the buying process. You've probably noticed that most surveys or warranty cards ask questions about how you heard about the product. These are just one tool marketers use to understand how consumers find information about their products.

> Marketers need to understand what types of needs, wants, or problems consumers are trying to solve when they choose their product.

3. **Evaluation of alternatives** is the stage in the buyer process in which the consumer considers all the information she has collected and compares the various products and brands under consideration. This can be a very simple process if the consumer is already familiar with the brands or with similar products, but it will be much more extensive if the buyer knew nothing about the products or the brands before beginning her research. Buyers in one of the problem-solving modes will often set up a chart of key attributes that are important to them and compare the various brands and their products. They will rank the alternatives and decide which product they intend to buy. Marketers need to study how consumers are comparing alternatives and what actually drives them to make their choice of product or brand. Once armed with this information, a marketer may determine that he must modify his product, improve the brand image among consumers, or improve the product image among consumers.

> Marketers need to study how consumers are comparing alternatives and what actually drives them to make their choice of product or brand.

4. The **purchase decision** is made after the evaluation of alternatives, but it may not be the product that ranked number one during the evaluation. Price, negative feedback from others about a choice, or even a bad sales experience can influence a person to decide to buy a different product then she intended to buy after evaluating the alternatives. Job loss may also impact a decision and the consumer could decide not to buy for a while. In fact, researchers have found that less than half the buyers who intend to buy a major consumer purchase actually go forward with the decision to purchase. Risks usually get in the way and delay, modify, or cancel the purchase decision. Most of these perceived risks relate to the amount of money at stake for the purchase or the possibility of job loss. Another key factor is the buyer's lack of confidence in his decision-making capability leads him to postpone a decision, especially if he is getting negative feedback about the purchase from his family or friends.

5. The **postpurchase behavior** involves what a consumer does after purchasing the product. Consumers will be either satisfied or dissatisfied with their choice. Satisfied consumers will probably continue to use the product or encourage their friends to buy the product. Marketers believe satisfied customers are their best advertisement. Dissatisfied customers will either return the product or complain to the company. Marketers should be prepared with strategies for how to deal with dissatisfied customers. Many companies that market high-end products will actually call consumers within a week or two

of their purchase to see if they are satisfied. If the consumers are not satisfied, marketers will ask what can be done to improve their satisfaction level.

New Product Adoption

If you are planning to introduce a totally new product to the market, then you will face a different buyer decision-making process. Researchers have found this process also has five steps: awareness, interest, evaluation, trial, and adoption. Awareness is the point at which the consumer hears about the innovation but doesn't have a lot of information about it. Interest is when the consumer is actually stimulated by what she hears to seek additional information. Evaluation is the point where the consumer considers whether he would like to try the product. Trial is when the consumer actually buys a small amount of the product to try or goes to a location where she can try the product. Adoption is when the consumer decides he likes the product and will use it regularly.

Everett Rogers, in his classic work *Diffusion of Innovations*, maps out the process of new product adoption: innovators, early adopters, early majority, late majority, and laggards.

- **Innovators** are the first 2.5 percent of the consumers who adopt the new product or idea. These are the people Rogers sees as adventuresome. They are not afraid to take the risk and try new ideas.
- **Early adopters** are the next 13.5 percent of the consumers who adopt the new product or idea. These people Rogers identifies as opinion leaders in their community. They are seen by their community to adopt new ideas early but carefully.
- **Early majority** are the next 34 percent of the consumers who adopt the new product or idea. While they may adopt the idea before the average person, they make decisions more deliberately and rarely take the lead for a new product.
- **Late majority** are the next 34 percent of the consumers who adopt the new product or idea. Rogers sees these consumers as skeptical. They will only adopt a new product after the majority of people have tried it.
- **Laggards** are the last 16 percent to adopt a new product or idea. Rogers sees these people as traditionalists. They only adopt a new

product or idea after it has been around long enough to have an air of tradition itself.

Marketers of new products must identify the potential innovators and early adopters and find ways to get them to try the product. For example, if you are introducing a new type of photographic accessory, you could attend meetings of photography clubs, identify the leaders and innovators, and offer them a sample of the new product to try. Companies that offer new products must be aware of this long process of adoption and plan financially for it, since it may be a long time before they see any profits.

Organizational Marketing

Organizations provide marketers with a different challenge than individual consumers. There are three types of organizational markets: industrial, reseller, and government. Organizational markets have fewer buyers and are usually more geographically concentrated. There are usually more people involving in the buying decision and the buyers are usually more professional.

> Organizational markets have fewer buyers and are usually more geographically concentrated.

The Industrial Market

The industrial market includes companies that buy goods and services in order to produce other goods and services, such as manufacturers, construction contractors, bankers, servicing organizations, farmers, and just about every type of business that offers a product or service. This market is huge and includes millions of businesses that spend trillions of dollars each year. This is the largest and most diverse organizational market. The buying process for the industrial market includes:

- **Users** are the departments that will actually use the product or service. Many times, these are also the initiators of the buying process. They will usually be involved in defining the product specifications.
- **Influencers** are the people who affect the buying decision by helping to define specifications and evaluate alternatives. Technical people are the most likely people in this group.

- **Buyers** are the people in the organization who have the actual authority to select the supplier and negotiate the terms of purchase.
- **Deciders** are the ones who have the power to pick or approve the supplier. In routine buying decisions, this will usually be the buyer, but in more complex situations the decision will be made at a higher level in the organization.
- **Gatekeepers** are the ones who control the flow of information. In many organizations, the purchasing group prevents salespeople from actually meeting directly with the users and deciders. In addition, secretaries and technical personnel can serve as gatekeepers.

Marketers need to know their contacts inside an organization and the role that person will play in the buying decision process. The actual buying process includes eight stages: problem recognition, general need description, product specification, supplier search, proposal solicitation, supplier selection, order routine specification, and performance review.

1. **Problem recognition** begins when someone in the organization identifies a problem that can be solved by buying a good or service. Most times, this occurs when a company decides to launch a new product or service, when a piece of equipment breaks down, when there are problems with a supplier, or when an opportunity is seen for a better price or quality of product.

2. **General need description** will be an evaluative process where the buyer determines the general attributes and quantity of the needed product or service. If the evaluation is complex, the buyer will work with engineers, users, and possibly even consultants to develop this description. Here, marketers can assist the buyer in understanding their product's characteristics and how it is differentiated from others in the marketplace. This can help the marketer get his or her foot in the door early in the buying process.

3. **Product specification** involves the development of the technical specifications for the product or service that will be bought. This is one point in the process where careful cost considerations can save a company a lot of money or the company can set standards to be sure they will get the quality they desire.

Influences on Resellers' Buying Decisions

AC Nielsen Company surveyed store managers to determine what influences their buying decisions. They asked the managers to rank different attributes on a three-point scale. Evidence of consumer acceptance was ranked the highest at 2.5, followed closely by advertising and promotion plans at 2.2. Next in line, at 2.0, were the introductory terms and allowances, followed at 1.9 by the reason the item was developed. The lowest-ranking attribute for selection by store managers was merchandising recommendations. Clearly, store managers look first for consumer acceptance and only then look at the advertising or promotion that will be given the product and the financial terms that will be offered. All these elements point to whether the store manager believes the product will sell well and offer her a profit-making opportunity. Marketers can greatly increase their share of the reseller market by focusing on these concerns when developing their marketing plan.

4. **Supplier search** includes the identification by the buyer of appropriate vendors. If the buyer is not already familiar with the suppliers, he can research them using trade directories, an Internet search, or by calling other professional buyers for recommendations.

5. **Proposal solicitation** involves inviting potential suppliers to submit a written proposal based on the product specifications. Good marketers realize these proposals should be marketing as well as technical documents. They are not just responding with price and technical specifications but must also market the company's capabilities and resources in order to compete with others.

6. **Supplier selection** involves an analysis of vendor proposals. This will not only include a look at pricing but also at supporting services, supplier reputation, customer responsiveness, product quality, credit terms offered, and interpersonal relationships between the buyer and the salespeople.

7. **Order routine specification** involves completion of the final order with the chosen supplier or suppliers. This will include specifying the number of products to be ordered, delivery schedule, return policies, warranties, and other specifications related to the product being ordered.

8. **Performance review** involves talking with users and asking them to rate their satisfaction with the supplier. At this point, the buyer could decide to continue the contract, modify it, or drop the supplier. Good marketers don't wait until the time of the performance review to find out if users are happy. They should attempt to gauge any signs of dissatisfaction as early in the process as possible so they can correct any problems.

The Reseller Market

The reseller market includes companies that buy goods or services for the purpose of reselling them or renting them to others. This marketplace includes both wholesalers (intermediaries between manufacturing groups and consumer retail outlets) and retailers who sell directly to the public. This group is responsible for most direct sales to the public. The only exceptions are those companies that choose to sell directly to the public themselves. For example, Dell computers are not sold in retail outlets.

The buying decisions process for resellers is similar to that in industrial markets, but they do differ in the types of buying decisions being made, who participates in those decisions, and how they make their actual choice. The key reason for this difference is that resellers are not buying for themselves, but instead are buying for their customers. Their aim is to satisfy their customers by having the products in stock that their customers will need or by having the ability to get those products for them as quickly as possible.

The Government Market

The government market includes local, state, and federal entities that purchase goods or services to carry out governmental functions. While the buying decision process includes participants similar to those in the industrial marketplace, there are some significant differences. Government buyers are watched not only by people inside their particular entity but also by outside political groups. At the federal level, they don't only answer to the head of the department, but also to Congress and the White House budget office.

Public interest groups will also jump into the mix if they believe that the buying process was not done fairly, allowing all interested parties that qualify to bid for a project. The controversy surrounding Halliburton and its contract for assisting with Iraq's reconstruction, which was awarded outside the normal government bidding process, is a good example of what can go wrong and of how outside groups will respond when the buying process is not carried out in the normal way. Millions of dollars in charges have been questioned, and Halliburton has agreed to repay many of them.

Selling to the government market requires more paperwork and an understanding of the complex bidding process. The Small Business Administration has an excellent resource online at *www.sba.gov/businessop/index.html.*

Analyzing the entity you are approaching requires more than just researching the data. You can see from reading about the buying process how important it is to understand the people involved and how they make their buying decisions.

> **Chapter 21**

Selecting Marketing Targets

Part One

Part Two

Part Three

Part Four

Part Five

Part Six

Defining Markets

Markets mean different things to different people. Originally, a marketplace was defined as a physical place where buyers and sellers go to exchange goods and services. Economists define it differently. They believe a market encompasses all transactions for a good or service without regard to the physical location. Marketers define markets even more broadly by including all actual and potential buyers of a product or service.

With the broad market definition assigned by marketers, it can be very difficult to measure the size of a market and forecast the potential demand. In this chapter, we'll review how to measure and forecast demand, how to segment your market, how to decide on your market targets, and how to position your company.

Measuring and Forecasting Demand

As you start to measure your market, the first thing you need to determine is what your potential market size is. It certainly won't be the total marketplace. There are numerous questions you must ask as you try to measure potential demand for your product. Three key factors must exist to form your potential market: interest, income, and access. Consumers must have an interest in the product you want to sell, they must have the income to be able to buy your product, and they must have access to be able to make that purchase.

The largest group may be those interested in your product. This group will become smaller when the price is known and they decide whether they can afford to spend the money. Next, your group will become smaller as interested consumers find out the product is not sold near their home. Others may not be qualified to buy. For example, if you are selling a product that requires consumers to be over the age of twenty-one, teenagers might be interested and might even have enough money to buy it, but they won't be qualified to make the purchase.

Next, as you build your market measurements, you have to determine where you want to serve your market. You can decide to introduce the product nationwide, but even a company with established nationwide brand identification will set their target market for a new product in a particular region of the country or in test cities.

If the market is already being served, you need to identify the number of your potential markets that are already being served by others. Finally, you must take out those who have already bought the product from someone else. As you take your measurements of potential customers, you must determine what percentage of the marketplace is already penetrated, what percentage is already being served by competitors, what percentage is not being served and is qualified to buy, what percentage is in the available market but is not qualified to buy, and finally, what percentage is in the total potential market but the product is not yet available. You can consider the possibility of marketing to consumers who have shown no interest in the product and you think you could convert.

Once these factors are considered, the company tries to measure current market demand. Marketing managers will measure total market demand, area market demand, and actual sales and market shares.

Total market demand represents the total sales volume of a product that would be bought by a particular consumer group in a certain geographic area during a specified period during a specific marketing environment within a defined level of product mix and marketing efforts. This is not a fixed number and it changes as any one of the conditions mentioned changes.

Area market demand involves selecting the best territories and allocating budgets among these territories. This can be done using two different measuring techniques: market-buildup method and market-factor index method. The market-buildup method identifies all the potential buyers in each market and estimates their potential purchases. This method is used when the potential customers are clearly defined, such as a paint manufacturer who is measuring total demand for his professional grade paints among professional painters. Most major consumer goods manufacturers use the market-factor index method for less-defined consumer groups. Calculations are done using a weighted-index of potential consumers in a particular area, considering disposable income, current retail sales, and population.

Actual sales and market shares involves gathering data of actual sales in the marketplace and the market shares of all the key players. The company can get industry figures from the industry's trade association, but it will have to estimate market share by reading various research reports about the industry and products involved.

> The market-buildup method identifies all the potential buyers in each market and estimates their potential purchases.

Using Forecasting Software

Numerous packages offer tools for forecasting. The one that has won the most praise is Business Forecast Systems (BFS) Forecast Pro line. This software package was named the number-one program by the *International Journal of Forecasting* because its expert-selection technique outperformed all other commercial and most academic models. The BFS's expert selection approach tests the data properties and then applies a rule-based system to select the most appropriate forecasting model. This allows people without backgrounds in statistics or economics to use the system and develop more accurate forecasts. You can learn more about this software at *www.forecastpro.com/products/fpfamily/index.html*.

Forecasting future demand is much more difficult with a lot more guessing and a lot fewer hard numbers. Most companies forecast demand by collecting information from the industry trade association about industry forecasts and then use that number to project their company sales forecast. Basically, a company is trying to forecast what buyers will do given a certain set of circumstances.

Companies use various techniques to forecast demand, including surveys of buyers' intentions, opinions of the sales force, expert opinions, market testing, time-series analysis, leading indicators, and statistical demand analysis.

- **Surveys of buyers' intentions** involve telephone, Internet, and in-person surveys of consumers asking questions about their intentions to buy a specific product over a specific period. For example, a telephone interviewer calls and asks if you intend to buy a computer in the next three months, next six months, or next year. The interviewer is conducting a survey of buyers' intentions for a particular company or industry trade association.
- **Opinions of the sales force** are collected regularly through sales reports on a monthly or weekly basis. The estimates are gathered into a composite to get a reading of the trends salespeople are seeing in the field.

- **Expert opinion** includes gathering sales trend data from experts, including dealers, distributors, suppliers, and marketing consultants.
- **Market testing** involves testing a product under market conditions to see how well consumers accept it. This is particularly useful for new product introductions.
- **Time-series analysis** uses historical sales data to forecast future sales.
- **Leading indicators** involve looking for outside economic conditions that seem to occur just prior to a change in the company's sales results. For example, an electrical contractor would look for an increase in the housing starts index as a sign that its sales volume will likely increase.
- **Statistical demand analysis** goes further than time-series analysis by looking for factors that impact the demand for a product.

Segmenting Markets

Once a market has been measured and the demand forecast, the next step is to segment that market. Segmentation primarily helps focus your marketing strategies based on the segments you decide to target. For example, you certainly don't want to be promoting retirement products to teenagers. That would not be a likely segment for your product or service.

Markets can be segmented in a number of ways, as discussed in Chapter 19, including by geography, demographics, psychographics, and behavior.

Geographic segmentation can be done by region, county, metropolitan area, city, or town. Density can also be a geographic group, such as urban, suburban, or rural. For example, a company may decide to place several sales offices in an urban setting, one sales office in a suburban setting, and hire a salesperson to serve a rural area. Climate can also be a factor, such as northern or southern, hot or cold.

Demographic segmentation can be done by age, sex, family size, family lifecycle, income, occupation, education, religion, race, or nationality. Grouping by age, family size, or income is purely by the numbers. Family lifecycle groupings can be by single, married with no children, married with children, married with children under six, married with teenagers, married with no

Researching Segments Online

Start your segmentation research online with statistics offered by various government agencies at no cost. Good resources include the U.S. Census Bureau (*www.census.gov*), which offers a page full of links to quickly find key demographic information; Fedstats (*www.fedstats.gov*), which links you to many key government agencies and their statistics; ZIPfind (*www.zipfind.net*), which helps you find population information, including how many people live in a particular zip code; and ClickZ Network (*www.clickz.com/stats/*), formerly CyberAtlas, with statistics about the Internet, including size, usage patterns, geographic, demographic, and other Internet marketing news. For a fee, you can also get the U.S. Industry and Trade Outlook (*www.ntis.gov*), prepared by the National Technical Information Service and Mc-Graw-Hill Companies. It gives an analysis of the major U.S. industries, industry specific outlooks for international trade, and geographical snapshots of industry and trade trends.

children under eighteen, and any other family grouping that makes sense within your marketing strategy. Educational groupings would include those with grade school or less education, some high school, high school graduates, some college, college graduates, some graduate school, advanced degrees. Occupational groups would include professional and technical, managers, business owners, clerical, sales, craftsmen, farmers, retirees, students, homemakers, and unemployed. Religious groups commonly include Catholic, Protestant, Jewish, Muslim, and other. Race groupings include Caucasian, African-American, Asian, and Latino. Nationality would be groupings according to the country of origin; such groups would include Americans, British, Italians, or Irish.

Psychographic segmentation is by social class, lifestyle, or personality. Social class would include lower lowers, upper lowers, lower middles, upper middles, lower uppers, and upper uppers. New lifestyle groupings are constantly being developed by psychologists depending on the type of product. Check with your industry trade associations to see if there has been a lifestyle breakdown for your industry. Personality groupings could include ambitious, compulsive, or authoritative.

Behavioristic segmentation occurs by purchase occasion, benefits sought, user status, user rate, loyalty status, readiness stage, or product attitude. Purchase occasion could be special occasion or regular occasion. Benefits sought could include quality, service, or price. User status could include non-user, ex-user, potential user, first-time user, and regular user. Usage rate could include light user, medium user, and heavy user. Loyalty status could include none, medium, or strong. Readiness stage could include unaware, aware, informed, interested, desirous, and intending to buy. Product attitude could include enthusiastic, positive, indifferent, negative, and hostile.

Segmenting for industrial markets is done a bit differently. They usually group their segments either by end users (such as commercial buyers, industrial buyers, or government buyers) or by customer size (such as major accounts or dealer accounts). Some may also segment regionally for the purpose of building sales territories.

In order for segmentation to be a useful marketing tool, the segments must be measurable, accessible, substantial, and actionable. You must be able to measure the segment to be able to gauge its size and purchasing potential. Your potential segment must be accessible, which means you must be able to reach the segment through some sales method. Don't get too creative about segmentation and then find out you've got the perfect segment, but don't know how to sell them your products. Your potential segment must be substantial enough to provide an opportunity that is worth the marketing effort. Your potential segment must be actionable, which means you must be able to develop effective programs to attract and serve the segment.

Targeting Your Market

Once you've grouped your potential market into segments, you then have to decide which segments you want to target. There are three potential strategies you can use to market to your target segments: undifferentiated marketing, differentiated marketing, and concentrated marketing.

Undifferentiated marketing essentially means your company decides to ignore the segment differences and instead decides to develop one market mix that it will promote to the entire market. If you decide to use this strategy, you will develop one marketing program that would be attractive to the broadest number of buyers. This certainly will save you a lot of money because you will need only one product with one set of attributes, one set of promotion materials, and one marketing and promotion plan. Marketers that use this strategy seek to attract the largest segments and ignore the smaller ones. These are also the segments that are most likely to attract the greatest number of competitors and that require the largest financial resources to compete in. With this strategy, you leave yourself open to the niche competitors and challengers who may decide to take over the smaller markets you are ignoring.

Differentiated marketing is when you decide on your target market segments and develop a market mix for each. In some cases, you may decide the same market mix will work for more than one segment. This type of marketing can be more costly because it may mean that you need to modify the product for certain segments, which will increase production and inventory costs. Administrative costs would also be increased to develop and monitor more than one marketing program. Promotion costs for these various programs could also be higher than the costs for an undifferentiated marketing approach. As long as these costs of differentiation result in higher sales and higher profits, they are worth it.

Concentrated marketing is used by companies with limited resources that decide to focus on getting a large share of one or two market segments, usually those being ignored by the big players. Niche players primarily use this strategy.

In choosing a marketing coverage strategy, you must consider a number of variables, including company resources; how homogeneous your product is (for example, types of fruit are homogeneous products and can be marketed easily with an undifferentiated strategy, while computers require a differentiated strategy because of all the variables in product attributes); product lifecycle stage (for example, new products are usually introduced using a concentrated or undifferentiated strategy; only after they have been on the market for a while would the more expensive differentiated strategy be used); how homogeneous your market is (for example, if you are selling a product that is used the same way by all, then an undifferentiated strategy makes the most sense); and competitive marketing strategies (if you are looking to enter a segment of the marketplace where everyone is using differentiated marketing strategies, you won't have a chance trying to use an undifferentiated strategy).

Once a company has identified its target market segments, it should start researching the segments to find out the current dollar sales, projected sales-growth rates, estimated profit margins, strategies of competitors, consumer buyer behaviors, and any other market research that will help it develop a strong marketing plan. Next, the company has to consider the information it has collected and compare it to the company's own strengths. For example, you may find that the government market segment is strong, but you have no one in the company who knows how to market in that arena. You would need to decide whether you want to build those resources or pick a different segment. You should always choose the markets that match well with your company's business strengths so you will have the greatest strategic advantage against your competitors.

Positioning Your Product

The position of your product is actually the way a consumer sees your product as it compares to other similar products on the market. Products can be positioned by desired features, benefits, occasion of use, product class, or against a competitor. The position your product gets in a consumer's mind will depend on a complex set of perceptions, impressions, and feelings about your product versus your competitors. While consumers will position your product with or without your help, marketing managers certainly don't want to leave that decision to chance, so they design their promotional campaigns based on the product position they believe will offer the greatest sales potential.

> Products can be positioned by desired features, benefits, occasion of use, product class, or against a competitor.

When a product is positioned by attributes, promotions will focus on low price, key features, or performance attributes. Products that are positioned to fill needs or desires will be promoted on the basis of the benefits they offer. For example, toothpaste is usually sold on the basis that it tastes good or reduces cavities or plaque. Products positioned to sell on special occasions will advertise around those time periods, such as cards for Christmas, New Year's, or other special occasions. Other marketers position their products based on user classes. One classic campaign was Johnson and Johnson's major increase in market share when it positioned its baby shampoo as a gentle shampoo that was good for adults who wanted to wash their hair daily.

Other companies decide to position their product against a competitor. A true classic is the Avis "We try harder" campaign, which is based on the fact that they are number two and working to beat Hertz. Another famous campaign was 7-Up's "Un-cola" campaign, which successfully built itself into the number three soft drink by competing directly against the top cola drinks Pepsi and Coca-Cola.

Positioning your product against another product class can also be successful, if you believe your product offers a good alternative. Margarine makers frequently sell their products against butter and cooking oils. Arm & Hammer successfully sells its baking soda for other home uses, such as a deodorizer for refrigerators. In fact, the company has a long history of repositioning its product to build its market share. In 1907, it was the first company to show its concern for the environment by using recycled paperboard for its products. In 1927, it started promoting its baking soda for kitchen and personal care uses. In the 1950s, Arm & Hammer added camping uses and baby care to its promotions, and in the 1970s, it again answered environmental concerns and was the first company to introduce nonphosphate laundry detergent.

In 1972, it began its classic campaign that encouraged users to put an open box of baking soda in their refrigerator and freezer to keep foods fresh and smelling good. In the 1980s, it introduced its carpet deodorizing and dental care products. In the 1990s, cat litter deodorizer was introduced to the market, and with its refrigerator usage so popular, the company repackaged baking soda in a special package just for the refrigerator and freezer. Now that's a marketing staff that knows how to reposition itself.

You can see that market positioning is limited only by your imagination. The one thing you must realize is that when you pick your positioning, you also need to determine who your direct competitors will be and they may not be people who are selling the exact same type of product. For example, when margarine makers take on butter, they are not only competing with other margarine products, they are competing with butter and oil producers are well.

> **Chapter 22**

Developing Your Product

Part One

Part Two

Part Three

Part Four

Part Five

Part Six

Making a Better Potato Peeler

How would you like to make a product that you could sell at a price seven times greater than most similar products, and that you could produce at a cost that is not nearly seven times as much? Entrepreneur Sam Farber did just that with the OXO Good Grips Swivel Peeler. Farber got the idea for this potato peeler as he watched his wife, who suffers from arthritis, struggle with existing kitchen tools. He decided to design a line of kitchen utensils that were not only more comfortable for her (and other arthritis sufferers) but were also more aesthetically pleasing. Farber's version was designed with customer needs in mind. The handle is easier to grip and more comfortable to handle, and the blade is curved to echo the shape of the handle. By looking for ways to meet customer needs, Farber created a successful company of specialty tools for which customers will pay a premium.

What Is a Product?

A product is more than just an object that has been developed to be sold. Products from the marketing viewpoint are anything that can be packaged for the purpose of gaining attention, use, or consumption in order to serve a need or want. This broad definition includes physical objects, as well as services, people, places, organizations, and ideas. In this chapter, we'll review product design, brand creation, naming a brand, packaging development, product lifecycles, pricing strategies, and product promotion.

Designing Your Product

In designing your product, you must think of it on three levels: *core product, tangible product,* and *augmented product.* From the marketing perspective, the core product relates to the role the object will have in fulfilling a customer's want or need. Is the buyer buying the product to fulfill a dream, perform a task, or enjoy a hobby? While the research and development arm of the company is concerned with the technical aspects of building the product, the marketer must determine what problem buying the product will solve in order to package it for the market.

You may even determine that your core product is different depending on the market segment. While hobbyists may be interested in your camera because they want to take pictures of their family and friends, professionals may be interested in the same camera in order to do their work. The core product could have different meaning and purpose for each of your market segments.

The tangible product is the actual entity or service that will be offered to the marketplace. This can include its quality level, features, styling, brand name, and packaging. The tangible product may have more than one form depending on the marketing mix. You may decide that different features, styling, or packaging will be needed for each of your target market segments, or you may develop only one tangible product for all your segments.

The augmented product includes all the benefits and costs the person will get or experience after buying your product. This could include training, customer service, delivery, installation, warranties, and other additional items you decide to offer in order to augment the experience the buyer will have when using your product.

Once you've decided on these three product levels, you then have to decide where the product fits within the various product classification schemes. The first three are *nondurable* (these are products usually consumed in one to five uses), *durable goods* (these are products that can be used many times), and *services* (these include any activities or benefits that aren't tangible goods).

You also must decide whether you are offering a consumer good or an industrial good. Consumer goods are grouped by *convenience goods* (usually purchased frequently for immediate use with little effect spent researching or comparing products), *shopping goods* (these are products for which the customer will compare price, quality, style, and other factors with competitors before making a selection), *specialty goods* (these are goods for which the buyer will make a special effort to purchase a particular brand because of its unique product—such as a particular luxury car or musical instrument), and *unsought goods* (products that consumers are unaware of and have no intention of buying until the product producer makes them aware—insurance and burial plans are two common examples of unsought goods). Industrial goods groupings include *materials and parts* (such as raw materials and manufactured parts that become a part of the new produced good), *capital items* (major items such as buildings or equipment), and *supplies and services*.

Creating a Brand

Almost all products go through a process of branding, starting from an unbranded state with the dream of moving to the final of six stages of branding: unbranded goods, brand as reference, brand as personality, brand as icon, brand as company, and brand as policy. Not all products make it to that sixth stage, and that final stage might not even be necessary for all products. First, we'll briefly review what each stage entails.

Unbranded

At this stage of the process, the goal of the manufacturer is simply to sell goods and the goal of the consumer is simply to buy goods that meet a particular need or want. Although introducing a product unbranded is rare, the introduction of most new products relates more to selling the need for the product than establishing a brand. This was not true before the Civil War, when most products were sold unbranded out of barrels and bins without any supplier identification. Today, most unbranded goods are found primarily in developing countries or in countries where brands were discouraged by the government, such as the former Soviet Union. Even though brands were not common there, Russians learned to identify codes on certain products that indicated where they were manufactured. Some codes represented higher quality expectations than others.

Brand as Reference

During this stage, marketers seek to position their brand based on unique functional benefits. It is critical to give the product a distinctive name that differentiates the product from others on the market and that can be protected through trademark registration, giving the company legal protection against imitators as well as a source of ownership. You achieve differentiation for your product by stressing its attributes. This process of differentiation is critical because during this stage most consumers are still learning about your product. This stage of the branding process gives the consumer more knowledge about your product. The goal is to get the consumer to identify and distinguish your brand from the competition. If successful, consumers will choose your brand quickly because of its known attributes rather than risk buying an unknown brand.

Brand as Personality

As brands in a product group become known for functionality and several brands meet consumer expectations for function, the next stage in the branding process is to give your product a personality. For example, water can be sold for its functional value to quench thirst, or it can serve as a lifestyle choice as we have seen with all the designer waters now on the market.

One classic brand as personality is Camel cigarettes and its Joe Camel personality, which RJ Reynolds has built on the concept of an ultrahip and cool cowboy. Joe Camel has helped RJ Reynolds improve Camel sales even at a time when tobacco smoking is under incredible political pressure to get people to stop smoking. Tobacco companies must find new ways to get existing smokers to switch brands. A product with a personality goes beyond its function, when marketing communicates that personality effectively, to a package of values found only in that brand. For example, Rolls-Royce is driven by the affluent while Ford is driven by the less affluent. Success is owning a Mercedes-Benz, while driving a dilapidated Ford connotes something else. Personality for a brand is not a constant. Marketers must keep a close watch on the marketplace and shift the brand personality to reflect changing social values and consumers' self-images or expressions. Developing a brand personality is not only a function of marketing, consumers will also respond with their own interpretations, which you will have to monitor so you can revise your brand personality to keep it up-to-date with the consumers' wants and desires.

Brand as Icon

At this stage, your brand is so widely accepted that it has come to stand for something on its own; it has become a symbol. For example, Rolls-Royce has become the epitome of luxury, quality, and status. Sometimes this can backfire, though. For example, people commonly use the term "to xerox something," even though they are actually copying it on some other brand of copier. Xerox lost its brand to some extent when it became an icon. Several business cases have been written about why Xerox lost its branding when it became an icon. Today it is repositioning itself with a new campaign—"The Document Company—Xerox." Once a brand has become an icon, companies start to look for a symbol that allows the consumer to quickly recognize the brand, such as the Harley

Branding a Car

The automobile industry is one of the most successful at creating a brand. Some decide to focus on luxury, such as Mercedes, BMW, Lexus, Cadillac, Lamborghini, Ferrari, and Porsche. Others seek to brand their cars based on a lower price with limited features, such as Hyundai, Honda Civic, or Toyota Corolla. Once a brand is established, it can be hard to reposition that brand for a different customer group. For example, even though Toyota is a well-developed and respected brand known for reliability, quality, and dependability, when the company wanted to move up to the luxury car market, it had to create a new brand called Lexus, which is essentially technically the same as one of its Toyota brand cars but repackaged as a luxury car with added features that are attractive to the luxury market.

Davidson eagle, the Coca-Cola hourglass bottle, the Mack truck bulldog, or the Mercedes star in a circle hood ornament. Sometimes this symbol will actually borrow on a celebrity image, such as with Michael Jordan and Nike.

Brand as Company

As the market matures, both consumers and management look for different and more sophisticated differentiation techniques. To continue building a brand, companies must find ways to communicate more interactively with their customers. Most companies at this stage will use various differentiation marketing techniques to design numerous marketing mixes so they can meet the needs of various segments in different ways. When companies get to this stage, they must also be more protective of their brand identity and aware of outside political forces that can threaten their brand. The company is more susceptible to boycotts or other consumer actions if some consumers believe the brand can be held accountable for some politically incorrect action.

> To continue building a brand, companies must find ways to communicate more interactively with their customers.

Not only is the product brand important but also the image of the company that makes that brand. Companies at this level also begin to package their brands differently as they no longer think of their products individually but instead as products plus services. For example, IBM does not only sell computers but positions its products as providing overall solutions for a company's needs, such as various software products bundled together to serve a company's marketing function or personnel functions. Companies and consumers engage in more two way communication, with consumers telling them what they want and companies responding with product design changes or even entirely new products or services. The service element becomes a large chunk of the branding process at this stage as a company looks for ways to include the customer in its process of creating added value for its products and brands. This not only improves a company's offerings, but it also builds a closer relationship between the consumer and the company.

Brand as Policy

At this stage, companies seek to move their brand into the policy arena by identifying the brand closely with social, ethical, or political issues. For example,

Benetton focuses on racial and ethnic unity through its "united colors of Benetton." Patagonia takes a strong environmental stance and seeks to reduce excess consumption with its zero growth policy. Arm & Hammer was the first brand to sponsor Earth Day, which fits with its policy of developing environmentally safe products. This can be a risky strategy, which may turn off more consumers than it attracts. But companies that choose this route have found that consumers will become advocates for the company and support the brand when controversy arises because they have more of a reason to be committed to the brand. To be successful, this branding stage must attract more committed consumers than it repels uncommited ones. This stage is still controversial and not many companies choose to take this route, even though social consciousness to improve company image is becoming more common. If a company does choose to take a political or social stance, it must be certain its products will support that stance. For example, Exxon would have a hard time building its brand on environmental protection since it is still closely tied to the *Valdez* oil spill. Logging, wood, and coal companies also would have a hard time taking a strong environmental stance given their activities.

Naming a Brand

Picking a brand name is a critical part of the product design process and can't be taken lightly. Before even beginning to think about names, a company should first identify the objectives and criteria for the name. It does this by listing all the product's features and benefits, its target market segments, and the proposed marketing strategeies. When thinking of the name, the company wants to find a word or possibly a group of words that best encompasses all these factors.

Once these lists are complete, the company holds a brainstorming session or possibly even an internal contest to search for the ideal name. In *Advertising Age* in 1983, Walter Stern wrote that you should have at least 100 names listed before beginning the process of choosing a name, and that list can sometimes go as high as 800 names for a major company. Next, the names should be prioritized and the list narrowed to 10 to 20 names that seem the most appropriate for further testing.

Then the company should test this narrower list of names by getting reactions from others inside the company as well as from external consultants or the

Deciding on Exxon

When Standard Oil decided it was time to pick a new brand name in 1972, it wanted something that could be used internationally and didn't mean anything in any language. It already had two mishaps with name choices. Enco meant "no go" in some languages, and Esso mean "stalled car" in Japanese. The company spent about $2 million to find just the right name and then tested it around the world. Part of this process was also coming up with a logo design, which was done by Raymond Loewy, who is an engineer responsible for designing some of America's great commercial logos, including Time, Lucky Strike, and Coca-Cola. Loewy came up with seventy-six rough sketches based on placing the visual emphasis on the double x to help ease the transition from the brand name Esso to the new name Exxon.

company's advertising agency. The list should then be narrowed to five to ten names and tested by getting consumer reactions to the names. Many companies do this by using focus groups so they can get an idea of what each name brings to consumers' minds and whether the name is actually getting across the message the company intends. This will narrow down the choices to two to five names, at which time the company should do a trademark search to be sure that no one else already owns the name and that it can be legally protected. The brand name is then selected from the names that still remain available.

Developing Effective Packaging

Once the brand name is chosen, the company must then decide how to package the product. How many products can you think of that have such distinctive packaging that you recognize them from a distance? The traditional Coca-Cola bottle comes quickly to mind, but that is rarely seen on store shelves today.

As more and more stores shift to self-service, even to the point of self-service supermarket checkouts, packaging becomes more than just an attractive face on the shelf. Not only must the packaging have certain codes for checkout, many types of product must include various government order verbiage. The challenge to design an effective package as well as a package that serves all its other purposes is getting more difficult.

People are willing to pay extra for convenience, so companies are now packaging food products as single lunch items or juice drinks for one-time use. New innovations even have packages coming to the market that are self-heating—a product that was developed for emergency purposes and deployed on a wide scale during the Iraq war. While you may not find them at your local store, it probably won't be long before they show up in our convenience-driven society.

Packaging plays an important role in the marketing mix and can be a key ingredient in the promotional marketing plan. In addition to designing the package for its attractiveness, the company must also be sure the design passes a number of tests. Engineering tests are needed so the company can be sure the package will stand up to abuses it will face getting to the marketplace, standing on the shelves, traveling to the home, and standing on the customer's shelves as it is being used. People get pretty angry when they are halfway through a product and have to throw out the rest because the package fails. Visual tests must be done to be sure the package is legible and the colors blend. Dealer tests are needed to be sure the stores find the packaging attractive and easy to work with. Finally, customer tests should be done to be sure the packaging gets a favorable response.

Understanding Product Lifecycles

Every product goes through the same basic lifecycle, starting with the product development phase, to introduction, followed by growth, maturity, and decline. During each phase of this product lifecycle, different marketing strategies are needed:

During the **product development** phase, marketing will be involved in estimating market demand, segmenting the market, selecting market targets, and forecasting demand. If all

Designing the Coca-Cola Bottle

The goal to design a new bottle for Coca-Cola in 1915 did not come from a marketing department. The recommendation actually came out of the legal department in a memo that stated, "We need a distinctive package that will help us fight substitutions . . . we need a bottle which a person will recognize as a Coca-Cola bottle even when he feels it in the dark. The Coca-Cola bottle should be so shaped that, even if broken, a person could tell what it was." The purpose of this memo was to encourage Coca-Cola management to develop a package that could be protected by trademark. The distinctive bottle we've all come to know and love was born in 1915 and designed by the Root Glass Co. of Terre Haute, Indiana. The design was inspired by the shape of an African kola nut, which is one of the ingredients that contributes to the soda's flavor, along with the South American coca leaf.

the numbers look good, the company will then go forward with all the phases of product design just discussed. While much of the actual work during this phase will be done by the technical side as they try to design and develop a marketable product, marketing should be involved throughout the process to be sure the end product will have the best possible chance of success when it is finally introduced.

Introduction is a period of slow growth when the primary focus of marketing is to introduce the product, its attributes, and benefits and work toward encouraging adoption by the innovators and early adopters. Much of the advertising and promotion budget will be spent on educating the public about the product. Profits during this phase are nonexistent because introduction expenses are so high.

Growth is the time in the lifecycle when the product is getting rapid market acceptance and profits are first seen. By this time, the innovators and early adopters have been sold on the product's value, and early majority consumers are beginning to step up and buy the product. Promotion is not as expensive because the product is better known. Money can be spent on expanding market share by added new target market segments or possibly even new accessories or services to the product line to increase profits. New distribution channels are also developed during this phase.

Maturity is a time when growth begins to slow because most of the potential buyers have already bought the product. The early majority are regular customers, and the late majority are jumping on the bandwagon. Some companies can just milk the profits if there isn't much competition and the profits will stabilize. Sometime during this phase, profits will stabilize and possibly even begin to decline as competitors challenge the company's leadership role in the marketplace. Product modification can sometimes extend the maturity phase. Finding new market segments that attract new users to the product is another way to extend this phase.

Decline is the period when product sales start to decrease either because the product is not as competitive with innovations on the market or because another product has been found that completely substitutes for the product you are selling, such as calculators replaced slide rules and computers replaced typewriters.

Developing Pricing Strategies

While price is just one part of the marketing mix and non-price factors frequently take a much more prominent role in planning the marketing mix, pricing strategy is still a very important part of the plan to bring a product to market as well as part of how a product will be positioned in the marketplace. Deciding on a product's price involves a number of both external and internal factors. Internally, the company must consider factors such as the marketing objectives, market mix strategy, and costs. Externally, the company must consider market demand, competitor's pricing and offers, the general state of the economy, the needs of its resellers, and government regulation. All of these factors can impact a product's price.

When determining a product's price as it relates to the target market and how to position that product in the market, a company must consider how it must price the product in order to survive financially by considering factors such as the marketing mix strategy and how much key parts of that mix will cost, its marketing coverage strategy, its desired role (such as market leader, market challenger, market follower, or market nicher), and the level of quality it plans to maintain. Also the company must consider whether to target the product to a high end user who is willing to pay a premium for the product or to a low end user who will only buy the product if it is cheap. All these factors are part of the marketing mix and will affect what price the company will actually charge.

Once the marketing mix decisions are made, the company must then price out its actual costs to carry out its marketing strategies. The company certainly doesn't want to sell the product without covering its costs as well as earning a reasonable profit. It must also calculate how costs will differ depending on sales volume. In addition, the company must decide who will have the authority to set pricing. Most companies will assign an executive that authority. He or she will include not only marketing in the price-setting process, but will also be certain that production, finance, and accounting managers will be included in the process. No matter how careful you are at finding the right price, the consumer will be the one who determines if the company has set the right price and that right price may vary depending on general economic conditions.

There are four basic pricing strategies:

> Once the marketing mix decisions are made, the company must then price out its actual costs to carry out its marketing strategies.

- **Premium pricing** is used to set a high price because you believe you are offering a unique product or service. This pricing strategy is most often used for luxury or specialty products or services.
- **Penetration pricing** is used to set artificially low prices in order to increase your market share. Once the market share goal is achieved, pricing will be increased to regain profitability.
- **Economy pricing** is used to sell a no-frills product at a no-frills price. To make a product profitable, the cost of marketing and manufacture is kept at a minimum. Supermarket store brands are a good example of economy pricing.
- **Price skimming** is used when a company has a substantial competitive advantage and decides to charge a high price. This type of pricing cannot be sustained for long because a high price will usually attract new competitors or the demand for your product will drop and you'll need to lower the price to attract buyers again.

In addition to these basic types of pricing, there are product mix pricing strategies such as *product-line pricing* (where pricing strategies are determined based on a line of products rather than just a single product), *optimal product pricing* (where a company sells options or accessories along with the main product—car manufacturers are a prime example), and *captive product pricing* (where the main product is priced low while continuing supplies are priced much higher—computer printers and their supplies are a good example). You can usually buy a computer printer at or even below its cost because the manufacturer then knows you are captive to the printer's needed supplies, which can be priced much higher than cost and are needed over a long period.

Industrial manufacturers also use a pricing strategy called *by-product pricing*, which is used to sell waste or by-products from the manufacture of its core products. Interestingly, oil was first discovered as a usable by-product when it was left over after companies made the desired product, kerosene. Today, oil has many by-products that are marketed successfully for other things. Plastics are produced from what was an oil by-product.

Even after a company sets its product price, the price must be constantly monitored to be sure it is the right price under current market conditions. During economic slowdowns, discount pricing may be needed to encourage sales, or companies may decide to offer discounts to a customer who buys a certain number of products at once to increase its sales volume. Seasonal discounts are common especially in the clothing industry when companies discount summer clothes to clear the shelves as the fall clothes hit the market.

Other types of pricing strategies are used for special situations:

- **Discriminatory pricing** is used when some customers will pay different prices for the same product or service. Museums and amusement parks are good examples of this type of pricing when they price tickets based on age. Theaters may price their products differently, depending on where you sit. Time can also be a pricing factor. For example, electricity is usually priced higher during peak usage times or seasons.
- **Psychological pricing** is used when consumer psychology actually plays a greater part in the price than the cost of the actual product. Perfumes are a prime example; the price of a bottle of a well-positioned brand is often set at a premium to its costs. A $100 bottle of perform could have as little as $3 of the actual perfume.
- **Promotional pricing** is used to set a low price temporarily during a special promotion period to encourage new users to try the product. Supermarkets also use this strategy to price a common product at a loss to get people into the store because they know the customer will then buy other items.
- **Geographic pricing** is used when a company charges more for a product that must be shipped a greater distance than for one that a customer can buy locally.

Pricing can play a major role in how you want to promote your product. Now, we'll briefly review some of the key considerations that impact how you will promote your product.

> Pricing can play a major role in how you want to promote your product.

Promoting Your Products

Product promotion is accomplished using four basic techniques:

Advertising—This includes any paid form of product promotion that presents or promotes your ideas, products, or services in which you are clearly identified as the sponsor. Decision-making involves a five-step process that includes setting objectives for the advertising, deciding how much you can spend, deciding on the message that you want to convey, deciding what medium or media you want to use to convey that message, and evaluating the advertising campaign after it has been completed. If the expense for the advertising is large, many companies will test an advertising message by using focus groups or even a test market to be sure the advertising campaign is effective before using the campaign more broadly.

Sales promotion—This includes incentives that encourage people to purchase your product or service. This can include many different strategies such as coupons, premiums contests, and buying allowances in order to stimulate sales.

Publicity—This includes product or service information that is reported in the media that presents your product in a favorable light, but for which you did not have to pay. You plan a publicity campaign by setting the objectives for the campaign, selecting your message, deciding on the vehicles you will use, implementing the campaign, and evaluating the results. Sponsoring a charitable event has been a common way to combine both advertising and promotion activities with publicity. The sponsorship may be considered advertising or a charitable donation depending on how the sponsorship is acknowledged. A brief note on a press release or a mention in a program is usually sponsorship that can be used as a charitable donation, while a sign at an athletic field for a sporting event, such as a tennis tournament held for charity, will likely be considered advertising rather than a donation. Whether it is advertising or a charitable donation, the opportunity for free publicity is great.

> Sponsoring a charitable event has been a common way to combine both advertising and promotion activities with publicity.

Personal selling—This includes any oral presentation of your product to one or more people for the purpose of making sales. Most companies use sales representatives as part of their promotion strategy. Since this is the most expensive type of promotion, careful planning of the sales force with a strong management component is crucial for its success. When setting up a personal selling force, the company must decide the objectives for the sales force; design the sales force strategy; determine its structure, size, and compensation; recruit and select its salespeople; develop an effective training program; and evaluate the program before and periodically after it has been established. Some of the facets of promotion that can only be done by a sales force include prospecting for new customers or clients, communicating information about the product or service on a personal level, selling and servicing the customers, and gathering information about the marketplace while in the field.

Marketers of consumer goods use this promotional mix differently than marketers of industrial goods. Consumer goods marketers will spend more heavily on advertising and sales promotion with less effort put into personal selling. Marketers of industrial products spend more heavily on personal selling and sales promotion with less time and money spent on advertising. Publicity has the lowest emphasis on both sides.

Developing your product is more than just creating something unique or different for the marketplace; it is an extensive process that not only includes product design, but also includes creating a brand, developing effective packaging, understanding the product lifecycles and marketing appropriately during those lifecycles, developing pricing strategies, and designing appropriate strategies for promoting the product.

> **Chapter 23**

Establishing Your Distribution System

Part One

Part Two

Part Three

Part Four

Part Five

Part Six

PART FIVE   MARKETING

■ CHAPTER 18 Understanding Marketing ■ CHAPTER 19 Developing Your Marketing Plan ■ CHAPTER 20 Analyzing Your Market Approach ■ CHAPTER 21 Selecting Marketing Targets ■ CHAPTER 22 Developing Your Product ■ CHAPTER 23 Establishing Your Distribution System

Getting to the Marketplace

You can do outstanding product design planning and develop the best product promotion plans, but if you haven't got a way to get that product to the marketplace, none of it will be worthwhile. Setting up an effective distribution channel is a critical part of any marketing plan. In fact, many leading marketers believe an effective distribution channel is one important way to differentiate your product and beat out your competition.

While some companies decide to manage the entire distribution process themselves and sell directly to the customer, few take this route. In this chapter, we'll review how distribution channels are set up and how to plan and manage physical distribution, and we'll explain the basics of both retailing and wholesaling.

Setting Up Distribution Channels

Marketing distribution channels are characterized by the number of levels within the channel. In a zero-level channel, the company sells directly to the consumer. In a one-level channel, the company sells to a retailer who then sells to the consumer. In an industrial market, the intermediary between a company and the customer would normally be a sales agent or broker. In a two-level channel, the company sells to a wholesaler who sells to a retailer who then sells to the customer. In an industrial market, the two levels in between the company and the customer would likely include an industrial distributor and a dealer. The three-level channel would include sales to a wholesaler to a jobber then to a retailer. In this structure, the jobber is the third party between the wholesaler and smaller retailers. The smaller retailer normally cannot buy directly from the wholesaler in this type of channel.

Problems within the channel occur because the company marketing the product has different needs than the others down the channel. While a manufacturer's only interest is selling his product, the primary interest of the wholesaler, jobber, or retailer is making a profit. If they can satisfy their customers with a different product and make a better profit, they most likely will push the product that offers them the best profit possibility. For example, a marketer for the manufacturer may realize that customer education is needed, but neither the wholesaler nor the retailer has the resources or the expertise to educate the customer. In this scenario, the marketer offer incentives to the retailer or wholesaler by bearing the costs of the education or offering the training for the wholesaler's or retailer's staff.

Manufacturers do risk conflicts with others in the channel and sometimes fall victim to conflict situations such as bait and switch and free riding. In bait-and-switch situations, manufacturer number 1 pays for customer education about a particular product, while manufacturer number 2, who sells the same type of product, does not. In exchange for paying those educational costs, manufacturer number 1 offers lower margins for the retailer selling the product. Since manufacturer number 2 is not paying those education costs, he can offer higher margins. The retailer, who is only interested in her bottom line, can use the educational programs to attract customers and then switch them to manufacturer number 2's products because her profit margins will improve.

> Manufacturers do risk conflicts with others in the channel and sometimes fall victim to conflict situations such as bait and switch and free riding.

In a free-riding situation, members in a distribution channel are expected to provide a certain level of service but find ways to avoid providing that level. For example, suppose a customer segment expects certain before-sales service and the requirements set for being part of a manufacturer's distribution channel are that a retailer must provide that service (such as measuring windows before selling window dressings). A retailer who free rides offers the product at a lower price without offering that expected service. Instead the free rider encourages the customer to get the service from another retailer that offers it. The free rider gets a higher profit margin by not having to offer the service. If manufacturers allow this type of free riding, eventually everyone in the chain will avoid offering the service. Ultimately the manufacturer's sales will decline because customers are not getting the service they expect.

In order to avoid bait and switch and free riding, manufacturers offer incentives or place restrictions on retailers, wholesalers, or distributors who want to sell their products. For example, in order to be given the opportunity to provide free customer education in the store, a manufacturer may stipulate that the retailer cannot carry certain competing product lines. Or in order to ensure a certain level of service, a manufacturer might stipulate that if the retailer fails to provide the service, the product line might be pulled from the store.

You might think that these kind of problems can be solved with a contract, but being able to write a contract that specifies all unwanted behavior can be difficult if not impossible and it is even more difficult to enforce.

Rather than police their channel, manufacturers look for self-enforcing agreements that are in the retailer's best interest to do what is best for the manufacturer.

Possible solutions include the following:

- **Subsidize specific services** that the manufacturer expects the retailer to provide for its products. Offer the subsidy only to retailers that provide the specific service. Coop advertising (sharing in the cost of advertising with the retailer) is a good example of a subsidy a manufacturer can offer to be sure the product is adequately advertised in local markets.
- **Monitor** retailers periodically to check on the services being offered. For example, the window dressing manufacturer could send in shoppers to be sure the measuring service is being offered. Franchises frequently use secret shoppers to check the required levels of service and quality of their franchisees.
- **Offer exclusive territories** to reduce the customer's ability to free ride and increase the retailer's incentives to maintain service levels. This can be much harder to do now that the Internet offers customers an easy way to bypass these geographic boundaries.

Vertical marketing systems are another way that companies are dealing with the conflicts that can arise in the marketing channel. In the traditional channel, each of the components is an independent entity that seeks to maximize its own profits. By contrast, vertical marketing systems involve the three entities acting as a unified system. This usually involves ownership by one member of the channel or through franchising agreements. There are three types of vertical marketing systems: corporate, contractual, and administered.

Corporate vertical marketing systems combine all parts of the marketing distribution channel under one corporate ownership. UPS just completed this process with its purchase of Mail Boxes Etc. so it controls the entire channel from the time the customer drops off the package to the time it is delivered to the intended recipient. Sears and Sherman-Williams are two good examples of this kind of system.

Contractual vertical marketing systems pull together independent entities at different levels of the distribution channel using a contractual agreement. Wholesaler-sponsored voluntary chains pull together retailers so they can compete with larger chain organizations. Retailer cooperatives organize so they can carry on wholesaling and possibly even manufacturing. Franchising is another example of this type of vertical marketing system.

Administered vertical marketing systems coordinate production and distribution not through common ownership or contractual ties, but instead because one member of the channel has the size and power to control the channel. Coca-Cola and Pepsi both use this type of system, as do most of the major consumer brand companies.

Designing a channel has some of the same components of other marketing planning. First, you must review your channel objectives and constraints by determining (1) customer characteristics (the expected buying behavior and the type of retailers you'll need), (2) product characteristics (such as perishable, bulky, non-standardized, or high unit value), (3) intermediary characteristics (so you can find the right person or company to service the other parts of the channel), (4) competitive characteristics (how your competitors have designed their channel so you can compete effectively), (5) company characteristics (such as size, financial resources, product mix, and marketing strategy), and (6) environmental characteristics (such as economic conditions or governmental regulations).

Then you must identify the types of intermediaries you want to have, such as direct to retailers, through wholesalers to retailers, or through wholesalers to jobbers to retailers. Finally, you'll have to decide on the terms for and the responsibilities of the members by establishing a pricing policy, setting sales roles, and determining territorial rights among distributors. Also you will have to determine how you will allocate responsibilities for mutual services.

Retailing with Ace

The retailer network of Ace Hardware is a good example of how retailers banded together to create a vertical marketing system. Ace Hardware focuses on the neighborhood retail niche with the goal of providing top-quality products at competitive prices. Retailers who want to own their own stores yet have the power of a known national brand join this network. Ace Hardware store-owners have the advantage of national advertising in addition to what they are doing locally. As local retailers, they also have the buying power of a national retailer; the retailers, with more than 5,000 stores, have banded together to buy from the manufacturers. Ace Hardware also offers start-up assistance, training, ongoing support, and state-of-the-art retailing tools. Ace Hardware posts on its Web site that the total investment to start a store ranges from $823,495 to $1,563,495, depending on size and other variables. Of that amount, Ace expects new retailers to come up with $150,000 to $250,000 in start-up cash.

Once you've mapped out your channel design, you will then have to select channel members that you think best match your needs and develop programs for motivating them. Companies with well-known products and a well-known brand will have channel members knocking at their door, but if you are trying to introduce a new product or are not known in the marketplace, you will find it much harder to get wholesalers or retailers interested in your product.

Motivating your channel depends primarily on helping your channel members maximize their profits. Just as with motivating your staff or stimulating your customer base, you must understand the needs of your channel members and find ways to meet them. Some companies use the carrot-and-stick approach to motivation, rewarding certain behaviors and punishing others. More sophisticated companies use a partnership approach by developing a good understanding of their distributor's wants and needs and finding ways to fill those needs. This approach will usually involve working together to solve problems related to market coverage, product availability, market development, account solicitation, technical assistance, services, and market information.

Once the channel is set up, the manufacturer can't just let the distribution channel operate and forget about it. Instead, the manufacturer must regularly evaluate its channel members by using measurements such as performance standards, sales quota allotments, inventory levels, customer delivery time, treatment of damaged or lost goods, and cooperation with the company and its training programs.

Planning and Managing Physical Distribution

Once you have the distribution channel designed and set up, your next step will be to plan how to get your goods into that channel. Distribution of your product must be done by carefully planning, implementing, and controlling the actual physical flow of your product as it makes its way from your factory to the customers' home or industrial setting.

The first step in the planning process is determining your costs. The biggest cost in the physical distribution process is transportation, followed by warehousing and inventory. Other smaller costs include receiving and shipping, packaging for shipment (you package your product so it is attractive on the shelf; for distribution purposes, however, it should fit in a standard box without being too concerned about how it might look to a customer), administration, and order processing.

Keeping control of your physical distribution costs or finding ways to lower them is an excellent way to reduce your overall product costs and, ultimately, the price you can offer your customers to stimulate sales. As long as the product gets to the store shelves when it's needed, the customer doesn't care how you got it there. Whatever you can do to trim costs while still being able to deliver the same quality product on time can help maximize your profits.

Basically, the objective of your physical distribution operations should be to get the right products to the right place at the right time for the lowest cost. Companies must coordinate different functions to be sure to maintain an effective physical distribution channel in-house. A traffic manager is concerned with costs of transportation alternatives (it's cheaper to send products by train than air), but the customer service manager may recognize the need to get the product to the customer faster, especially if there has been a problem at the retailer location. This can cause internal conflict and policies must be established to deal with these conflicts when they arise.

Another potential area of conflict can occur when the shipping manager, who is concerned with the costs of shipping materials, wants to use a cheaper, less sturdy box, but the wholesaler or retailer complains that these cheaper materials are causing major damage to the products and making it more difficult to manage the physical distribution process.

As you can see from these two examples, decisions made among managers within the physical distribution channel will affect others in the channel either negatively or positively. Careful planning and coordination throughout the channel that includes an opportunity for each to impact the final decision-making process can go a long way to improving your physical distribution system and lowering its costs.

Physical Distribution the Wal-Mart Way

Wal-Mart, the number-one U.S. retailer, believes that successful inventory management is the key to physical distribution and is an important part of its ability to maintain low prices. In order to efficiently manage its operations, the company turned to technology in the early 1980s. In the beginning, technology was used to collect and analyze sales data, and then transmitting orders to suppliers was added to the technology mix. By the 1990s, Wal-Mart was collaborating electronically with thousands of its suppliers. Suppliers used modems to dial into the Wal-Mart database and get up-to-date, store-by-store information on sales and inventory for their products. Using this system, Wal-Mart suppliers were able to work with the company's buyers to manage inventory in the stores and help with forecasting, planning, producing, and shipping products. Today that network uses Internet technology rather than dial-up modems, which makes it easier and cheaper for Wal-Mart to work with its international suppliers.

There are many points along the physical distribution channel that can slow down its efficient operation. Order processing is where physical distribution begins. The order-processing department is responsible for making multiple copies of the order and sending it to the various departments that will fill the order. If this department gets backed up, the entire physical distribution channel will stop.

Warehousing and location of those warehouses is critical to your ability to deliver the product on time. A nationwide company with only one warehouse would have to ship all goods from that location. A company located in Pennsylvania, for example, would only need a day to get products to the Northeast, but several days to get them to the West Coast. Most companies carefully plan their warehouse locations to minimize the time it takes to travel from the warehouse to the customer.

Warehousing can also save a lot of money for a manufacturer, especially if its product line comes from various producers. The manufacturer can have each producer deliver its part of the line to the warehouse; the warehouse combines the various products and ships it to the wholesalers or retailers. This saves the costs of shipping each part of the product separately to each retailer. Proper planning of your warehousing operation can be a good source of cost savings if planned and managed properly. We've already discussed inventory management in Chapter 12, so we won't revisit that here, but it is another spot along the physical distribution process in which cost savings can be found.

Understanding Wholesaling

Wholesaling is a $1.9 trillion industry in the United States with over 300,000 wholesaling establishments that employ more than 6 million people. This is known as a highly competitive area and companies won't hesitate to eliminate a wholesaler from an established channel if they are not performing up to expected standards. There are basically two types of wholesalers: merchant intermediaries and full-service wholesalers. Functional intermediaries also sometimes play a role in the distribution process without taking title to the products being distributed, but instead just helping to facilitate distribution.

Merchant intermediaries buy products and sell them. More than 80 percent of the wholesalers fall into this category, and they represented about half of all wholesale sales. Full-service wholesalers offer a broad range of functions including general merchandise (handle a wide mix of unrelated products but limited depth), limited line (handle a few products but an extensive assortment), specialty line (handle a narrow range of products), and rack jobbers (handle specialty product lines, own and manage display racks, and take back unsold products). Limited-service merchant wholesalers provide some of the marketing functions and include cash-and-carry wholesalers (customers pay cash for the products and furnish their own transportation with no credit extended), truck wholesalers (operate rolling warehouses and sell a limited line of primarily perishable products directly from their trucks to customers using regular routes), drop shippers (also known as desk jobbers, who negotiate sales but do not take physical possession of the goods), and mail-order wholesalers (who use catalogues instead of a sales force).

Functional intermediaries do not actually take title to the products; instead they expedite the exchanges between producers and resellers and are compensated with fees or by commission. These include agents and brokers who serve as third parties to bring buyers and sellers together. They are usually compensated based on a commission structure. Agents represent buyers on a permanent basis, while brokers represent buyers and sellers on a temporary basis. Over half of all agents are manufacturer's agents, which represent two or more sellers and offer customers complete lines. Selling agents market either a specific product line or a manufacturer's entire product offering. They do everything a wholesaler would do except actually take title to the product. Many times, selling agents are used in place of a marketing department. A selling agent can represent more than one product line so long as they are not competing lines. A commission merchant focuses on selling. They receive goods on consignment from local sellers and negotiate sales in large central markets. Auction companies provide a place that companies can store their products for inspection and then sell the product to the highest bidder. Brokers perform the fewest intermediary functions. They just help negotiate exchanges and they assume no risk.

> Selling agents market either a specific product line or a manufacturer's entire product offering.

Understanding Retailing

Retailing is even a larger part of the U.S. industrial work force than wholesaling. In fact, it is the second largest industry nationwide. Over 23 million

Americans are employed at the retail sector, which boasts more than $3 trillion in sales annually. The largest single retailer in the United States is Wal-Mart, which employs more than one million people and had approximately $255 billion in sales in 2003.

About 95 percent of all retailers in the United States are single mom-and-pop businesses, but they only generate about 50 percent of all retail store sales. The gross margin for most retail outlets falls between 31 and 33 percent on average, but this varies widely depending on the types of products being sold.

Building a distribution system is such a critical part of the marketing plan, that business schools usually offer an entire course on the process. You can see from just the few key points made here, that a properly designed and implemented distribution channel can offer you not only a strong competitive edge, but an opportunity to control costs, maximize your profits, and offer your products for a competitive price.

> **Chapter 24**

Forming Strategic Alliances

PART SIX   LOOKING OUTSIDE THE BOX

■ CHAPTER 24 **Forming Strategic Alliances**   ▨ CHAPTER 25 Going International

eBay Partners with Microsoft

Strategic partnerships are not just small companies partnering with large corporations. One partnership announced in 2001 involved a project to expand Microsoft's online presence and improve eBay's e-commerce experience for consumers. The two firms worked together to develop software solutions that would enable buyers and sellers to use the Internet to interact across multiple Web sites and other applications around the world. eBay offered Microsoft a community-based commerce engine so it could further develop its software and make that software available to a huge base of customers. Microsoft offered eBay access to its marketplace of Web properties including its Internet service worldwide. eBay was able to improve its back-end software operations, and Microsoft was able to introduce its software offerings to a much larger network of users and prove the viability of its software potential in a broad international effort using eBay's customer base.

What Is a Strategic Alliance?

As the world becomes more complex and knowledge of various technologies, control of marketing channels, and massive production capabilities are needed to get products to market, more and more companies are looking for partners to help share the costs and the risks. Strategic alliances are becoming one common way that companies are combining their forces to succeed in this ever-changing world. In this chapter, we'll introduce you to the concept of strategic alliance, give you things to think about to determine if they are right for your business, talk about the basics you need to know to manage a strategic alliance, and review the possible end scenarios for a strategic alliance.

A strategic alliance can take many forms, but it is basically a partnership formed by two companies that believe that in working together they will be able to grow their business more effectively either by developing and getting a new product to market or by serving their current customer needs better.

One of the most common forms of a strategic alliance is when a small company that has developed a new product looks to a major manufacturing company for a partnership to get that product to the marketplace. The advantage for the small company is that they will gain the power of a large distribution and manufacturing network to get their product to market more quickly and cheaply than if the small company tried to build that capacity itself. The advantage for the major manufacturer is that they have access to the new product without having to spend the money to research and develop it.

When I was in business school, my master's thesis was on corporate strategic alliances, how they operated and what made them most successful. One of the companies I studied was a small technical development company that developed a unique color copier. This company partnered with a Japanese manufacturing company to get the product to market.

Today these types of partnerships are happening at all levels of business. Almost every day the newspaper carries the announcement of the formation or the dissolution of a strategic partnership. IBM partners with small software developers to help serve its customers from the problem solution standpoint. Small biotechnology firms partner with major pharmaceutical manufacturers to get new and innovative drugs to market.

Do They Make Sense for Your Business?

While a strategic alliance may sound like an exciting way to grow your business, this is not a decision you should make lightly nor should you make it without strong legal advice. First, both you and your potential partner must consider the advantages and disadvantages of this partnership. Both partners must see clear advantages for the partnership to work. Only win-win situations in which both partners see a clear growth or profit potential will sustain a long-term relationship.

Before even starting the process of finding a partner, you need to determine your company's objectives for the potential relationship. What needs are you looking for your partner to fulfill? Is the partnership the best way to fulfill this need? If not, what other possibilities should you consider?

You must understand your company's capabilities and decide what you can commit or contribute to the partnership. Assess your company's strengths and weaknesses honestly. Be sure the partnership you are considering will bring value to your customers.

Once you make the decision that finding a partner is the best choice for your company, you should search carefully for the right partner. Choosing the wrong partner will create problems when something goes wrong. You must do a careful assessment of your potential partners, and not only look at short-term objectives. Take the time to understand the potential partners you are considering and realize that a partnership does not happen quickly but is something that is built slowly over time.

Even before making contact with a potential partner, you should assess its strategic behavior in the marketplace and see how that behavior will meld with your company culture. You must be sure your methods of operations are compatible with your potential partner. Talk with other companies that have worked with the partner you are considering to understand both the positives and negatives of working with that potential partner. Also talk with your potential partner's competitors to get a good idea of how that partner operates in the marketplace. Be sure you understand your partner's objectives, incentives, motivations, capabilities, and level of commitment.

There are numerous questions you should ask before even starting contract negotiations. You must determine potential problems with the partnership from your prospective and the prospective of your existing customers. While you might see greater profit potential, if the partnership results in customer dissatisfaction because your customers are not happy with the partner you have chosen, the loss of customers will kill any potential profit advantage.

Next you must look at the time frame for the agreement. Are you comfortable with its terms? Does it last long enough to make it worthwhile to commit to the partnership, or is your commitment to your partner so long you are concerned that if things don't work out as well as you expect you'll have a business obligation that doesn't make sense?

Also you must consider whether the agreement is too narrow or too broad. If the agreement is too narrow, it will not allow the partnership room to grow. If it is too broad, you may be giving your partner too much latitude to control the situation. The agreement must clearly spell out how conflicts will be resolved. While you might not want to think of potential conflicts as you are forging a new relationship, conflicts and differences are part of human nature. You need to establish a process on which you can both agree for settling any conflicts that may arise.

Additionally this agreement must clearly lay out the responsibilities each partner will take in order for the partnership to thrive and grow. If these responsibilities are not clearly defined, you may find that you are taking on more than you expected and that the additional resources you must put into the partnership to make it successful are eating up the profit potential for your company.

You should definitely contact a legal adviser who has experience drafting strategic alliance contracts in order to be sure your contract takes into consideration all the possible pitfalls. Although this procedure may increase the costs of establishing the partnership, it will certainly be worth the money in the long run to protect your company and its assets.

Managing a Strategic Alliance

When managing a strategic alliance, you should create a formal process that incorporates alliance integration, management responsibilities, negotiation tools, and a method to assess the success of the agreement. Assessment plans should include self-assessment of your activities as well as an assessment by your partner. This assessment should be a two-sided street and needs to be built into the overall management process to be sure any problems are discovered quickly and corrected.

Any strategic alliance is going to introduce new problems and you'll need new solutions. You'll learn a lot as the partnership develops and you want to have a mechanism in place to capture what you learn so you can improve the alliance and its management in the future. You may want to start with a set of incentives and penalties that are tied to successful completion of certain alliance activities. This will help you decide on any tasks that need to be performed and who will perform them, and it will also help you and your partner begin to think along organizational lines.

> Any strategic alliance is going to introduce new problems and you'll need new solutions.

The next step is to develop a thorough business plan with adequate details of how the alliance will operate. You should also create a team within your organization that is dedicated to the success of the strategic alliance. In finding the right people for this assignment, you should look for employees who offer a strong strategic vision as well as good operational and interpersonal traits. They must be people who can accept change, can persuade others, and can quickly adapt to new and challenging situations.

You must also be sure that the strategic alliance is adequately funded. Give the same time to developing a budget for the strategic alliance as you would to any other capital project. Recognize the amount of time and resources it will take to succeed and be sure you have the financial and other internal resources to fully support the alliance. Set up various stages in the alliance at which you or your partner could pull the plug if resources far exceed initial expectations.

Establish ways to measure your progress. These could include performance measurements such as new customers, increased market share, development of new products, improved time to get products to market, increased quality, or increased customer satisfaction. Decide on a baseline for measuring these activities and track progress from the baseline. You shouldn't focus solely on revenue or profitability, because, as with any new product, a new partnership will take time to add to your bottom line. While revenue and profit goals are important, the first step for the strategic alliance will likely be either introducing a new product or expanding the customer base.

Setting Milestones Is Important

Establishing milestones early in the lifecycle of a strategic alliance is important. IBM's general manager of Developer Relations Robert Timpson says, "It all begins with a clear understanding of exactly what you can do for your partner, and what your partner can do for you. Agreeing on precise objectives and milestones, on both sides, with names and dates assigned, is key to avoiding gaps between expectations and reality." He should know because IBM maintains more than fifty-five relationships with leading independent software vendors (including Siebel, SAP, i2, Ariba, PeopleSoft, Vignette, and JD Edwards). These partnerships collectively generate over $1 billion annually for IBM and its partners.

Contributions to these measurements should be collected throughout your company. Involve all who might be impacted by the partnership, including executives, sales managers, engineering, and production. Not only will this spread accountability, it will also help involve key players early in the process so there is less resistance to the changes that may be needed to support the partnership.

No matter how you set up your measurements, the key goal you must achieve is an early warning system that allows you to detect problems that could drive the alliance to an unexpected end. These problems could include budget cutbacks, layoffs, an unusually high turnover, a delay in project completion, cancellation of projects, and the worst of all, lost customers. Any of these warnings signs should be heeded and acted on quickly.

Obviously, the main goal of any strategic partnership arrangement should be to generate a profit for both parties. This can only be realized if both partners provide strong support for the partnership and work to execute the action plan developed before the start of the partnership, while making changes as necessary as problems are recognized.

Both partners must educate their employees to the goals and objectives of the partnership so there is internal support on both sides. Companies can sponsor various types of activities to share the knowledge of the alliance using management information systems, educational seminars, and periodic functions with alliance teams. Not only should these opportunities be available separately within each company, but the teams involved with the alliance should be given opportunities to share their experiences and build a good working relationship. Ultimately, companies want to make the alliance part of the culture within their business structure so they can increase the possibility of success. Without offering these information-sharing opportunities, both companies risk the possibility that managers will not understand or incorporate the goals of the alliance within their departments, which increases the chance of failure for the project.

Possible End Scenarios

Most strategic partnerships are planned for a set time period or a set number of objectives to be met. Once that time comes, the partners will have to decide on the next steps, which can be to formalize the relationship into a long-term permanent partnership or possibly even to merge. Not all strategic partnerships will work out, and sometimes the decision will be just to end the relationship.

Exit strategies should be a part of the discussion even before the partnership begins. Most strategic alliance agreements will specify a number of different scenarios depending on the success of the partnership. Whatever you do, try to set up exit strategies that will not destroy the relationship between the companies even if you decide this particular partnership didn't work. Both companies have learned a lot about each other and their cultures, and you may find that while this particular project didn't work out, another type of partnership or project may be a better match.

If the partnership is clearly not working, companies should not hesitate to terminate the project early rather than continue to throw resources at something that will never work. Seek to end the partnership while both companies are still on good working terms and treat the exit as something positive for all involved. Concentrate on the successes and the knowledge gained and the aspects of the partnership that helped each company rather than focus on the failure.

Many times failures occur because not enough planning went into the early stages of the partnership or even before the partnership was formalized. Companies seeing challenges from the competitors that cannot be met with internal resources may rush too quickly into a partnership in order to respond to the challenge. This can almost guarantee a failed partnership.

Formal Partnership

Some successful strategic partnerships end with negotiations to form a long-term, permanent partnership. In this case, both companies will remain as separate entities with their own operations, but they will continue to manage and grow the strategic partnership into a permanent business of its own. Many times this business is ultimately grown to the point where the partners actually sell stock for this new entity, which becomes a separate company in its own right.

Splitting Up

Total failure usually results in splitting up the partnership. If done at the right point, the companies will still be able to work together on other business opportunities. Unfortunately, companies often try to keep a strategic alliance going until both are so frustrated with each other and with the failure that they part ways and decide never to work together again.

Merger or Acquisition

Sometimes the partners will merge or one partner will decide to acquire the other partner. This happens most often when small companies partner with large corporations. The great risk the large corporation takes when it acquires the small company is that the key players who designed the new product in the first place will leave, deciding they don't want to work for the large corporation. This can cause a loss of needed technical skills and may actually hurt the long-term development of the product line.

When partnerships are properly designed and executed, they can close gaps in a company's operation and increase the chance of success for both partners. By maintaining adequate support levels, measuring success throughout the project to quickly find and fix any problems, and building a good mutual understanding and implementation of goals, strategic alliances can help companies become stronger players in their markets, which ultimately will benefit their partners, their customers, and their shareholders.

> **Chapter 25**

Going International

Part One

Part Two

Part Three

Part Four

Part Five

Part Six

PART SIX   LOOKING OUTSIDE THE BOX

■ CHAPTER 24 **Forming Strategic Alliances**   ■ CHAPTER 25 **Going International**

Moving into the Global Marketplace

For many U.S. companies, once they have saturated the U.S. market, the dream of selling their products internationally is the best way to grow their company. More and more companies today operate in many countries. Even small companies are jumping into the international marketplace.

There are many pitfalls companies must overcome before deciding to operate in another country, including financial issues, exchange rates, political and operating risks, management considerations, and marketing opportunities and concerns. In this chapter, we'll introduce you to the issues you'll need to understand before expanding internationally, but if you are thinking of moving into the international sphere, you'll definitely need to do a lot more research on the subject.

Financial Issues

First and foremost, before even starting to research international opportunities, a company must determine whether it has the financial resources to succeed. Not only will a company need to increase staff, it will also need to increase the skills available in-house.

Language ability is important even to begin talking with potential customers outside the United States. You will either have to hire someone who is conversant in the language of the country or countries you plan to consider marketing in or, at the very least, a competent interpreter.

Understanding cultural differences is also critical as you try to understand the costs involved in shifting to international marketing. What you have found works successfully in this country for promoting and selling your product could actually be a turnoff in your target country. Marketing will need considerable resources to research and develop its marketing plans.

> Understanding cultural differences is also critical as you try to understand the costs involved in shifting to international marketing.

Accounting will need to set up an entirely new process for managing international sales, and finance will need to develop new and possibly different kinds of financial resources to operate outside the country. Studies of operational costs in each country under consideration will also be a major role for accounting and finance.

Budgeting will take on an entirely new personality as you try to determine whether you have the financial resources to actually move into the international arena.

Exchange Rates

These financial plans will be complicated by the need to understand exchange rates and how they fluctuate, sometimes as often as hourly or even more frequently depending on the volatility of the currency in the United States and in the target countries. Managing your company finances will be much more complicated as you try to estimate the impact various exchange rate changes will have on your project's profitability and chances of success.

Political and Operating Risks

Each country will have its own types of political and operating risks. Many major corporations have spent time developing a market in a country and then find that they lose their entire operations when the political tides turned and the new government decides to nationalize its industries.

Even if the company is allowed to maintain its operations, the company may find that staying in that country requires operating under security risks that no longer make the market viable economically and that cut into expected profits. For example, many oil companies are looking forward to the prospect of getting a foot in the door in Iraq, which has the second largest untapped oil reserves in the world, but most are waiting to see what will happen politically before making any major financial commitment to the country.

Even the companies already in Iraq are finding it difficult to secure the assets related to the oil industry. While the United States and local Iraqi oil company officials initially expected to be able to get the oil industry back to prewar production levels by the end of 2003, the deadline for meeting that goal keeps slipping into the future. Oil companies have lost their investments in many countries when control of the government shifted politically, so they will enter the Iraq market slowly.

As part of your research of a potential foreign market, be sure you understand both the political and operating risks you could be facing in that marketplace. These risks can include:

China: Its Risks and Rewards

Most companies see China as the next major growth marketplace. U.S. companies have already invested billions in developing the Chinese marketplace, as well as producing cheap products for resale here in the United States. In order for this to happen, China had to be granted most-favored-nation status (MFN), which allows its products to more easily enter the United States at the lowest prevailing tariffs. In 2001, China was also granted membership in the World Trade Organization. At this time, however, it is still not operating according to WTO standards. Many in the United States are questioning whether China should keep its MFN status because of its human rights policies, its sales of nuclear materials, and its failure to protect copyrights and other intellectual property. WTO membership could also be at risk if China does not make steady progress to meet these standards. If either designation is lost, the chances of success for foreign companies attempting to operate in China and distribute products manufactured there will be much lower and the profit margins could become much slimmer.

- Changes in tax regulations or exchange controls, especially when a country institutes these changes to protect its own homegrown companies.
- Stipulations by the host country in order to protect its own local production companies, product sourcing, or jobs for its populace.
- Discrimination by possible customers who prefer to buy products made in their own countries.
- Restrictions on access to financial resources from local institutions.
- Interference by the government in privately negotiated contracts.
- Riots or other political unrest that could result in harm to your personnel or your facilities.
- A takeover of your company and its foreign assets by the host country.

Management Considerations

Managing foreign operations can also be a challenge. While you initially may want to send over a manager who has been with your company a long time and who knows your company culture and how it operates, you will also need to realize that each country has its own types of corporate cultures and management styles.

If you do decide to go forward with operations in a new country, your greatest chance of success will probably be found if you recruit and hire managers who have worked in that country before. In some cases, you may be able to hire managers who ran operations for other U.S. companies or managers who have operated divisions of foreign companies selling the same type of product in the country you plan to target.

Marketing Opportunities and Concerns

There is no question that new markets offer marketers new opportunities to grow their market share. Almost every company wants to find new target markets for its products. Developing an international marketing plan requires the same steps as any other marketing plan, plus some additional research and planning to understand the target country's culture and buying behavior. Also the development of promotional campaigns will need to reflect this different culture and behavior.

> Almost every company wants to find new target markets for its products.

One of the best ways to learn about the challenges you will face marketing in a new country is to review the advertising and promotional tools used by other companies currently operating there. You will see major differences not only in the style of ads, but also in what is socially and culturally acceptable in each of the markets. One of the most fascinating rooms in the Coca-Cola Museum is the one that offers you an opportunity to try its various international products and to view how differently it must advertise and promote its products in each country. Find out if your trade association, or even one of your competitors, has a similar display that will help you research the market.

Gather whatever information you can about similar products and their market structure for whatever country you are targeting. Use that information to decide not only whether to enter that country but also to develop your own marketing plan more effectively.

There are many resources you can use online to begin your research on the international marketplace. The U.S. Commerce Department is one of the best places to start. They have extensive information available about trade opportunities for U.S. businesses *(www.commerce.gov/trade_opportunities.html)*. The U.S.

State Department provides excellent information about countries and regions you may want to research *(www.state.gov/countries).* The trade association for your industry is another good resource to check for both online resources and private industry reports.

The international marketplace is certainly worth investigating to determine if the move makes sense for your business. Research all the factors mentioned here so you can be sure the opportunities are there; if the answer is yes, consider hiring a consultant familiar with the country or countries you want to target, so your resources used for developing that market will be well spent in an effective and efficient manner.

Glossary

APPENDICES

■ **APPENDIX 1** **Glossary** ■ APPENDIX 2 **Resources**

A

Accounts payable tracks all bills paid for obligations of less than one year.

Accounts receivable tracks all items sold on credit.

Administered vertical marketing systems coordinate production and distribution not through common ownership or contractual ties, but instead because one member of the channel has the size and power to control the channel.

Assets are items the company owns.

B

Balance sheets detail items the company owns, commonly called assets, and claims that are made against the company, which include liabilities (claims made by debtors) and owners' equity (claims made by owners or investors). A balance sheet is actually a snapshot of a business's financial position at some set point in time.

Behavioral management theory is concentrated on individual attitudes and group processes. Behavioral management came into vogue in the 1930s and 1940s and was driven by the birth of industrial psychology and the human relations movement.

Bonds are essentially IOUs. The company borrows money from bond investors and agrees to pay interest on that money, as well as repay the principal at some future date.

C

Capital markets are markets for long-term debt and corporate stocks.

Cash disbursements journals track all outgoing cash transactions.

Cash receipts journals track all incoming cash transactions.

Classical management theory is based on two primary ideas: scientific management, which focuses on employees and how to improve their productivity, and classical organization, which focuses on the total organization and how to make it more efficient and effective.

Common stock represents a partial ownership in a company with full voting rights and the right to share in the profits of the company through dividends, if the company chooses to pay dividends rather than retain earnings. Many growth companies pay no dividends at all. Instead they reinvest profits in the business's continuing expansion.

Consumer credit includes markets for loans for consumers, including for items such as autos, appliances, vacations, and education.

Contractual vertical marketing systems pull together independent entities at different levels of the distribution channel using a contractual agreement.

Convertible securities are bonds or preferred stock that can be exchanged for common stock at the option of the holder under terms and conditions specified at the time the convertible is issued. Unlike warrants, convertibles do not have the potential of bringing additional cash into the firm, but do have the advantage of lowering expenses of interest (if a bond is converted) or dividends (if preferred stock is converted).

Corporate vertical marketing systems combine all parts of the marketing distribution channel under one corporate ownership.

Corporations are businesses that are treated as a separate legal entity in the courts. They provide the greatest liability for the company founders because they cannot be sued personally for a corporation's actions or face collection from the corporation's creditors. Most major corporations are C corporations. The S corporation is a designation for small companies that want to avoid corporate taxes, but still want the other protections of a C corporation. The S corporation is solely an IRS designation, not a unique legal entity.

D

Demand encompasses the behavior of buyers. Buyers' demand for a product is based on price. As the price for a product rises, demand for that product will likely fall. For example, when gas prices are relatively cheap (in 2003, that was probably about $1.30 per gallon), demand for gas increases, but when prices near $2 per gallon, demand drops off considerably.

Diversification involves a decision to grow your company by starting up an entirely new product line outside your current market focus (such as introducing a line of floor coverings for the home improvement market if your product has been totally focused on tools) or looking to reach totally new market segments (such as introducing tools for professional builders if your current tools are made primarily for the home repair market).

E

Economy pricing is used if you are selling a no-frills product at a no-frills price. To make a product profitable, the cost of marketing and manufacture is kept at a minimum. Supermarket store brands are a good example of economy pricing.

Equilibrium encompasses the outcome of supply and demand on the market. When there is lack of demand because buyers see the price of the product or service as too high, the quantity that is supplied will exceed the quantity that is demanded. This will create a surplus of the product. Sellers will respond by lowering the price to get rid of the product. At some point, the price will drop too low, at which time producers will no longer want to make the product. At that point, supplies will dry up and there will likely be a shortage of the product. This shortage allows sellers to raise prices. When the price is just right with no surplus and no shortage, that particular product is considered to be in equilibrium—the quantity demanded equals the quantity supplied.

Equity represents the portion of the company owned by its shareholders, sole proprietor, or partners.

F

Financial Accounting Standards Board (FASB), which has been the designated organization in the private sector since 1973, sets financial reporting standards. The FASB is recognized as the authoritative source for this information by the Securities and Exchange Commission (SEC) and the American Institute of Certified Public Accountants (AICPA).

Futures establish a fixed price for an asset the day the future contract is issued, which guarantees that the asset can be sold or purchased at some time in the future at the fixed price. No matter how high or low the price goes, the parties on both sides of the future must carry out the contract at the agreed-on price. This differs from options, in which the buyer of the option has the right to buy or sell the option, but is not required to do so.

G

Government market includes local, state, and federal entities that purchase goods or services to carry out government functions.

I

Income statements provide information about a company's revenues and expenses and any taxes associated with those expenses for a given financial period, whether the report is for a month, a quarter, or a year, or possibly some other accounting period that makes business sense.

Inventory control focuses on finding the optimum level of inventory to avoid shortages, lost sales, and customer complaints without having too much product on hand.

L

Liabilities include all debts owned by the company.

Limited liability companies (LLCs) are businesses run as partnerships or sole proprietorships that enjoy some of the benefits of limited liability afforded corporations. While these entities are not corporations, they fall somewhere between a corporation and a sole proprietorship or partnership. LLCs are state entities and the degree to which your legal liability is limited depends on the state in which your LLC is organized. In most states, an LLC is given the same protection from liability as a traditional corporation.

M

Macroeconomics looks at the big picture of the economy. Macroeconomists seek to learn why the economy is growing or declining and about what impacts economic cycles.

Management information systems (MIS) focus on the information provided to managers, usually using an integrated database on a computer system that aids managers with decision-making. MIS enable the flow of information in a company, allowing managers to request reports about company operations depending on their clearance level, such as line supervisor, middle management, and executive management. The amount of information available to a manager depends on his or her level of access. For example, marketing managers can get basic information about production and inventory levels without needing to call the department heads; this saves time for both the marketing managers and the production and inventory managers.

Management science focuses on the development of mathematical models to solve problems and make decisions, most commonly in production settings. For example, a mathematical model will be developed on different variables whose values can fluctuate. As each value changes, a manager can use the model developed to determine the impact on the production process.

Managerial accounting provides a series of reports to assist managers with planning effectively, directing day-to-day operations, and solving problems through analyzing data and developing alternative methods. By helping managers stay on target and providing alternative solutions when problems arise, managerial accountants can become a critical function for the success of all departments.

Market development is used to find new market segments for the company's products. This can be done by looking for new demographic markets, such as developing a marketing campaign to attract teens or seniors to a product not currently used by them. Another way to develop new markets includes institutional marketing, such as working with complementary businesses that might agree to sell your product.

Market penetration is used to find new market opportunities by finding ways to increase sales of its current product without changing that product. Market penetration is most commonly accomplished by switching users of similar products made by another company to its product.

Microeconomics tracks the behavior of individual entities, such as people or businesses. This branch of economics seeks to understand how individual households will respond to changes in prices or wages. Microeconomists also want to understand how individual businesses make decisions regarding product production and pricing.

Money markets include debt securities with a maturity date of less than one year.

Monopoly exists in the marketplace when only one company controls the market for a particular product.

Mortgage markets include markets for loans on residential, commercial, and industrial real estate, as well as farmland.

Oligopolies exist in the marketplace when a few companies control a particular product and tend to control its prices.

Operations coordination focuses on what materials and services are needed in order to efficiently do the work of the company. In setting up controls, companies must determine the materials and parts needed for production operations, and then determine the level of inventory the company should keep on hand and at what point more materials or parts should be ordered. Next, a schedule is set up for parts deliveries and lead times as needed.

Operations design focuses on how work facilities (such as equipment and job assignments) are constructed, arranged, and coordinated.

Operations management, which is less mathematical than management science, is used more broadly in the management of the organization and is not tied as directly to production management. Tools that fall within this category include network modeling, queuing theory, break-even analysis, and simulation. While these techniques are commonly used in production, they can also be used in finance, marketing, and personnel management.

Opportunity costs are the costs involved when a company must decide among various options. By deciding to spend the money on one option, the opportunity cost will be the cost of not being able to spend on another option. This can be a much larger cost than anticipated if by having money tied up in the first decision, management then must pass on the newer and possibly better opportunity. Each time a company spends money on a project, it risks the possibility of missing a future opportunity.

Options are contracts that give a holder the right to buy (or sell) an asset at some predetermined price within a specified period. Both warrants and convertibles are types of options.

P

Partnerships are businesses owned and run by two or more people.

Penetration pricing is used when you set artificially low prices in order to increase your market share. Once the market-share goal is achieved, pricing will be increased to regain profitability.

Physical assets markets include markets for tangible assets, such as grains, autos, real estate, electronics equipment, machinery, and so on.

Preferred stock falls somewhere between a bond and common stock. While a preferred stockholder has an ownership share, he or she does not have voting rights. In exchange for the loss of voting rights, the preferred stockholders are paid dividends before common stockholders. If the company goes bankrupt, preferred stockholders will be paid their share of the remains before common stockholders.

Premium pricing is used when you plan to set a high price because you believe you are offering a unique product or service. This pricing strategy is most often used for luxury or specialty products or services.

Price skimming is a strategy that can be used when a company has a substantial competitive advantage and decides to charge a high price. This type of pricing cannot be sustained for long because a high price will usually attract new competitors or the demand for your product will drop and you'll need to lower the price to attract buyers again.

Primary markets include markets for new securities.

Product development involves deciding to grow your business by improving your existing products or introducing new products to the market segments in which you are already successful.

Pro forma statements are sometimes used by companies to emphasize their results using either current or projected figures. These statements do not necessarily meet standards set by the FASB and usually should not be used when making decisions about whether to invest in a company.

Q

Quality control focuses on maintaining the level of quality that keeps customers happy. A number of techniques are used to control quality. The two most commonly used are acceptance sampling of finished goods and in-process sampling during production to be sure quality is maintained.

Quantitative management theories are an outgrowth of techniques learned during World War II related to the movement of troops and equipment, as well as the deployment of submarines. Basically, quantitative management theory depends on quantitative techniques to solve workplace problems and make management decisions. There are three distinct areas of quantitative management: management science, operations management, and management information systems.

R

Reseller market includes companies that buy goods or services for the purpose of reselling them or renting them to others. This marketplace includes both wholesalers (middlemen between manufacturing groups and consumer retail outlets) and retailers that sell directly to the public.

S

Secondary markets include markets where existing securities are bought and sold.

Sole proprietorships are businesses owned and run by one person.

Statement of cash flows gives information about a company's cash position. This statement has three parts: operating activities, investment activities, and financial activities.

Strategic Business Units are parts of a company that have their own mission. They can include a single unit or a set of related units. An SBU will have its own set of competitors and its own unique strategy.

Sunk costs are costs already incurred that cannot be changed. For example, the construction of a facility or purchase of equipment is a sunk cost. Even if the decision is later determined to have been a mistake, the cost of the equipment or facility has been made and cannot be part of a differential analysis to correct that mistake in the future. Differential analysis only looks at the costs that can be changed.

Supply encompasses the other side of the market—the behavior of sellers and producers. The quantity of a product produced and offered for sale will depend on the price that buyers are willing to pay for that product. The more buyers are willing to pay for the product, the more incentive there is to increase the supply. For example, looking at the price of oil from the producers' perspective, if a barrel of oil sells for only $10, not many producers are going to seek out new sources of oil, but when the price of a barrel rises to $30, many more producers are willing to take the risks of looking for more oil supplies.

W

Warrants are a type of option that gives the owner the right to buy a stated number of shares of the company's stock at a specified price. These are generally distributed with debt instruments to entice investors to buy a firm's long-term debt. Warrants do have the potential of bringing additional capital to the firm if the warrant owners decide to purchase stock at some future date.

> **Appendix 2**

Resources

APPENDICES

■ APPENDIX 1 Glossary ■ APPENDIX 2 Resources

Useful Government Internet Sites

The **Census Bureau** *(www.census.gov)* offers you a page full of links organized in a way to quickly find key demographic information.

The **Commerce Department** *(www.commerce.gov/trade_opportunities.html)* has a page with extensive information about trade opportunities for U.S. businesses.

The **Department of Labor** *(www.dol.gov)* has extensive resources online regarding all labor issues.

The **Federal Reserve** *(www.federalreserve.gov/rnd.htm)* has links to economic statistics.

Fedstats *(www.fedstats.gov)* links you to many key governmental agencies and their statistics.

The **National Technical Information Service** *(www.ntis.gov)* provides you with the largest central resource for government-funded scientific, technical, engineering, and business-related information available today.

The **Small Business Administration** *(www.sba.gov)* has excellent resources online for small businesses.

The **State Department** *(www.state.gov/countries/)* has a page that provides excellent information about countries and regions you want to research.

The **White House Economic Statistics Briefing Room** *(www.whitehouse.gov/fsbr/esbr.html)* is an excellent place to find the most current statistics on employment, income, money, prices, production, output, and transportation.

Useful Non-Government Internet Sites

Bonds Online *(www.bondsonline.com)* is a good site for information on bonds and bond trading.

The **Chicago Board Options Exchange Learning Center** *(www.cboe.com/Learn Center)* is a good place to learn more about options and options trading.

ClickZ Network *(www.clickz.com/stats/)*, formerly CyberAtlas, provides you with statistics about the Internet, including size, usage patterns, and geographic, demographic, and other Internet marketing news

The **Commodity Futures Trading Commission** *(www.cftc.gov)* is a good place to start if you want to learn more about futures.

CPA and PERT project management techniques can be learned at *www.mindtools.com/critpath.html.*

The **Ethics Resource Center** *(www.ethics.org)* is a nonprofit education and research organization based in Washington, D.C., that collects and distributes information about business ethics.

Financial Accounting Standards Board *(www.fasb.org)* is where you can find information about requirements for financial statements.

Gantt charts can be explored at *www.smartdraw.com/resources/centers/gantt/tutorial1.htm.*

Stocks and mutual fund information can be found at Morningstar *(www.morningstar.com),* Standard and Poor's *(www.standardandpoors.com),* and Value Line *(www.valueline.com).*

Zipfind *(www.zipfind.net)* helps you find population information including how many people live in a particular zip code.

Recommended Business Reading

Competitive Advantage: Creating and Sustaining Superior Performance by Michael Porter (Free Press, 1998).

Competitive Strategy: Techniques for Analyzing Industries and Competitors by Michael Porter (Free Press, 1998).

Corporate Taxation: Examples and Explanations, 2nd edition, by Cheryl D. Block (Aspen, 2001).

Designing Organizations: An Executive Guide to Strategy, Structure, and Process Revised by Jay Galbraith (Jossey-Bass, 2001).

The Essential Drucker: The Best of Sixty Years of Peter Drucker's Essential Writings on Management by Peter Drucker (HarperBusiness, 2003).

The Financial Numbers Game: Detecting Creative Accounting Practices by Charles Mulford and Eugene Comiskey (Wiley & Sons, 2002).

Innovative Reward Systems for Changing the Workplace, 2nd edition, by Thomas Wilson and Rosebeth Moss Kanter (McGraw-Hill Trade, 2002).

Operations Management, 7th edition, by Jay Heizer and Barry Render (Prentice Hall, 2003).

Real Change Leaders: How You Can Create Growth and High Performance at Your Company by Jon Katzenbach (Three Rivers, 1997).

Strategic Corporate Tax Planning by John E. Karayan, Charles W. Swenson, and Joseph W. Neff (Wiley & Sons, 2002).

➤ Index

A

K

Kamins, Michael, 284
Kanigel, Robert, 185
Karayan, John, 126
Katzenbach, Jon, 223
Koch Industries, 159
Kroc, Ray, 257, 258
Kroll, Karen, 149

L

Lawler, Edward, 226, 227, 229
Leadership. *See also* Management
in general, 226, 230–233
market leaders, 270–271
Leadership Potential Equation, 230
Leasing. *See also* Financing
capital lease, 165
combination lease, 166
compared to loan, 166–167
discussed, 165–167
operating lease, 165
sale/leaseback, 165
Legal issues, 45. *See also* Business law; Business structure
liability issues, 3, 8, 12
product liability, 14
Levy, Michael, 21
Liabilities. *See* Accounting system

Limited liability company (LLC), discussed, 8–11
LLC. *See* Limited liability company
Lockheed-Martin, 31
Loewy, Raymond, 312
Long Island Lighting Company, 145, 152

M

Mail Boxes Etc., 266
Management. *See also* Business structure; Employees; Financial management; Leadership; Planning
authority and delegation, 214–216
behavioral management
in general, 187
industrial psychology, 187–188
centralized vs. decentralized, 216–217
classical management, 184–187
contemporary management, 191–194
by exception, 215
in general, 184, 191
of groups
in general, 233–236
group dynamics, 236
styles, 234–235

human relations
movement, 189–190
by objectives, 200
quantitative management, 190–191
management information system, 190
management science, 190
operations management, 190
tall vs. flat, 217–219
X, Y, Z theories, 191–194
Marcus, Bernard, 217
Market segment. *See also* Marketing
determining, 268
Market. *See also* Marketing
defining, 296
Market research, discussed, 273–277
Market segmentation
behavioristic, 300
demographic, 299–300
in general, 299
geographic, 299
psychographic, 300
Market targeting
concentrated marketing, 302
determination, 269
differentiated marketing, 301–302
in general, 301
undifferentiated marketing, 301

STREETWISE® BOOKS

Newest Arrivals!

Crash Course MBA
$19.95 (CAN $29.95)
ISBN 1-59337-210-8

Structuring Your Business
$19.95 (CAN $29.95)
ISBN 1-59337-177-2

Also Available in the *Streetwise*® Series:

24 Hour MBA
$19.95 (CAN $29.95)
ISBN 1-58062-256-9

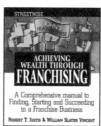

Achieving Wealth Through Franchising
$19.95 (CAN $29.95)
ISBN 1-58062-503-7

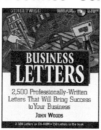

Business Letters with CD-ROM
$29.95 (CAN $47.95)
ISBN 1-58062-133-3

Business Valuation
$19.95 (CAN $31.95)
ISBN 1-58062-952-0

Complete Business Plan
$19.95 (CAN $29.95)
ISBN 1-55850-845-7

Complete Business Plan with Software
$29.95 (CAN $47.95)
ISBN 1-58062-798-6

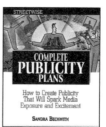

Complete Publicity Plans
$19.95 (CAN $29.95)
ISBN 1-58062-771-4

Customer-Focused Selling
$19.95 (CAN $29.95)
ISBN 1-55850-725-6

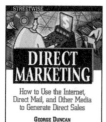

Direct Marketing
$19.95 (CAN $29.95)
ISBN 1-58062-439-1

Do-It-Yourself Advertising
$19.95 (CAN $29.95)
ISBN 1-55850-727-2

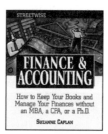

Finance & Accounting
$19.95 (CAN $29.95)
ISBN 1-58062-196-1

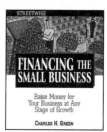

Financing the Small Business
$19.95 (CAN $29.95)
ISBN 1-58062-765-X

Human Resources Management
$19.95 (CAN $29.95)
ISBN 1-58062-699-8

Independent Consulting
$19.95 (CAN $29.95)
ISBN 1-55850-728-0

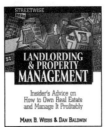

Landlording & Property Management
$19.95 (CAN $29.95)
ISBN 1-58062-766-8

Low-Cost Marketing
$19.95 (CAN $31.95)
ISBN 1-58062-858-3

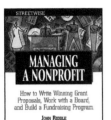

Managing a Nonprofit
$19.95 (CAN $29.95)
ISBN 1-58062-698-X

Managing People
$19.95 (CAN $29.95)
ISBN 1-55850-726-4

Marketing Plan
$19.95 (CAN $29.95)
ISBN 1-58062-268-2

Maximize Web Site Traffic
$19.95 (CAN $29.95)
ISBN 1-58062-369-7

Project Management
$19.95 (CAN $29.95)
ISBN 1-58062-770-6

Relationship Marketing on the Internet
$17.95 (CAN $27.95)
ISBN 1-58062-255-0

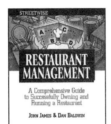

Restaurant Management
$19.95 (CAN $29.95)
ISBN 1-58062-781-1

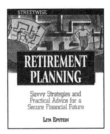

Retirement Planning
$19.95 (CAN $29.95)
ISBN 1-58062-772-2

Selling Your Business
$19.95 (CAN $29.95)
ISBN 1-58062-602-5

Small Business Start-Up
$19.95 (CAN $29.95)
ISBN 1-55850-581-4

Time Management
$19.95 (CAN $29.95)
ISBN 1-58062-131-7

Available wherever books are sold.
For more information, or to order, call 800-872-5627 or visit www.adamsmedia.com
Adams Media, an F+W Publications Company, 57 Littlefield Street, Avon, MA 02322

About the Author

Lita Epstein, who earned her MBA degree from Emory University's Goizueta Business School, worked for about ten years in various management positions before returning to her passion—writing. Today she translates the complex worlds of money and politics through her writing. Her books include *Streetwise® Retirement Planning*, *Trading for Dummies*, and a number of books in the *Complete Idiot's Guide* series including *Accounting, Politics of Oil, Tax Breaks and Deductions, Federal Reserve,* and *Supreme Court*.